Kieler Studien · Kiel Studies 319
Horst Siebert (Editor)
Kiel Institute for World Economics

Springer
Berlin
Heidelberg
New York
Hong Kong
London
Milan
Paris
Singapore
Tokyo

Ludger Wößmann

Schooling and the Quality of
Human Capital

Springer

Dr. Ludger Wößmann
Institut für Weltwirtschaft
Abteilung Entwicklungsökonomie und weltwirtschaftliche Integration
Forschungsgruppe Humankapital und Wachstum
D-24100 Kiel
woessmann@ifw.uni-kiel.de

ISSN 0340-6989

ISBN 3-540-43882-3 Springer-Verlag Berlin Heidelberg New York

Library of Congress Cataloging-in-Publication Data applied for
Die Deutsche Bibliothek – CIP-Einheitsaufnahme

Wößmann, Ludger: Schooling and the quality of human capital / Ludger Wößmann. – Berlin;
Heidelberg; New York; Hong Kong; London; Milan; Paris; Singapore; Tokyo: Springer, 2002
  (Kieler Studien; 319)
  ISBN 3-540-43882-3

Springer-Verlag Berlin Heidelberg New York
a member of BertelsmannSpringer Science+Business Media GmbH

http://www.springer.de

© Springer-Verlag Berlin Heidelberg 2002
Printed in Germany

The use of general descriptive names, registered names, trademarks, etc. in this publication
does not imply, even in the absence of a specific statement, that such names are exempt from
the relevant protective laws and regulations and therefore free for general use.

Hardcover-Design: Erich Kirchner, Heidelberg

SPIN 10885923   42/2202-5 4 3 2 1 0 – Printed on acid-free paper

Preface

This study investigates macroeconomic consequences and microeconomic determinants of the quality of human capital, as reflected in the academic achievement of students at school. Many people become pessimistic about our future when looking at today's students. The following quotations exemplify this attitude:

"The children now ... have bad manners, contempt for authority; they show disrespect for elders ... They no longer rise when elders enter the room. They contradict their parents, chatter before company, gobble up dainties at the table, cross their legs, and tyrannize their teachers."

However, these quotations do not spring from our days, as one might expect. They are ascribed to Socrates (470–399 B.C.)—and apparently, the subsequent generations were not all that bad after all. For example, they included Aristotle (384–322 B.C.), who is not generally viewed as a basket case—and who is reported as saying:

"I do not have any hope whatsoever for the future of our country when one day the youth of today are the men of tomorrow. Our youth is unendurable, irresponsible, and appalling to look at."

Mankind has evolved despite this assessment, and probably any generation has viewed the subsequent one as a lost case. Maybe, then, the pessimistic assessment of the coming generation is not so much caused by the dire straits of the youth as by the lack of understanding and of the willingness to change on part of the older generation. Thus, my view of the young generation is not that pessimistic at all. Instead, today's young generation is as good as any before it, full of potential, and inevitably the foundation for our future, but we, the older generation of today, have to fulfill our duty to ensure that the young generation has the basis and the possibilities to strive in the future. One central element in this foundation is the youth's schooling, and this study tries to add to our understanding of how we can equip the young generation with the knowledge which is the prerequisite for future prosperity.

Saying has it that the day we stop learning, we are dead. Thus, just as students learn at school, which is the focus of this study, I myself learned a lot while working on it. I had the privilege of benefiting from many other people's knowledge. To all of them, I am deeply grateful, as I think that to strive for the advancement of our knowledge is in itself the most satisfying work of all.

My special thanks go to Professors Horst Siebert and Johannes Bröcker, who led me through the work on this study. Likewise, Professor Rolf J. Langhammer was most helpful in ensuring a concise argumentation. Most of all, I would like to thank Erich Gundlach, who guided my work on the economics of human capital and economic growth right from my start at the Kiel Institute for World Economics. With his constant criticism of any argument I would advance with and his in-depth discussion of any thought I would bring up, he focused my attention on the most interesting topics and made the Kiel Institute's research environment a stimulating place. The best of this freedom of research in Kiel is also reflected in the Thursday lunch-time jogging rounds which ensured regular thought exchanges with some of my most formidable colleagues. (Who needs a brown-bag seminar to sit in at lunch time when you can move your legs while discussing the most challenging subjects which economics has to offer?)

Many researchers from other institutions working on similar issues advanced my knowledge in the field. Even at the risk of making serious omissions, I would like to name Professors John H. Bishop, Eric A. Hanushek, Caroline M. Hoxby, George Psacharopoulos, Xavier Sala-i-Martin, and Jon Temple, whose comments on different parts of this work were both helpful and encouraging.

Michaela Rank provided skillful research assistance in the preparation of the data and the construction of the figures. Ingrid Gleibs, Melanie Grosse, Sabine Hübener, and Kerstin Stark helped with the careful editing of the manuscript. My thanks go to all of them.

Last but not least, I wish to thank my parents, who made me value learning and made my studies possible, my other family members, and Esther, for keeping my spirits high during my work on this study and suffering most in the trade-off between work and the more important parts of life. This work is dedicated to them.

Kiel, September 2002   Ludger Wößmann

Contents

List of Tables

List of Figures

List of Abbreviations

2SLS	two-stage least squares
BA	bachelor of arts
CPI	consumer price index
CPI-S	consumer price index for services
CRLR	clustering-robust linear regression
CSPS	community, social, and personal services
EBRD	European Bank for Reconstruction and Development
EIB	European Investment Bank
GDP	gross domestic product
HLM	hierarchical linear models
IAEP	International Assessment of Educational Progress
IDB	Inter-American Development Bank
IEA	International Association for the Evaluation of Educational Achievement
ISCED	International Standard Classification of Education
ISIC	International Standard Industrial Classification of all Economic Activities
IV	instrumental variable
MA	master of arts
NAEP	National Assessment of Educational Progress
OECD	Organisation for Economic Co-operation and Development
OLS	ordinary least square
PGS	producers of government services
PhD	doctor of philosophy
PPP	purchasing power parity
PSU	primary sampling unit
PWT	Penn World Tables
SNA	System of National Accounts
STAR	Student/Teacher Achievement Ratio (Tennessee Project)
TIMSS	Third International Mathematics and Science Study
UN	United Nations
UNDP	United Nations Development Programme
UNESCO	United Nations Educational, Scientific and Cultural Organization
WEI	World Education Indicators
WLS	weighted least squares

List of Symbols

Chapter 2

a	attainment index
A	total factor productivity
A_{high}	highest possible working age
A_{low}	lowest possible working age
ATT	attainment census method
C	cost of schooling
d	drop-out rate
D_0	school-entrance age
D_a	duration of attainment level a
DD	de la Fuente–Doménech dataset
e	enrollment ratio
E	enrollment
g	grade index
h	human capital per worker
h^{HJ}	human capital per worker based on Hall–Jones specification
h^M	human capital per worker based on Mincer specification
h^Q	quality-adjusted human capital per worker
h^r	human capital per worker based on country-specific rates of return
hig	higher attainment level
$high$	higher level of schooling
H	stock of human capital
i	country index
I	investment
k	physical capital per worker
K	stock of physical capital
l	adult literacy rate
low	lower level of schooling
L	labor force (number of workers)
M_A	literates in the adult population
MRW	Mankiw–Romer–Weil dataset
n_0	fraction of the labor force without schooling
n_a	fraction of the labor force with a as highest attainment level
N_a	number of workers with a as highest attainment level

p	survival probability
P_A	adult population
P_g	population at grade g
P_w	population at working age
PIM	perpetual inventory method
pri	primary attainment level
PRO	projection method
Q	index of educational quality
r	rate of return to education
r_g	ratio of repeaters to enrollments in grade g
s	average years of schooling in the labor force
S	total years of schooling in the labor force
sec	secondary attainment level
t	time index
T	year index
W	annual earnings (wage) after t years of schooling
y	output per worker
Y	output
α	production elasticity of physical capital
γ	growth rate
δ	depriciation rate
ϕ	efficiency of labor

Chapter 3

a	age-group index
b	subtest index
B	family background
$CUREXP$	current educational expenditure
d^{US}	deviation of OECD-sample test scores from U.S. test score
H	hypothesis
i	subscript: sector index
i	superscript: country index
I	instruments
L	labor
n	sample size
O	subscript: index for other sector

O	superscript: OECD sample
p	price of output
PERFIR	percentage of expenditure spent at the first level of education
PERSEC	percentage of expenditure spent at the second level of education
Q	schooling quality
r	rate of productivity growth
R	resources
s	subject index
S	subscript: index for schooling sector
S^i	original test score of country i
Ser	index for other service industries (except for schooling)
STUPFIR	students enrolled at the first level of education
STUPSEC	students enrolled at the second level of education
t	time index
T^i	transformed test score of country i
U^i	test score of country i relative to US test score
w	wage per unit of labor
x_S	educational expenditure per student
Y	output
Δ	annual rate of change
σ	standard deviation

Chapter 4

A	ability
Aut	school autonomy
AutPro	school autonomy in process and personnel decisions
AutSta	school autonomy in standard setting and performance control
B	benefits
c	cost parameter
C	costs
CenExa	central examinations
C_G	costs of school inputs to the government
C_S	costs of student's effort
d	share of diverted spending
E	student effort
G	government index

I	school effectiveness index
j	intrinsic rewards for learning
l	extrinsic rewards for learning
P	political priority for schooling quality
ParInf	parental influence
PrivSc	private school management
Q	schooling quality
R	resources employed in teaching
S	student index
TeaMet	teachers' influence on teaching methods
TeaScr	teachers' scrutiny of performance examination
TeaUni	influence of teacher unions
TeaWor	teachers' influence on work load and rewards
w	total rewards for learning
X	educational expenditure
α	elasticity of schooling quality Q with respect to student effort E
β	elasticity of schooling quality Q with respect to effective spending IR
μ	elasticity of student costs C_S with respect to student effort E
Δ	$= \mu - \beta\mu - \alpha$
η_{xy}	elasticity of x with respect to y

Chapter 5

A	variable containing missing values
B	student background
c	school index
d	design effect
F	"fundamental" explanatory variables for data imputation
i	student index
I	institutions
m	number of observations in primary sampling unit
n	number of primary sampling units
Q	schooling quality (as measured by TIMSS test score)
R	resources
S	set of students with available data
V	variance-covariance matrix
w	sampling weight

W	diagonal matrix of sampling weights
X	explanatory variables
ε	error term
μ	school error component
ν	student error component
ρ	intra-cluster correlation coefficient
σ^2	error variance

1   An Economic Analysis of Schooling

1.1   The Issue

Human capital is the most important resource in the modern knowledge economy. With lifelong learning becoming essential in a rapidly changing global environment, it is not so much the specialized knowledge of specific higher-education courses which determines the long-run fates of individuals and societies. Instead, the basic knowledge learned early in schools is the essential enduring resource which forms the "scaffolding" (World Bank 1999a: 40) of a society's knowledge. Since "[e]arly learning begets later learning" (Heckman 2000: 5), the knowledge base formed in schools provides a lasting foundation on which later specialized learning can build. Thus, the quality of basic education has a substantial impact on the potential future prosperity of individuals and countries.

This study first demonstrates empirically that the quality of schooling, as indicated by students' performance on international comparative achievement tests, is important for economic development, and then goes on to analyze what determines the quality of schooling. Evidence reported in the literature and new evidence presented here both suggest that merely increasing the resources available within existing schooling systems does not increase the quality of schooling. Following a theoretical model which stresses the importance of institutionally set incentives for the outcome of educational production within schools, this study presents microeconometric evidence, based on an extensive international student achievement test, which demonstrates the large effects of institutions on the quality of schooling. The results imply that international differences in educational institutions, rather than differences in schooling resources, explain the large international differences in schooling quality.

By establishing the basis of people's entire education, schooling is vital for the quality of a nation's economically usable stock of human capital. The basic idea that education is an investment embodied in human beings and is thus of central importance for economic development was already advanced by Adam Smith ([1776]1976: 118) in his classical *Inquiry into the Nature and Causes of the Wealth of Nations*:

A man educated at the expence of much labour and time to any of those employments which require extraordinary dexterity and skill, may be compared to [an] expensive machin[e]. The work which he learns to perform, it must be expected, over and above the usual wages of common labour, will replace to him the whole expence of his education, with at least the ordinary profits of an equally valuable capital.

And Alfred Marshall ([1890]1922: 564) stated in his *Principles of Economics* that "[t]he most valuable of all capital is that invested in human beings." While these citations demonstrate an early awareness of the importance of human capital, it was not until the second half of the twentieth century that economists such as Theodore W. Schultz (1961), Gary S. Becker ([1964]1993), and Jacob Mincer (1974) developed the economics of education and human capital more thoroughly. With the emergence of the new theories of endogenous growth, in which human capital plays an important role (e.g., Lucas 1988; Romer 1990a), and with the neoclassical revival in growth economics, which augments the Solow model by human capital (Mankiw et al. 1992), education is also one of the central topics in the new wave of empirical evidence in growth economics (Temple 1999a).

Because of new comprehensive technologies in the information industry, a knowledge economy is emerging today in which the quality of human capital is even more important. In this "new economy," human capital is the decisive production factor, and it is central to the productivity and growth prospects of a country. Hence, Siebert (2000b: 32–33) concludes that "[h]uman capital formation ... is at the core of economic policy in the new economy." If countries are to participate in the benefits of the new economy, it is vital that they have a national human capital formation system which works efficiently.

Accordingly, in the United States, one of the major current policy debates focuses on the efficiency of the system of primary and secondary schooling. In the 2000 presidential election campaign, schooling was one of the most important issues, with one candidate supporting increased spending on schools as they are, and the other candidate proposing structural reforms to the education system which would introduce competition, choice, and accountability (*The Economist* 2000). In a Gallup poll, 91 percent of the U.S. public ranked education as "very" or "extremely" important, making education more important than any other issue mentioned in the poll, even including the economy, health care, or national defense (Gallup 2000). In the last election in the United Kingdom, Prime Minister Blair famously declared that his three top priorities in government would be "education, education and education" (*The Economist* 1997).

In its annual report for 2000/01, the German Council of Economic Experts (Sachverständigenrat 2000: 185–186) stresses the central role of a vital and efficient education system for the needs of the new economy and points out the poor educational standard of many school-leavers in Germany. In its 1998/99 report, the Council provided an encompassing analysis of the reforms needed in the German system of higher education (Sachverständigenrat 1998: 247–256). Because the current system of higher education, which is traditionally controlled by the state in Germany, is alleged to exhibit a high degree of inefficiency, the Council proposed far-reaching reforms based on market-economy principles which would make higher education competitive, allow colleges and universities freedom from bureaucratic interventions, and give the actors involved incentives for superior performance and quality, e.g., through performance-related pay for professors. No similar reforms have been proposed as yet for the system of primary and secondary education, in which the necessary foundation for the future learning activities of school-leavers is laid.

All the international development agencies have recently embraced the importance of high-quality basic education for countries' growth prospects. Basic education was a central topic in the World Bank's (1999a) *World Development Report* 1998/99 on "Knowledge for Development," and in his draft *Proposal for a Comprehensive Development Framework*, World Bank President James D. Wolfensohn (1999: 13) stressed that "[a]ll agree that the single most important key to development and to poverty alleviation is education." Both the African Development Bank (1998) and the Asian Development Bank (1998) made human capital formation the topic of their 1998 development reports. Likewise, the European Bank for Reconstruction and Development focused its *Transition Report* 2000 on the creation of skills (EBRD 2000), and the Inter-American Development Bank (IDB) recognized differences in education as constituting the primary cause for differences in income in Latin America in its 1998/99 report (IDB 1998). And the governors of the European Investment Bank (EIB) decided in 1999 that financing investments in education should become a permanent EIB financing objective (EIB 2000).[1]

In studying the economic forces at work in schooling systems, one is easily led to the simple production-function argumentation that more inputs such as smaller classes, higher teacher salaries, or more teaching materials should lead to higher schooling output in the form of improved educational quality. However, this would require the efficient use of resources in the sense that given inputs are used in a performance-maximizing way. In other sectors of the economy, this is ensured by firms trying to maximize their profits under the constraints of competition. In the education sector, however, which tends to be run publicly everywhere in the world, there is neither much competition nor are schools subject to a stringent performance maximization objective (Hoxby 2000b). It is, thus, not very surprising that the empirical evidence overwhelmingly shows that schooling systems throughout the world operate highly inefficiently. At given levels of expenditures, an increase in the amount of resources used does not generally lead to

---

[1] Additionally, the annual *World Education Report*, published since 1991 by the United Nations Educational, Scientific and Cultural Organization (UNESCO 2000b), and the annual Human Development Reports launched in 1990 by the United Nations Development Programme (UNDP 2000) focus on basic education.

an increase in educational performance (Hanushek 1996a). This makes the quest for the determinants of educational quality in schools a quest for the determinants of the (in)efficiency of schooling systems.

The problem at the current state of the literature is that "nobody can describe when resources will be used effectively and when they will not" (Hanushek 1997b: 148). The central hypothesis underlying this study is that it is the differing institutions which distinguish more effective schooling systems from less effective ones. While public provision of schooling may generally be associated with inefficiencies, public schooling systems nevertheless differ substantially across countries in their institutional structures with respect to educational decision-making processes. They give different amounts of decision-making power to the different actors involved in educational production, which creates different incentives for their behavior. These differences in institutions and incentives affect the actors' decisions on resource allocation and thereby the effectiveness of resource use in schooling systems, which ultimately determines the quality of the education produced. Coase (1984: 230) once stressed that "[t]he choice in economic policy is a choice of institutions." This study argues that the same holds for schooling policy, and it presents evidence which reveals which institutions have the most favorable influence on efficiency in educational production.

1.2   Overview

Chapter 2 motivates the study by showing that schooling quality, as measured by students' educational performance, is a key determinant of long-run economic development. The remainder of the study shows how the quality of schooling is determined. Increased educational expenditure as the most intuitive determinant does not explain variations in the quality of schooling (Chapter 3). Consequently, Chapter 4 presents a model of the schooling system which elaborates the central role of institutions and incentives in educational production and which implies the possibility that positive resource effects may be lacking within actual current schooling systems. Microeconometric evidence corroborates the importance of international differences in educational institutions in explaining the large international differences in schooling quality (Chapter 5). Chapter 6 concludes by discussing what the findings imply for schooling policy. The following paragraphs summarize the scientific procedures and main results of each chapter.

Chapter 2 starts with a review and critique of the measures of human capital currently used in empirical growth research, including adult literacy rates, school enrollment ratios, and years of schooling embodied in the labor force. Based on human capital theory, it is shown that these measures proxy only poorly for the stock of human capital. The simple use of the most common proxy, average years of schooling of the working-age population, is found to misspecify the relationship between education and the stock of human capital because it implicitly assumes constant returns to each year of education in the human capital production function and uniform quality of the education systems. The specification of human capital is then extended to allow for decreasing returns to education and for differences in the quality of a year of schooling. Applying this improved measure of the stock of human capital in a cross-country development-accounting framework reveals that the different specifications of the human capital variable can lead to diverging conclusions on the development effects of human capital. When adjusted for differences in schooling quality, cross-country differences in human capital account for about half of the worldwide dispersion of levels of economic development and for virtually all of the development differences across OECD countries. The results favor the human-capital-augmented neoclassical growth model as an explanation of the cross-country dispersion in development levels. The chapter concludes with an assessment of the potential benefits of high-quality education for different objective areas of economic policy.

Given the importance of the quality of schooling for economic development, the remainder of the study analyzes the determinants of schooling quality. Chapter 3 gathers evidence on the empirical link between schooling expenditure and measures of student performance. First, a review of the literature on within-country cross-section estimates of education production functions shows that at the expenditure levels currently reached in developed countries, increased educational expenditure does not seem to have positive effects on the quality of schooling. This result holds even after accounting for potential reverse causality from student performance to available resources. Second, the cross-country evidence also shows that differences in the amount of schooling resources used cannot explain the large international differences in student performance. Third, new within-country time-series evidence on the relationship between schooling expenditure and schooling quality is presented. Real changes in schooling expenditure per student over time are calculated using price deflators for schooling derived on the basis of Baumol's (1967) cost-disease model, and changes in average schooling quality over time are calculated by combining U.S. time-series student performance evidence with cross-country student performance evidence at different points in time. The evidence reveals that substantial increases in the amount of schooling resources per student over the past 15 to 25 years have not lead to increased schooling quality in most OECD countries and in selected East Asian countries. In sum, neither the within-country cross-section evidence nor the international cross-section evidence nor the within-country time-series evidence suggests that resource endowment is a major determinant of schooling quality.

To shed light on the missing empirical input-output relationship in schooling, Chapter 4 develops a model of the schooling system, elaborating the central role of institutions and incentives. In the education process, a network of principal-agent relationships exists, relationships which entail conflicts between the multifarious interests of different actors and serious problems of monitoring due to informational advantages of self-interested agents. This creates adverse incentives and leeway for the agents to act opportunistically, leading to inefficiencies in resource utilization. By setting the incentives faced by the actors in educational production, institutions determine the relative costs and benefits of different behaviors. Based on Bishop's (1998) economic theory of educational production in schools, the chapter develops a model of the impact of different institutional settings on the incentives which the different actors have. Students, who are the agents in the presented model, choose the level of learning effort which maximizes their net benefits, while the government as the principal in this model chooses the level of educational spending which maximizes its net benefits. The model predicts that several institutions have a positive impact on the behavior of students and the government by tilting their incentives in favor of increased student performance, resulting in superior schooling quality. Among these institutions are central examinations, school autonomy in process and personnel-management decisions, an intermediate level of administrative decision-making, teachers' influence on teaching methods, teachers' scrutiny of their students' educational achievement, parental influence on the education process, and competition from private schools. In contrast, school autonomy in standard-setting, performance-control, and budgetary decisions, teachers' influence on their salary levels and on the size of their work load, and political power of teacher unions have a negative impact on the quality produced in the schooling system by setting detrimental incentives.

Chapter 5 estimates empirically the effects of institutions on schooling quality predicted by this model. Drawing on the Third International Mathematics and Science Study (TIMSS), a student-level data set is constructed for more than 260,000 students from 39 countries. This new data set combines students' test score performance with data on student-specific family and schooling background, including resource provision in the respective classroom and the institutional settings governing the education process. A microeconometric estimation of student-level education production functions reveals strong positive family-background effects on student performance, while different categories of resource inputs have no clear positive impact. Many institutional features show strong and significant effects on schooling quality. Positive effects on students' educational performance stem from centralized examinations and control mechanisms, school autonomy in personnel and process decisions, competition from private educational institutions, scrutiny of achievement, and teacher influence on teaching methods. A large influence of teacher unions on curriculum scope is found to have negative effects on student performance. Estimation of country-level education production functions reveals that sparsely specified models can explain three-quarters of the international variation in mathematics achievement and two-thirds of the international variation in science achievement when institutional effects are taken into account, whereas previous studies which constrained themselves to family and resource effects found only up to one-quarter of explained variation. The findings imply that the large differences in schooling quality, as measured by students' performance in cognitive achievement tests, which exist across countries are not caused by differences in schooling resources, but are mainly determined by differences in educational institutions.

Chapter 6 concludes the study by drawing policy implications from the findings. The results underscore that schooling policy is growth policy, and that it is the quality of schooling rather than the quantity of schooling which matters for economic performance, especially in developed countries. Increasing the resources spent on education within the present schooling systems will not ensure higher educational quality. Instead, educational politicians and administrators have to be aware of the incentives which govern the behavior of all actors in the schooling sector. School autonomy in operational areas is beneficial to a high level of schooling quality, at least as long as schools are made accountable for their performance. Central examinations, external standard setting, and external evaluation can help to focus their incentives on schooling quality. Likewise, it is vital to bring teachers' incentives in line with students' educational performance. Introducing possibilities of choice between schools exposes the schooling system to competition and helps in assuring a high quality of schooling.

2 The Quality of Human Capital and Economic Development

2.1 The Measurement of Human Capital in Growth Empirics

The fundamental question of economic development, namely why some countries are so rich and others are so poor, has occupied the economics profession throughout its existence. The economists' theoretical answer to this question is straightforward: Differences in income levels stem from differences in the amount of factor inputs used in production and from differences in the productivity of the use of these inputs. It is then an empirical question to what extent differences in the accumulation of inputs or differences in total factor productivity contribute to the international variation of per capita income.

Investing in human capital is one way of accumulating inputs. The acquisition of knowledge and skills is an investment in the sense that people forego consumption for it in order to increase future income. Because workers have invested in themselves to different extents through prior education, one hour of labor input does not yield the same output across all workers. Education increases future labor productivity and future income and can thus be seen as an investment in human capital, which is then embodied in the human being. As demonstrated by the citation in Section 1.1, early awareness of this idea of education as an investment in human capital can be traced at least as far back as Adam Smith. However, it was not before the second half of the twentieth century that economists such as Theodore W. Schultz, Gary S. Becker, and Jacob Mincer developed a thorough theory of human capital.

This chapter[2] reviews attempts to derive a measure of the stock of human capital in empirical work and provides some extensions, focusing on education as the central means to accumulate human capital. In his review article of the new empirical evidence in the economics of growth, Temple (1999a: 139) points out that "[t]he literature uses somewhat dubious proxies for aggregate human capital." There are two types of measurement errors in the measurement of any variable which can lead to unsatisfactory proxies. Data recording errors con-

---

2   An earlier version of this chapter was circulated as Kiel Working Paper 1007 (Wößmann 2000b).

stitute one reason for mismeasurement. But even when the data is perfectly recorded, the measured variable may still be a poor measure of the true variable. The present study focuses on this second type of measurement errors due to using an imperfect proxy for the true stock of human capital.

The main reason for the use of poor proxies of the stock of human capital is that in most empirical growth studies, the choice of the human capital measure is hardly reflected upon and depends very much on data availability. Instead of being based on an ad hoc choice, however, the search for a measure of the stock of human capital should be led by economic theory. Human capital theory offers a specification of the human capital function which represents the stock of human capital, expressed in money units, as a function of the observed level of education, expressed in units of time. Therefore, the task of deriving a viable measure of the stock of human capital embodied in the labor force is mainly a task of correctly specifying the form of the relationship between education and human capital. The objective of this chapter is to improve on the specification of the human capital measure, to expose the potentially huge specification errors in the human capital measures used in applied work, and to show the central role which the quality of schooling plays in economic development.

Section 2.2.1 reviews the measures of the stock of human capital used in the literature from early growth accounting to the cross-country growth regressions of the 1990s. These measures include education-augmented labor input, adult literacy rates, school enrollment ratios, and average years of schooling of the working-age population, which is currently the human capital proxy most commonly employed in growth empirics.

Human capital theory can be used to show that the stock of human capital is misspecified by the simple use of the proxy "average years of schooling" because this includes an incorrect specification of the functional form of the education-human capital relationship (Section 2.2.2). Therefore, some extensions of the specification of human capital are presented which yield measures which accord to human capital theory. A first extension, proposed by Bils and Klenow (2000), is to account for decreasing returns to investment in education by combining years of education with rates of return to education in a Mincer specification of the function linking education to human capital. Further extensions, based on Gundlach et al. (2002), try to account for cross-country differences in the quality of education, especially through the inclusion of a cognitive-skill index from Hanushek and Kimko (2000) into the human capital function. Section 2.2.3 compares the various proposed specifications empirically.

With the improvements in the measure of the stock of human capital, the research question of effects of human capital on economic development can be addressed in a development accounting analysis (Section 2.3). The results reveal that the differences in the specifications of the human capital variable have a large impact on the share of the international variation in levels of economic development attributed to cross-country differences in accumulated human capital. The misspecification of the human capital function leads to a severe understatement of the development impact of human capital. Human capital, when adjusted for the quality of schooling, accounts for about half of the dispersion in income levels in the world and for nearly the whole income dispersion across OECD countries. Hence, once it is acknowledged that the quality of schooling constitutes a central aspect of the investment in human capital, this evidence corroborates Becker's ([1964]1993: 12) contention that "few if any countries have achieved a sustained period of economic development without having invested substantial amounts in their labor force."

The specification error introduced by disregarding differences in educational quality is found to be far greater than the recording errors in the data on educational quantity which have been stressed recently in studies by Krueger and Lindahl (2001) and de la Fuente and Doménech (2000). With regard to theories of the international dispersion in levels of economic development, my results favor a human-capital-augmented neoclassical growth model where the stock of human capital has *level* effects due to its accumulation as a factor input, relative to those models of endogenous growth in which the stock of human capital has *growth* effects because it facilitates technical progress.

Section 2.4 concludes the chapter by expanding the focus to further potential benefits of high-quality education in addition to its impact on long-run economic growth and development. It is suggested that ensuring a high quality of education might render positive impacts in the areas of unemployment, distribution, and worldwide locational competition.

2.2   The Specification of the Stock of Human Capital

2.2.1   A Review of Human Capital Specification in Growth Research

2.2.1.1   *Education-Augmented Labor Input in Early Growth Accounting*

The only factor inputs which were accounted for in the earliest growth accounting studies—beginning with Tinbergen (1942)[3]—were physical capital and la-

---

3   Tinbergen's (1942) article deserves credit for being the first to divide the sources of economic growth between investment and productivity (Griliches 1996; Jorgenson 1995). However, neither Solow in his famous 1957 paper nor anybody else in the

bor. Thus, the total labor force, which is the linear sum of all workers, was the only measure of input embodied in human beings, implying the assumption that workers are homogeneous. Schultz (1961: 3) dismissed this notion as patently wrong: "Counting individuals who can and want to work and treating such a count as a measure of the quantity of an economic factor is no more meaningful than it would be to count the number of all manner of machines to determine their economic importance either as a stock of capital or as a flow of productive services." In his pioneering growth-accounting work which used only physical capital and labor as factor inputs, Solow (1957: 317, footnote 8) was also already aware of the importance of skill accumulation as a form of capital formation, conceding in passing that "a lot of what appears as shifts in the production function must represent improvement in the quality of the labor input, and therefore a result of real capital formation of an important kind."

Subsequent growth-accounting studies tried to account for the heterogeneity of labor by considering differences in the quality of labor input. Labor input was augmented by considering differences across workers with respect to several categories of characteristics, including education in addition to gender, age, and occupational characteristics. In that sense, human capital specification has its predecessors in early growth accounting. Denison (1967) augmented labor input to reflect differences in the quality of labor by adjusting total employment for hours worked, age-sex composition, and levels of education. The effect of differences in the gender, age, and educational composition of hours worked upon the average quality of labor was estimated by the use of earnings weights. Assuming that wage differences reflect differences in the productivity of labor, differences in the wages earned by different groups of the labor force made it possible to measure differences in their human capital. By using data on the distribution of the labor force across worker categories and weighting each category by its relative average wages, an aggregate labor quality index was constructed which reflected differences in the labor force with respect to the categories, weighted by market returns.

Denison (1967) argued that not the whole wage differential by level of education represents differences which are due to differences in education, because some of the wage differentials may represent rewards for intelligence, family background, or credentialism. Therefore, he did not use average wages directly as educational weights, but instead made the ad hoc assumption that only three-fifths of the reported wage differentials between the group with eight years of education and each other group represents wage differences due to differences in education as distinguished from other associated characteristics. As education

---

emerging growth-accounting literature at that time seems to have been aware of Tinbergen's paper, which was published in German in *Weltwirtschaftliches Archiv*.

weights, Deninson and many subsequent studies used the ensuing compressed income differentials. Denison (1967) also made some allowance for differences in days of schooling per year.

Jorgenson and co-authors elaborated on this specification of education-augmented labor input in numerous contributions, many of which are collected in Jorgenson (1995). After constructing constant quality indices of investment goods and of labor inputs, where the latter was based on wage differences between workers with different levels of educational attainment, Jorgenson and Griliches (1967) found that the role of residual total factor productivity in postwar U.S. economic growth was negligible once factor inputs were accurately accounted for. In later research (see especially Jorgenson et al. 1987), the analysis was disaggregated to the level of individual industries and the labor input was broken down not only by gender, age, and education, but also by such characteristics as employment status and occupational group. This led to a myriad of labor input categories which were then aggregated on the basis of wage weights to yield a constant quality measure of overall labor input.

The detailed data required for these calculations are only available in a few advanced countries. Since most of the early growth-accounting literature was interested mainly in within-country intertemporal comparisons of indices of the quality of labor, difficulties in cross-country comparisons, stemming mainly from informational deficiencies and measurement differences, were not addressed. Therefore, measures of total labor input adjusted for quality differences, and especially education-augmented labor input, are available only for very few countries.[4]

2.2.1.2 Adult Literacy Rates

The availability of national accounts data for a large number of countries and years in the Penn World Table compiled by Summers and Heston (1988, 1991) has initiated a huge literature of cross-country growth regressions, which from the outset considered the inclusion of a measure of human capital. The early contributions to the literature specified the stock of human capital in the labor force by proxies such as adult literacy rates and school enrollment ratios. In most studies, this choice of specification reflects ease of data availability and a broad coverage of countries by the available data (usually coming from UNESCO, *Statistical Yearbooks*) rather than suitability for the theoretical concept at hand. It

---

[4]   Gundlach (1994) computes the relative stocks of human capital for a limited sample of developing countries relative to the United States in 1980 by using the method suggested by Krueger (1968). This method is based on a cross classification of the populations by years of schooling, age, sex, and place of residence and the marginal products of each population group from the United States as a reference country.

soon became apparent that the specification by these proxies does not yield very satisfactory measures of the stock of human capital available in production.

Studies such as Azariadis and Drazen (1990) and Romer (1990b) use the adult literacy rate as a human capital proxy. Literacy is commonly defined as the ability to read and write, with understanding, a simple statement related to one's daily life. The adult literacy rate then measures the number of adult literates (e.g., in the population aged 15 years and over) as a percentage of the population in the corresponding age-group:

$$(2.1) \quad l = \frac{M_A}{P_A},$$

where l is the adult literacy rate, M_A is the number of literates in the adult population, and P_A is the total adult population.

There has been some discussion about the international comparability of the thus defined variable because it is not easily applied systematically, but adult literacy rates certainly reflect a component of the relevant stock of human capital. However, they miss out most of the investments made in human capital because they only reflect the very first part of these investments. Any educational investment which occurs on top of the acquisition of basic literacy, e.g., the acquisition of numeracy, of logical and analytical reasoning, and of scientific and technical knowledge, is neglected in this measure. Hence, using adult literacy rates as a proxy for the stock of human capital implicitly accepts the assumption that none of these additional investments directly adds to the productivity of the labor force. Therefore, adult literacy rates can only stand for a minor part of the total stock of human capital.[5]

2.2.1.3 School Enrollment Ratios

School enrollment ratios, a further human capital proxy used in the literature, measure the number of students enrolled at a grade level relative to the total population of the corresponding age-group:

$$(2.2) \quad e_g = \frac{E_g}{P_g},$$

where e_g is the enrollment ratio at grade level g, E_g is the enrollment (the number of students enrolled) at grade level g, and P_g is the total population of the age-

---

5   Accordingly, adult illiteracy rates $(1-l)$ have later been used in the construction of school attainment measures to proxy for the percentage of the population without any schooling (Section 2.2.1.4).

group that national regulations or custom dictate would be enrolled at grade level g.[6] These enrollment ratios have been used to proxy for human capital in the seminal studies of Barro (1991) and Mankiw et al. (1992)[7] and in the sensitivity study by Levine and Renelt (1992), among many others.

Although some researchers interpret enrollment ratios as proxies for human capital stocks, they may be a poor measure of the stock of human capital available for current production. Enrollment ratios are flow variables, and the children currently enrolled in schools are by definition not yet a part of the labor force, so that the education they are currently acquiring cannot yet be used in production. Current school enrollment ratios, therefore, do not necessarily have an immediate and stable relationship to the stock of human capital embodied in the current productive labor force of a country. The accumulated stock of human capital depends indirectly on lagged values of school enrollment ratios, where the time lag between schooling and future additions to the human capital stock depends on the ultimate length of the education phase and may be quite long.

Enrollment ratios may thus be seen as proxies of the flow of human capital investment. However, the stock of human capital is changed by the net additions to the labor force, which are determined by the difference between the human capital embodied in the labor force entrants and the human capital embodied in those who retire from the labor force that year. Therefore, enrollment ratios may also proxy only poorly for the relevant flows. First, they do not measure the human capital embodied in the entrants into the labor force that year, but the human capital acquired by current students who might enter the labor force at some time in the future. Second, the education of current students may not at all translate into additions to the human capital stock embodied in the labor force because graduates may not participate in the labor force and because part of current enrollment may be wasted due to grade repetition and dropping out. Third, net investment flows would have to take account of the human capital content of the workers who are retiring from the labor force that year. In sum, enrollment ratios may turn out to be a bad proxy for changes in the human capital stock, especially during periods of rapid educational and demographic transition (Hanushek and Kimko 2000).[8]

---

6   Gross enrollment ratios take the total number of students enrolled at the grade level as the numerator in equation (2.2), while net enrollment ratios take only those students enrolled at the grade level who belong to the corresponding age-group P_g.

7   Mankiw et al. (1992) use the proportion of the working-age population enrolled in secondary schools as their proxy, obtained by multiplying secondary school enrollment ratios by the fraction of the working-age population which is of school age.

8   See Pritchett (2001) for an illustration why enrollment ratios can—and in reality seem to—be *negatively* correlated with true accumulation rates of human capital; see

2.2.1.4 Levels of Educational Attainment and Average Years of Schooling

Both adult literacy rates and school enrollment ratios seem to have major deficiencies as proxies for the concept of human capital highlighted in theoretical models. Since the inadequacies of these proxies have motivated improvements in the specification of the human capital stock, it cannot be recommended to use either of them as a human capital measure. When looking for a measure of the stock of human capital that is used in the production of output, it seems sensible to quantify the accumulated educational investment embodied in the current labor force. Therefore, several studies have tried to construct data on the highest level of educational attainment of workers in order to quantify the average years of schooling in the labor force. Educational attainment is clearly a stock variable, and it takes into account the total amount of formal education received by the labor force. So average years of schooling have by now become the most popular and most commonly used specification of the stock of human capital in the literature, including studies such as Barro and Sala-i-Martin (1995), Barro (1997, 1999), Benhabib and Spiegel (1994), Gundlach (1995), Islam (1995), Krueger and Lindahl (2001), O'Neill (1995), and Temple (1999b).[9]

Three main methods have been used in the construction of data sets on years of educational attainment in the labor force, each building in one way or another on the data on enrollment ratios discussed previously. The three methods are the projection method, the perpetual inventory method, and the attainment census method.

Projection Method

The first method to get from school enrollment ratios to average years of schooling is the projection method, which is the simplest and most ad hoc method. The method, implemented by Kyriacou (1991), builds on information on average years of schooling in the labor force available for the mid-1970s from Psacharopoulos and Arriagada (1986) based on direct census evidence of workers' attainment levels (see below). Data on lagged enrollment ratios are then used to project (superscript *PRO*) average years of schooling in the labor force, s, for further countries and years, T:

---

also Gemmell (1996) for a critique of the use of enrollment ratios as human capital measures.

[9] For an application which uses data on levels of educational attainment directly, see Temple (2001a).

(2.3) $s_T^{PRO} = \alpha_0 + \alpha_1 e_{pri,T-15} + \alpha_2 e_{sec,T-5} + \alpha_3 e_{hig,T-5}$,

where $e_{a,t}$ is the enrollment ratio at attainment level a (primary *pri*, secondary *sec*, and higher *hig*) at time t, and the α's are estimated in a regression of the value of the attainment-data based years of schooling in the mid-1970s (i.e., between 1974 and 1977) on prior enrollment rates:

(2.4) $s_{1975}^{ATT} = \alpha_0 + \alpha_1 e_{pri,1960} + \alpha_2 e_{sec,1970} + \alpha_3 e_{hig,1970} + \varepsilon$,

where ε is an error term.[10]

Kyriacou (1991) finds that this relationship is rather strong across the 42 countries in the mid-1970s for which the respective data are available, with an R^2 of 0.82. For the projection, it has to be assumed that the relationship between average years of schooling in the labor force and lagged enrollment ratios is stable over time and across countries.

Perpetual Inventory Method

The second method to get from school enrollment to years of schooling is the perpetual inventory method, which was used by Lau et al. (1991) and refined by Nehru et al. (1995). If sufficiently long data series on school enrollment ratios are available, the perpetual inventory method (superscript *PIM*) can be used to accumulate the total number of years of schooling, S, embodied in the labor force at year T by

(2.5) $S^{PIM} = \sum_{t=T-A_{high}+D_0}^{T-A_{low}+D_0} \sum_g E_{g,t+g-1}(1 - r_g - d)p_{g,t+g-1}$,

where $E_{g,t}$ is total (gross) enrollment at grade level g at time t as in equation (2.2), A_{high} is the highest possible age of a person in the labor force, A_{low} is the lowest possible age of a person in the labor force, D_0 is the age at which children enter school (typically six), r_g is the ratio of repeaters to enrollments in grade g (assumed to be constant across time), d is the drop-out rate (assumed to be constant across time and grades), and $p_{g,t}$ is the probability that an enrollee at grade g at time t will survive until the year T.[11] By assuming $A_{low} = 15$ and $A_{high} = 64$, the studies count all persons between age 15 and 64 inclusive as con-

---

[10]   Kyriacou (1991) does not give an explicit rationale for the lag structure chosen between years of schooling and enrollment rates, or specifically for choosing the same lag for the enrollment ratios at the secondary and higher level, but only reports that he heuristically found a strong relationship of the form of equation (2.4).

[11]   Note that the perpetual inventory formula given in Nehru et al. (1995) is erroneous.

stituting the labor force. The probability of survival, $p_{g,t}$, is calculated on the basis of age-specific mortality rates in each year, which implicitly assumes that the mortality rate is independent of the level of schooling attained. The total number of years of schooling S can then be normalized by the population at working age P_w to obtain the average years of schooling of the working-age population, s:

$$(2.6) \quad s^{PIM} = \frac{S^{PIM}}{P_w}.$$

Much of the data on enrollment rates, repeater rates, age-specific mortality rates, and drop-out rates necessary to implement the calculation on the basis of the perpetual inventory method are not available and have, therefore, been "statistically manufactured"; e.g., enrollment ratios and repeater rates have to be extrapolated backwards, and data gaps have to be closed by interpolations. Both problems are especially severe in the case of tertiary education. Age-specific survival rates have been constructed for a "representative" country in each world region only.

Attainment Census Method

The third method applied in the construction of attainment data sets is to use direct measures of levels of educational attainment from surveys and censuses. Psacharopoulos and Arriagada (1986) collected information on the educational composition of the labor force from national census publications for six levels of educational attainment, a: no schooling, incomplete primary, complete primary, incomplete secondary, complete secondary, and higher. Based on these direct data on attainment levels (superscript *ATT*), average years of schooling, s, in the labor force can be calculated as

$$(2.7) \quad s^{ATT} = \sum_a \left[n_a \sum_{j=1}^{a} D_j \right],$$

where n_a is the fraction of workers in the labor force for whom attainment level a is the highest level attained ($n_a = N_a / L$, with N_a as the number of workers for whom a is the highest level attained and L as the labor force) and D_a is the duration in years of the ath level of schooling.[12] For fractions of workers in the

---

[12] Several studies use years of schooling at the different levels separately (e.g., Barro and Sala-i-Martin 1995; Barro 1997). This seems problematic since, e.g., years of primary schooling can only increase up to universal coverage. The variation across countries with basically universal coverage is mainly caused by cross-country differ-

labor force who have achieved an attainment level only incompletely, half the duration of the corresponding level is attributed. The main shortcoming of the data set of Psacharopoulos and Arriagada (1986) is that the year of observation varies greatly across the countries covered, with most of the countries providing only one observation, so that a cross-country analysis is hard to obtain.

Barro and Lee (1993) apply basically the same methodology based on census and survey data on educational attainment levels, but they are able to greatly extend the coverage of countries and years. The greater coverage is partly achieved through focusing on the adult population as a substitute for the labor force (they use $n_a = N_a / P_A$, with P_A as the total adult population), so that their s^{ATT} represents average years of schooling in the working-age population, i.e., the population aged 25 (or 15) years and over, instead of the actual labor force. Barro and Lee's (1993) attainment levels are based on UNESCO's International Standard Classification of Education (ISCED) and are: no schooling, incomplete first level, complete first level, entered first cycle of second level, entered second cycle of second level, and entered higher level.

Barro and Lee (1993) also use data on adult illiteracy rates, $(1-l)$, from equation (2.1), to estimate the fraction of the working-age population with no schooling in those instances where direct data from censuses or surveys is not available. Since they observe a high correlation between the no-schooling fraction n_0 and adult illiteracy rates $(1-l)$—the correlation coefficient is 0.95 for the 158 observations where both data are available—they estimate missing values of the fraction of the working-age population with no schooling n_0 at year T for countries which report both a value for the no-schooling fraction n_0 and a value for adult illiteracy, $1-l$, in another year, $T\pm t$, based on

$$(2.8) \qquad n_{0,T} = (1 - l_T)\frac{n_{0,T\pm t}}{(1 - l_{T\pm t})}.$$

When measured at four broad attainment levels (no schooling, first, second, and higher level), 40 percent of all possible data cells (for a total of 129 countries at six points in time) are filled out by available census or survey data, and an additional 16 percent of the cells are filled out by using adult illiteracy rates.

Barro and Lee (1993) go on to estimate the missing observations in their data set based on data on school enrollment ratios. They use the perpetual inventory method (see above), starting with directly observed data points as benchmark stocks and estimating changes from these benchmarks on the basis of school

---

ences in the duration of the primary level D_{pri}, which will depend primarily on an education system's classification of different levels. Therefore, it is not quite clear what, e.g., estimated coefficients on level-specific years of schooling in a growth regression really show.

enrollment ratios and data on population by age to estimate survival rates. In Barro and Lee (1993), repeater ratios, r, and drop-out rates, d, were neglected in the estimation (equation (2.5)), while the revised version of the data set in Barro and Lee (1996) takes account of them. Barro and Lee (2001) additionally account for variations in the duration, D_a, of schooling levels over time within a country.

De la Fuente and Doménech (2000) point out that there are still a lot of data recording and classification errors in the available data sets, giving rise to severe differences in country rankings across data sets and to implausible jumps and breaks in the time-series patterns. They construct a revised version of the Barro and Lee (1996) data set for OECD countries, relying on direct attainment data and using interpolation and backward projection instead of the perpetual inventory method with enrollment data to fill in missing observations. They collect additional attainment data from national sources, reinterpret some of the data when data points seem unreasonable, and choose the figure which they deem most plausible when different estimates are available. Their treatment of data inconsistencies includes a fair amount of subjective guesswork, so that their heuristic method falls short of an "ideal" scientific methodology. Nevertheless, their revised data set may give an indication of the extent to which previous data sets are plagued with data recording errors.

Evaluation of the Construction Methods of Data Sets on Years of Schooling

Before coming to a fundamental critique of the specification of human capital by years of schooling in Section 2.2.2.1, some further criticism of the methods used to construct years-of-schooling data sets and of their implementation is warranted. The first method (*projection method*) is based on the assumption that the relationship between average years of schooling in the labor force and lagged enrollment ratios is a stable one. The available data on school attainment in the labor force from censuses and on school enrollment ratios gives ample evidence that this relationship varies over time and across countries, leaving the assumption erroneous and the projections unreliable. In addition to the limited availability of the data necessary to implement the second method (*plain perpetual inventory method*), another severe shortcoming is its lack of benchmarking against the available census data on educational attainment. By disregarding the only direct information available on the variable of interest, it is inferior to the third method which combines the perpetual inventory method with census information.

Given these shortcomings of the first two methods, the *attainment census method* seems to be the most elaborate one. However, even the Barro and Lee data set has some measurement weaknesses. It represents average years of schooling in the adult population, but not in the labor force. It, therefore, includes adults who are not labor force participants and it may exclude some of the members of the labor force (Gemmell 1996). The step from reported attainment levels to average years of schooling includes mismeasurement because it is only known whether a person has started and/or completed any given level. For people not completing a level, it is simply assumed that they stayed on for half the years required for the full cycle. For higher education, Barro and Lee (1993) simply assume a duration D_{hig} of four years for all countries. Furthermore, the original censuses and surveys often use varying definitions for the variables collected (Behrman and Rosenzweig 1994).

A direct data-recording problem of the Barro and Lee (1993) data set is the poor coverage of the basic data. While 77 of the 129 countries in their data set have three or more census or survey observations since 1945, only nine countries have more than four observations of the 9 potential data points from 1945 to 1985, and only three countries more than five. For any given five-year period since 1960, the number of countries for which census or survey data are available ranges from a minimum of 14 countries (in the period surrounding 1985) to a maximum of 78 (1980) out of the 129 countries in the data set. To give an example from the de la Fuente and Doménech (2000) data set, only 40 (or 27 percent) of the 147 observations (21 countries times 7 points in time) on secondary attainment in the data set are original observations taken directly from censuses or surveys, while the rest is interpolated in one way or the other. It would be reasonable to conclude that such a coverage does not provide a sensible basis for panel estimation. Accordingly, Krueger and Lindahl (2001) substantiate severe data measurement errors in panel data on average years of schooling. Hence, de la Fuente and Doménech's (2000: 12) conclusion is correct that "a fair amount of detailed work remains to be done before we can say with some confidence that we have a reliable and detailed picture of worldwide educational achievement levels or their evolution over time." By contrast, basically all observations in the OECD sample for 1990 are direct census or survey observations, allowing for a reasonable data quality at least for this sample at this specific point in time.

2.2.2   Human Capital Specification: A Critique and Two Extensions

2.2.2.1 *Critique of Schooling Years as a Specification of Human Capital*

Apart from the problems of *recording* average years of schooling in the labor force, there are more fundamental problems with the *specification* of the stock of human capital by average years of schooling (Mulligan and Sala-i-Martin 2000).

Although it is the most commonly employed measure, using the unweighted sum of schooling years linearly as a measure of the stock of human capital lacks a sound theoretical foundation. There are two major criticisms which render years of schooling a poor proxy for the human capital stock. First, one year of schooling does not raise the human capital stock by an equal amount regardless of whether it is a person's first or seventeenth year of schooling. Second, one year of schooling does not raise the human capital stock by an equal amount regardless of the quality of the education system in which it has taken place.[13]

As for the first point, specifying human capital by average years of schooling implicitly gives the same weight to any year of schooling acquired by a person. That is, productivity differentials among workers are assumed to be proportional to their years of schooling. This disregards the findings of a whole microeconometric literature on wage rate differentials which shows that there are decreasing returns to schooling (Psacharopoulos 1994). Therefore, a year of schooling should be weighted differently depending on how many years of schooling a person has already accumulated (Section 2.2.2.2).

As for the second criticism, using years of schooling as a human capital measure gives the same weight to a year of schooling in any schooling system at any time; i.e., it is assumed to deliver the same increase in skills regardless of the efficiency of the schooling system, of the quality of teaching, of the educational infrastructure, or of the curriculum. In cross-country work, a year of schooling in, say, Papua New Guinea is assumed to create the same increase in productive human capital as a year of schooling in, say, the Netherlands. Instead, a year of schooling should be weighted differently depending on the quality of the education system in which it has taken place (Section 2.2.2.3). In Sections 2.2.2.2 and 2.2.2.3, I propose specifications of the human capital stock which deal with these two criticisms.

2.2.2.2 The Mincer Specification and Decreasing Returns to Education

Mincer's Log-Linear Specification of the Human Capital Earnings Function

The stock of human capital embodied in the labor force is a variable expressed in money units. To transform a measure of education measured in units of time into the stock of human capital expressed in units of money, each year of schooling should be weighted by the earnings return it generates in the labor market. Human capital theory offers a straightforward specification of the functional

---

[13] Additionally, using average years of schooling assumes perfect substitutability of workers across attainment levels and a constant elasticity of substitution across subgroups of workers at any time and place (Mulligan and Sala-i-Martin 2000).

form of this relationship between education and the stock of human capital, the human capital earnings function (Mincer 1974; Chiswick 1998). Annual earnings, W, after t years of schooling are equal to annual earnings with $t-1$ years of schooling plus the return on the investment into the additional year of schooling, which is given by the cost, C, of the investment times the rate of return, r, on that investment:

(2.9)' $W_t = W_{t-1} + r_i C_t$.

Assuming that the total cost, C, to an individual of investing into an additional year of schooling lies in the earnings which he or she foregoes during that year, ($C_t = W_{t-1}$), this equation can be expressed as

(2.9)" $W_t = (1 + r_t)W_{t-1}$.

By mathematical induction, it follows that earnings after s years of schooling are given by

(2.9)''' $W_s = W_0 \prod_{t=1}^{s}(1 + r_t)$.

Taking natural logarithms and applying the approximation that, for small values of r, $\ln(1+r) \approx r$, yields

(2.9)'''' $\ln W_s = \ln W_0 + \sum_{t=1}^{s} r_t$.

For $r = r_t$ being constant across levels of schooling, this is equal to

(2.9) $\ln W_s = \ln W_0 + rs$.

Thereby, the relationship in equation (2.9)' between earnings and investments in education measured in money units is converted into the relationship in equation (2.9) between the natural logarithm of earnings and investments in education measured in time units. That is, the logarithm of individuals' earnings is a linear function of their years of schooling. This log-linear formulation suggests that each additional year of schooling raises earnings by r percent.

Mincer (1974) estimated the rate of return to education, r, for a cross section of workers as the regression coefficient on years of schooling in an earnings function like (2.9), controlling for work experience of the individuals. A large microeconometric literature has confirmed that this log-linear specification gives the best fit to the data (Card 1999; Krueger and Lindahl 2001). To be able to interpret the schooling coefficient in an earnings function as the rate of return to education, however, the assumption must hold that total costs of investment in the tth year of schooling, C_t, are equal to foregone earnings, W_{t-1}. If the opportunity cost of schooling were a full year's earnings, this would imply that there are no direct costs such as tuition, school fees, books, and other school supplies. Furthermore, the regression coefficient in the earnings function method is a biased measure of the rate of return if age-earnings profiles are not constant for different levels of education.

Therefore, rates of return estimated by the elaborate discounting method, which can account both for the total costs of schooling and for variable age-earnings profiles, are superior to estimates based on the earnings function method. The elaborate discounting method consists in calculating the discount rate, r, which equates the stream of costs of education to the stream of benefits from education:

$$(2.10) \quad \sum_{t=1}^{s}(C_{high,t} + W_{low,t})(1+r)^t = \sum_{t=s+1}^{A_{high}}(W_{high,t} - W_{low,t})(1+r)^{-t},$$

where C_{high} is the resource cost of schooling incurred to achieve a higher level, *high*, from a lower level, *low*, W_{low} is the foregone earnings of the student while studying, $(W_{high} - W_{low})$ is the earnings differential between a person with a higher level of education and a person with a lower level of education, s is years of schooling, and A_{high} is the highest possible working age.

By counting both private and public educational expenditures as the cost of schooling, C, the elaborate discounting method is able to estimate social rates of return to education. Social—as opposed to private—rates of return are the relevant choice when dealing with questions from a society's point of view. The estimated rates of return are "narrow-social," taking account of the full cost of education to the society (including public expenditure) while disregarding any potential external benefits. Recent studies by Heckman and Klenow (1997), Acemoglu and Angrist (2000), and Ciccone and Peri (2000) show that there is little evidence in favor of such external returns to education.[14]

As first suggested by Bils and Klenow (2000), the micro evidence derived from the log-linear Mincer formulation can be used to specify the aggregate human capital stock in macro studies as

$$(2.11) \quad H^M = e^{\phi(s)}L \quad \Leftrightarrow \quad h^M = e^{\phi(s)},$$

---

[14] Note that if there were signaling effects in the private rate of return, the social rate of return might be overstated (Weiss 1995). See Temple (2001b) for a discussion of the issues involved.

where H^M is the stock of human capital based on the Mincer specification, L is labor as measured by the number of workers,[15] and $h \equiv H/L$ is the stock of human capital per worker. The function $\phi(s)$ reflects the efficiency of a unit of labor with s years of schooling relative to one with no schooling. With $\phi(s) = 0$, the specification melts down to one with undifferentiated labor as in the earliest growth-accounting studies (Section 2.2.1.1). Furthermore, the derivative of this function should equal the rate of return to education as estimated in the labor literature, so that $\phi(s) = r$. In the simplest specification, this would imply

$$(2.12) \quad \phi(s) = rs.$$

Thereby, a human capital measure can be constructed for every country by combining data on years of schooling with rates of return estimated in micro labor studies which weight each year of schooling by its market return.[16] This approach of specifying human capital stocks based on the Mincer regression has already been used in several studies, including Bils and Klenow (2000), Klenow and Rodríguez-Clare (1997b), Hall and Jones (1999), and Jovanovic and Rob (1999).[17] Note that this approach is similar to weighting worker categories by relative wage rates as applied by the growth-accounting literature in the construction of education-augmented labor input (Section 2.2.1.1).

Decreasing Returns to Education

In addition to taking account of the log-linear relationship between earnings and schooling, this specification can also be used to include decreasing returns to education. While the original work by Mincer entered schooling linearly over the whole range of schooling years, international evidence by Psacharopoulos (1994) suggests that rates of return to education are decreasing with the acquisition of additional schooling. Therefore, one year of schooling should be weighted differently depending on whether it is undertaken by a student in primary school,

---

[15]   Note that in this work, no adjustment is made for differences in hours worked, as was done in the early growth-accounting studies (Section 2.2.1.1).

[16]   In addition to rates of return to each year of education, Bils and Klenow (2000) introduce an influence of teachers' education, measured by the stock of human capital 25 years earlier, into their measure of human capital. However, it is not clear why teachers' education should have an influence on the level of human capital apart from the one reflected in the returns to education. They also include a wage effect of experience, measured by age less years of schooling less 6, whereas my study focuses on human capital accumulated through education.

[17]   Topel (1999) and Krueger and Lindahl (2001) also specify the relationship between income and years of schooling in a log-linear way.

in high school, or in college. The available evidence allows a piecewise linear specification for the primary, secondary, and higher level of schooling:

$$(2.13) \quad \phi(s) = \sum_a r_a s_a \quad \Rightarrow \quad H_i^M = e^{\sum_a r_a s_{ai}} L_i \quad \Leftrightarrow \quad h_i^M = e^{\sum_a r_a s_{ai}},$$

where r_a is the rate of return to education at level a and s_{ai} is years of schooling at level a in country i.[18]

Barro and Lee (2001) argue that there are potential problems with the available estimates of returns to education because of biases through unmeasured characteristics like ability and because of disregard of social benefits. However, ample research in the modern labor literature has shown that the upward ability bias is offset by a downward bias of about the same order of magnitude due to measurement error in years of education (Card 1999). Estimates based on siblings or twin data and instrumental variable estimates based on family background or institutional features of the school system are of about the same magnitude as rates of return to education estimated by cross-sectional regressions of earnings on schooling, suggesting that rates of return to education reflect real productivity enhancements. Furthermore, recent studies have found no evidence in favor of externalities to education (see above).[19]

2.2.2.3 The Quality of Education

While several studies have by now taken on the Mincer specification to deal with the first criticism, the second criticism of qualitative differences in one year of

---

[18] Bils and Klenow (2000) suggest decreasing returns to schooling of the form $\phi(s) = [\alpha/(1-\beta)]s^{1-\beta}$, $\beta > 0$, which in applied terms becomes broadly equivalent to the piecewise linear specification of (2.13) because the parameters α and β are also estimated on the basis of the international data from Psacharopoulos (1994).

[19] Mulligan and Sala-i-Martin (1997) also suggest a measure of human capital based on labor income, namely the ratio of the average wage of the labor force to the wage of a person without any schooling. This wage of a person with zero years of schooling is measured as the exponential of the constant term α_0 from a Mincer regression like equation (2.9). This method weights different segments of the labor force by the income at different levels of education. While Mulligan and Sala-i-Martin (1997) calculate stocks of human capital for the states of the United States, the lack of the detailed labor-income data necessary to pursue this method in most countries of the world will make it impossible to apply such measures in cross-country research in the near future. In any event, for the calculation of the aggregate stock of human capital, this approach should yield estimates equivalent to using estimated rates of return to education in equation (2.13). Mulligan and Sala-i-Martin (2000) further expand on the idea of aggregating heterogeneous workers into a stock of human capital based on their educational attainment, yielding optimal index numbers for human capital stocks which minimize an expected-error function.

schooling has as yet not led to a generally accepted refinement in human capital measurement. However, it is not just the *quantity* of education, i.e., the average years of schooling, *s*, embodied in the labor force, which differs across countries, but also the *quality* of each year of schooling, i.e., the cognitive skills learned during each of these years. One year of schooling is not the same everywhere because one unit of *s* may reflect different amounts of acquired knowledge in different countries. Estimated development effects of human capital based on merely quantitative measures may be strongly misleading if qualitative differences do not vary with years of education. Therefore, differences in the quality of education should be introduced into the human capital measure in addition to differences in the mere quantity of education to account for how much students have learned in each year. In what follows, three suggestions are made as to how to adjust the specification of the human capital function for quality differences. They rely, respectively, on measures of educational inputs, country-specific rates of return to education, and direct measures of cognitive skills.

Educational Inputs

The first attempt to account for differences in educational quality is to use proxies for the quality of educational inputs. These measures of the amount of inputs used per student in the education system are then entered as separate explanatory variables in growth regression analyses, presumably reflecting an additional effect of human capital. Barro (1991) already added student-teacher ratios to his analysis as a crude proxy for the quality of schooling, Barro and Sala-i-Martin (1995) use the ratio of government educational spending to GDP, and Barro and Lee (1996) collect data on educational expenditure per student, student-teacher ratios, teacher salaries, and length of the school year to proxy for the quality of educational inputs.

However, it has repeatedly been shown that such measures of educational inputs are not strongly and consistently linked to acquired cognitive skills, rendering them a poor proxy for educational quality (Hanushek 1996a, 1996b; see Chapter 3 of this study). The input measures disregard the huge differences in the effectiveness with which inputs are put to use in different schooling systems, caused mainly by differences in institutional features of the education systems such as centralization of examinations, extent of school autonomy, or competition in the schooling system (Chapter 5).

Country-Specific Rates of Return to Education

Because of the lack of a systematic relationship between resource inputs and educational quality, a second specification to account for qualitative differences in a year of schooling can be thought of as building on country-specific rates of return to education. Under the assumptions that global labor markets are perfectly competitive, that labor is perfectly mobile internationally, and that employers are perfectly informed about the human capital quality of workers, differences in the quality of education of the work force would be captured by differences in the rates of return to education. Therefore, country-specific rates of return may already reflect differences in the quality of education across countries. A quality-adjusted measure of the human capital stock could then be specified as

$$(2.14) \quad h_i^r = e^{\sum_a r_{ai} s_{ai}},$$

where h_i^r is the stock of human capital per worker (based on country-specific measures of r) in country i, r_{ai} is the rate of return to education at level a in country i, and s_{ai} is average years of schooling at level a in country i.

Unfortunately, the data which are available on country-specific rates of return to education seem to be plagued with a high degree of measurement error and may presumably contain more noise than information. The figures collected by Psacharopoulos (1994) show a degree of variation which is difficult to interpret in terms of differences in schooling quality (Section 2.2.3). Furthermore, the three assumptions mentioned which underlie the hypothesis that country-specific rates of return to education capture cross-country differences in the quality of human capital are undoubtedly wrong. In many countries, labor markets are not thoroughly exposed to the market mechanism, given collective bargaining mechanisms and uniform wage setting, labor is highly immobile across countries, and employers are not perfectly informed about the acquired skills of potential employees. Consequently, qualitative differences in education are probably not well captured by the available data on country-specific rates of return to education.

Direct Tests of Cognitive Skills

Neither educational input measures nor country-specific rates of return appear to give good proxies for accumulated cognitive skills. Therefore, the most promising way to introduce an adjustment for differences in the quality of education builds on direct measures of the cognitive skills of individuals obtained from tests of cognitive achievement. There are two international organizations which have conducted a series of standardized international tests in varying sets of countries to assess student achievement in the fields of mathematics and natural sciences. The International Assessment of Educational Progress (IAEP), which builds on the procedures developed for the main national testing instrument in the United States, administered two international studies in 1988 and 1991, both encompassing mathematics and science tests. The International Association for the Evaluation of Educational Achievement (IEA), an agency specializing in comparative education research since its establishment in 1959, conducted cross-country mathematics studies in 1964 and 1981, cross-country science studies in 1971 and 1984, and the Third International Mathematics and Science Study (TIMSS) in 1995. Most studies include separate tests for students in different age-groups (primary, middle, and final school years) and in several subfields of the subjects.

Hanushek and Kimko (2000) combine all of the available information on mathematics and science scores up to 1991 to construct a single measure of schooling quality for each country. All together, they use 26 separate test score series (from different age-groups, subfields, and years), administered at six points in time between 1965 and 1991, and encompassing a total of 39 countries which have participated in an international achievement test at least once. To splice these test results together for each country, they first transform all test scores into a "percent correct" format. To account for the different mean percent correct of the test score series, their quality index $QL2^*$ makes use of intertemporally comparable time series information on student performance in the United States provided by the National Assessment of Educational Progress (NAEP). These national tests establish an absolute benchmark of performance to which the U.S. scores on international tests can be keyed. Thus, the results of the different test series are combined by allowing the mean of each international test series to drift in accordance with the U.S. NAEP score drift and the U.S. performance on each international comparison. The constructed quality measure is a weighted average of all available transformed test scores for each country, where the weights are the normalized inverses of the country-specific standard errors of each test, presuming that a high standard error conveys less accurate information. By combining student achievement tests from the relevant time range when current workers were students, the measure tries to approximate the cognitive skills embodied in the current labor force.[20]

To incorporate the thus measured cross-country differences in schooling quality into measures of the stock of human capital, I normalize Hanushek and Kimko's (2000) educational quality index for each country relative to the measure for the United States (Gundlach et al. 2002). This measure of relative quality can then be viewed as a quality weight by which each year of schooling in a country can be weighted, where the weight for the United States is unity. Using the United States as the reference country seems warranted by the fact that the returns to schooling should be relatively undistorted on the competitive U.S.

---

[20] Hanushek and Kimko (2000) show that such quality measures of education matter more in growth regressions than quantity measures, a finding also confirmed by Barro (1999).

labor market. To obtain a quality-adjusted human capital specification, I combine the quality and quantity measures of education with world-average rates of return to education at the different education levels in a Mincer-type specification of the human capital function:

$$(2.15) \quad h_i^Q = e^{\sum_a r_a Q_i s_{ai}},$$

where r_a is the world-average rate of return to education at level a and Q_i is Hanushek and Kimko's (2000) educational quality index for country i relative to the U.S. value.[21]

One virtue of this quality adjustment of the human capital specification is that one may think of the quality of human capital as potentially rising continually and without an upper bound. By contrast, the growth in pure quantity specifications of human capital is bounded because educational attainment is asymptotically a constant. Such a specification is hard to reconcile with most models of economic growth, where the stock of physical capital also has no natural upper bound. A further virtue of the final specifications of h_i^r and h_i^Q is that they yield one single human capital variable. Since human capital is embodied in the labor force, it is more natural to think of it as one combined factor of production, rather than as several independent factors. By combining information on the labor force, quantity of education, rates of return to these educational investments, and quality of this education, the final quality-adjusted human capital specification is more readily interpreted in growth and development applications.

2.2.3   Comparison of the Different Human Capital Measures

Human Capital Data

To be able to compare the different specifications of human capital proposed in the literature, Table A2.1 in Section 2.5 presents estimates of human capital stocks for the different specifications for 1990 or the most recent year available. To facilitate comparisons of the different specifications, values are reported relative to the United States, while the first row in each column shows the absolute U.S. value. Countries are ranked according to output per worker.

Adult literacy rates, l, and school enrollment ratios, e, are taken from the *World Education Indicators* (UNESCO 2000a). Adult literacy rates, l, refer to

---

[21] Note that due to the lack of Mincer-type evidence on earnings effects of the measure of educational quality, the choice of a linear functional form to enter the quality weight next to years of schooling is arbitrary. It assumes that the earnings effect of the quality weight is equal to the earnings effect of the quantitative measure of education.

the population aged 15 years and over and are for both sexes in 1990. School enrollment ratios, e, are gross enrollment ratios in primary, secondary, and tertiary education for both sexes in 1990. e^{MRW} refers to the indicator used by Mankiw et al. (1992), which is the average percentage of the working-age population enrolled in secondary school for 1960–1985.

Average years of schooling calculated by the projection method s^{PRO} are Kyriacou's (1991) projected average years of schooling for 1985, as reported in Benhabib and Spiegel (1994). Average years of schooling calculated by the perpetual inventory method s^{PIM} are for total (primary, secondary, and tertiary) education in 1987 as calculated by Nehru et al. (1995). Average years of schooling based on the attainment census method s^{ATT} are taken from Barro and Lee (2001) and refer to years of total (primary, secondary, and higher) education in the total population aged 15 and over in 1990. s^{DD} is the revision of Barro and Lee's average years of schooling in 1990 for OECD countries by de la Fuente and Doménech (2000).

In calculating the human capital specifications proposed in Section 2.2.2, I use average years of schooling s_a^{ATT} separately at the primary, secondary, and higher level for 1990 from Barro and Lee (2001). Years of schooling in the population aged 15 and over are taken because this age-group corresponds better to the labor force for most developing countries than the population aged 25 and over. The rates of return to education r_a used in h^M and h^Q are world-average social rates of return at the primary, secondary, and higher level of education estimated by the elaborate discounting method. As reported by Psacharopoulos (1994: Table 2), the world-average social rate of return to education is 20.0 percent at the primary level, 13.5 percent at the secondary level, and 10.7 percent at the higher level.

Instead of using equation (2.13) as the function $\phi(s)$, which links the stock of human capital to average years of schooling in equation (2.11), Hall and Jones (1999) and Gundlach et al. (2002) use

$$(2.16) \quad \phi^{HJ}(s) = \begin{cases} r^{pri}s & \text{if } s \leq D_{pri} \\ r^{pri}D_{pri} + r^{sec}(s - D_{pri}) & \text{if } D_{pri} < s \leq D_{pri} + D_{sec} \\ r^{pri}D_{pri} + r^{sec}D_{sec} + r^{hig}(s - D_{pri} - D_{sec}) & \text{if } s > D_{pri} + D_{sec} \end{cases}$$

$$\Rightarrow \quad h^{HJ} = e^{\phi^{HJ}(s)}.$$

Hall and Jones (1999) additionally assume that $D_{pri} = D_{sec} = 4$ for each country. This equation yields a biased allocation of level-specific rates of return to respective schooling years. For example, all the schooling years in a country whose average years of schooling are less than 4 will be weighted by the rate of return to primary education, although presumably some of the years which make up the total stock will have been in secondary or higher education. By just looking at the average and not splitting down the acquired years of education into those acquired at the primary, secondary, and higher levels, this method allocates the wrong rates of return to a substantial part of the acquired schooling years. Furthermore, Hall and Jones (1999) employ private rates of return to education calculated on the basis of the earnings function method, also reported in Psacharopoulos (1994), using the ad hoc assumption that the rate of return to primary education equals the average rate of return in Sub-Saharan Africa (13.4 percent), the rate of return to secondary education equals the world-average rate of return (10.1 percent), and the rate of return to higher education equals the average rate of return in OECD countries (6.8 percent).[22] To be able to compare my estimates of h^M, h^r, and h^Q to the method used by Hall and Jones (1999), I also report their measure as h^{HJ}, updated to 1990 with years of schooling from Barro and Lee (2001).

In calculating h^r, country-specific social rates of return to education at the three levels estimated by the elaborate discounting method—on which the world-average rates used in h^M and h^Q are based—are taken. However, the country-specific rates of return reported by Psacharopoulos (1994) include an implausible range of values, with rates of return to primary education ranging from 2 percent in Yemen to 66 percent in Uganda. Yemen's low figure makes it the country with the lowest h^r in the sample, while Uganda's and Botswana's high figures make them the countries with the highest h^r. Morocco's high figure stems from a reported rate of return to primary education of 50.5 percent, which compares to a regional average of 15.5 percent and an income-group average of 18.2 percent. These implausible results make a sensible use of country-specific rates of return virtually impossible.

As the quality measure for the quality-adjusted human capital specification, h^Q, I use Hanushek and Kimko's (2000) index of educational quality QL2*, relative to the U.S. value. To obtain a full set of human capital estimates, some values for s and Q (and for r in h^r) have been imputed. The imputation takes the mean of the respective regional average and the respective income-group average for any country with a missing value on one of these variables, using the World Bank's (1992) classification of countries by major regions and income groups.[23]

---

[22] Note that while, in general, narrow-social rates of return must be lower than private rates, the reported narrow-social estimates based on the elaborate discounting method are larger than the reported private estimates based on the earnings function method.

[23] The regions used are Asia, Latin America, Sub-Saharan Africa, North Africa, Middle East, Eastern Europe, and the OECD. The income groups are low, lower-middle, upper-middle, and high income.

Comparison

The human capital estimates in Table A2.1 show that the different specifications can yield very different measures of the human capital stock of a country. Even among the different estimation methods of average years of schooling, s, large differences exist; e.g., while Mauritania's s^{ATT} is 2.42 years and Switzerland's s^{ATT} is 10.14 years, their s^{PIM} is about the same (6.66 and 6.96 years). Likewise, Spain's s^{PRO} of 9.70 years is 3.26 years higher than its s^{ATT} of 6.44 years, while Taiwan's s^{PRO} of 4.67 years is 3.31 years lower than its s^{ATT} of 7.98 years. Even between the two measures based on the attainment census method (s^{ATT} and s^{DD}), France shows a difference of 3.92 years.

To allow for an overall comparison of the different specifications, Table 2.1 reports correlation coefficients for the 11 human capital measures. Because the data sets cover different samples of countries, the number of countries covered jointly by each pair of measures is reported in brackets below the correlation coefficients. For example, there is no country jointly covered by the l and s^{DD} data sets, because the UNESCO does not report adult literacy rates, l, for advanced countries and de la Fuente and Doménech's (2000) data set s^{DD} is available only for OECD countries.

The correlation between the enrollment ratio, e, and the three broad-sample schooling years variables, s^{PIM}, s^{PRO}, and s^{ATT}, is fairly high (between 0.83 and 0.90), suggesting that enrollment ratios may not be an altogether bad proxy for the quantity of schooling after all. The correlation between the three broad-sample schooling-years variables, s, ranges from 0.88 to 0.90, showing a comparable broad-sample distributions. When compared to the revised OECD sample data set s^{DD}, however, the correlation is very low (0.35, 0.47, and 0.79, respectively). Both s^{DD} and h^r in general show a low correlation to all other human capital specifications. Barro and Lee's (2001) s^{ATT} and the Mincer specification h^M are highly correlated (0.97), as are the two measures based on the Mincer specification, h^M and h^{HJ} (0.98). The correlation between the quality-adjusted human capital specification h^Q and most other specifications is relatively low.

In sum, there seem to be substantial differences between the different measures of the stock of human capital, and even between those measures which do not take into account differences in the quality of education. Given that the human capital specification which takes account of international differences in the quality of schooling is relatively weakly related to the other specifications, international differences in the schooling quality seem to introduce a substantial amount of additional information into the measure of human capital. The differences in the human capital measures may lead to largely different results in an

Table 2.1: Correlation between Different Measures of Human Capital

		[1]	[2]	[3]	[4]	[5]	[6]	[7]	[8]	[9]	[10]	[11]
		l	e	e^{MRW}	s^{PIM}	s^{PRO}	s^{ATT}	s^{DD}	h^{HJ}	h^{M}	h^{r}	h^{Q}
[1]	l	1 [96]										
[2]	e	0.828 [67]	1 [103]									
[3]	e^{MRW}	0.738 [83]	0.817 [90]	1 [117]								
[4]	s^{PIM}	0.770 [55]	0.858 [69]	0.863 [81]	1 [83]							
[5]	s^{PRO}	0.846 [79]	0.902 [83]	0.872 [108]	0.878 [79]	1 [111]						
[6]	s^{ATT}	0.841 [77]	0.830 [86]	0.819 [102]	0.890 [76]	0.896 [96]	1 [108]					
[7]	s^{DD}	– [0]	0.300 [21]	0.383 [21]	0.345 [21]	0.471 [20]	0.791 [21]	1 [21]				
[8]	h^{HJ}	0.789 [96]	0.809 [103]	0.806 [117]	0.863 [83]	0.872 [111]	0.999 [108]	0.789 [21]	1 [152]			
[9]	h^{M}	0.759 [96]	0.736 [103]	0.753 [117]	0.822 [83]	0.819 [111]	0.973 [108]	0.697 [21]	0.976 [152]	1 [152]		
[10]	h^{r}	0.395 [96]	0.447 [103]	0.344 [117]	0.373 [83]	0.361 [111]	0.574 [108]	0.579 [21]	0.558 [151]	0.554 [151]	1 [151]	
[11]	h^{Q}	0.562 [96]	0.576 [103]	0.623 [117]	0.695 [83]	0.661 [111]	0.846 [108]	0.503 [21]	0.845 [151]	0.916 [151]	0.510 [151]	1 [151]

Note: Correlation coefficients; number of joint observations in brackets below.

empirical application of the different measures, and thus to diverging conclusions on the importance of human capital for economic development.

2.3 Quality-Adjusted Human Capital and Economic Development

The ultimate aim of specifying the stock of human capital was to assess its relevance for cross-country differences in the levels of economic development. Research on economic growth in general deals with three related but conceptually distinct central issues: world growth, country growth, and dispersion in income levels (Klenow and Rodríguez-Clare 1997a). Research on the first issue tries to explain the continuous growth of income per capita in the world economy. Research on the second issue deals with cross-country differences in growth rates. And research on the third issue tries to answer why some countries are significantly richer than others at a given point in time.

In this chapter, I deal with the third issue—explaining levels rather than explaining growth—which is called "development accounting" by King and Levine (1994) because it looks for sources of differences in levels of economic development across the countries in the world. The focus on dispersion in levels of development is chosen because they are arguably the ultimate reason why research is interested in economic growth in the first place. Differences in development levels capture differences in long-run economic performance which are directly relevant to welfare, while recent studies show that differences in growth rates are largely transitory (Hall and Jones 1999).

2.3.1   Two Theoretical Views on Human Capital and Economic Development

Human capital takes a central role in most theories of economic growth and development. Both the augmented neoclassical growth model and most models of endogenous growth stress the importance of human capital for development in one way or another. However, the different models can be summarized into two distinct groups of theoretical views on the relationship between human capital and economic development (Aghion and Howitt 1998; Benhabib and Spiegel 1994). In the first view, the accumulation of human capital as a factor of production only has a transitory impact on growth rates because the marginal product of each input is diminishing, but differences in levels of human capital cause differences in output *levels* across countries (the "neoclassical view"). In the second view, a greater human capital stock permanently affects the rate of economic growth, mainly by facilitating innovation and adoption of new technologies, so that differences in levels of human capital cause differences in rates of output *growth* across countries (the "technical-progress view").

The "Neoclassical View"

The first view—that human capital levels should only be connected to levels of income—can easily be depicted on the basis of the human-capital-augmented neoclassical model of growth and development, where human capital enters as a factor of production.[24] In his neoclassical growth model, Solow (1956) uses a

---

[24]   Models of endogenous growth in the spirit of Lucas (1988), which also view human capital as an input factor in the production function, share the same result.

macroeconomic Cobb–Douglas production function with labor as a homogeneous factor and with physical capital as the only factor of production which can be accumulated. Mankiw et al. (1992) augment this model by introducing human capital as an additional factor of production which can be accumulated, acknowledging that labor is not an homogeneous factor. The level of output, Y, produced in a country, i, is then given by

$$(2.17) \quad Y_i = K_i^\alpha (A_i h_i L_i)^{1-\alpha},$$

where K_i is the stock of physical capital in country i, α is the production elasticity of physical capital, and A_i is the level of (Harrod-neutral) total factor productivity in country i.

The output level per worker $y_i \equiv Y_i / L_i$ is then given as

$$(2.18) \quad y_i = k_i^\alpha h_i^{1-\alpha} A_i^{1-\alpha} \quad \Leftrightarrow \quad y_i = \left(\frac{k_i}{y_i} \right)^{\alpha/(1-\alpha)} h_i A_i,$$

where $k_i \equiv K_i / L_i$ is the ratio of physical capital to labor. Thus, the *level* of output is a function of the *level* of human capital.

The "Technical-Progress View"

The second view—of effects of human capital levels on the rate of economic growth—is the central part of many models of endogenous growth, and it goes at least as far back as Nelson and Phelps (1966). In this "technical-progress view," the growth of total factor productivity depends on the stock of human capital (Benhabib and Spiegel 1994). This may be either due to effects of human capital on the domestic production of technological innovation (Romer 1990b) or due to effects of human capital on the adoption and implementation of new technology from abroad (Nelson and Phelps 1966). In either case, the growth of total factor productivity in country i, $\gamma_{A_i} \equiv \Delta A_i / A_i$, is a positive function of the country's average level of human capital, h:

$$(2.19) \quad \gamma_{A_i} = \psi(h_i), \quad \psi'(h_i) > 0.$$

This relationship implies that output *growth* is a function of the *level* of human capital.

Knowledge Advances and Cross-Country Income Distribution

This second class of models emphasizes the endogenous nature of technical progress. In that sense, the main contribution of these models of endogenous growth is to give an explanation of economic growth over time, usually by suggesting microfoundations for technological advances. As noted above, this issue is conceptually distinct from the development accounting question raised in the present study. Specifically, technological differences across countries should be transitory since technological knowledge is fairly free to move across countries as long as a country is open to the adoption of technological advances from abroad. As is directly evident from the Nelson and Phelps (1966) model of technological catch-up, the effect of the human capital stock on the growth of total factor productivity is a short-run effect of catching up to the technological leader. In the long run, total factor productivity in any country grows again at the growth rate of the world technological frontier, which in that model is exogenous. And while the innovation models endogenize the growth rate of the world technological frontier, this does not have an effect on the long-run income distribution across countries as long as catching-up through technological diffusion is taking place.

One of the central ideas of the innovation models is actually that technological knowledge is a nonrival and nonexcludable good. Therefore, by the very nature of technological knowledge, all countries should in principle have access to the same technologies, and even at a relatively modest cost (Olson 1996). The only way in which the knowledge available for productive use may differ across countries is through the knowledge embodied in people, i.e., through the available stock of human capital. Topel (1999) suggests that in that sense, the differences between the two views may be more semantic than real because human capital, when defined broadly, may encompass the creation of knowledge in a person and the ability of human beings to apply new knowledge. The nonrivalry and nonexcludability of technological knowledge implies that the "technical-progress view," while providing a possible explanation of worldwide advances in knowledge, should not be a major factor in the explanation of cross-country differences in development levels.

In contrast, the "neoclassical view" takes worldwide technical progress as given and explains differences in economic development as a function of the accumulated stocks of factor inputs.[25] Therefore, I use the neoclassical growth specification of equation (2.18) to account for the relative contributions to the cross-country dispersion in levels of economic development by the stock of

---

[25] Since neoclassical models and models of endogenous growth are thus able to answer distinct research questions, they should be viewed as complements (Mankiw 1995).

human capital, the stock of physical capital, and the level of total factor productivity.

2.3.2   Worldwide Development Accounting Results

Methodology and National Accounts Data

Since the empirical interest is in the contribution of differences in human capital stocks to cross-country differences in levels of economic development, I use the "covariance measure" proposed by Klenow and Rodríguez-Clare (1997b) to decompose the international variance in output per worker (the measure of the level of economic development) into the relative contributions of differences in human capital stocks, in physical capital stocks, and in levels of total factor productivity.[26] Assuming a macroeconomic production function with Harrod-neutral productivity as in equation (2.18) and assuming that countries are near their steady state,[27] the variance in output per worker can be divided into three covariance terms between output per worker and the factors which are constant in steady state, namely the stock of human capital, the physical capital-output ratio, and total factor productivity:

$$(2.20)' \quad \text{var}(\ln(y)) = \text{cov}(\ln(y), \ln(y))$$

$$= \text{cov}(\ln(y), \ln(h)) + \text{cov}\left(\ln(y), \ln\left((k/y)^{\frac{a}{1-a}} \right) \right)$$

$$+ \text{cov}(\ln(y), \ln(A)).$$

This decomposition allows the measurement of the relative contributions of the three factors as percentages:

$$(2.20) \quad \frac{\text{cov}(\ln(y), \ln(h))}{\text{var}(\ln(y))} + \frac{\text{cov}\left(\ln(y), \ln\left((k/y)^{\frac{a}{1-a}} \right) \right)}{\text{var}(\ln(y))} + \frac{\text{cov}(\ln(y), \ln(A))}{\text{var}(\ln(y))} = 1.$$

The three terms on the left-hand side equal the coefficients from regressing $\ln(y)$ on the logs of each of the three factors separately. Applying this method gives

---

[26] The basic methodology used in Section 2.3.2 was first presented in Gundlach et al. (2002).

[27] While the global evidence may be affected by the potential violation of the steady-state assumption in some newly industrializing countries, the assumption seems warranted for the sample of OECD countries analyzed in Section 2.3.3.

the respective average fraction of output dispersion across countries which can be statistically attributed to international differences in human capital stocks and in physical capital-output ratios, leaving the rest to be explained by residual total factor productivity. The three terms can be interpreted precisely as the percentage of one percent which the respective input in a given country can be expected to be above the mean across countries, conditional on output per worker in that country being one percent above the mean across countries.

As a robustness test for the results of the covariance measure, the "five-country measure," which is based on a calculation in Hall and Jones (1999), focuses on the highest and lowest part of the sample distribution. It shows, also in percentage terms, how much of the difference in output per worker between the five most developed and the five least developed countries (in terms of output per worker) is due to differences in the three input components:

$$
(2.21) \quad \frac{\ln\left(\prod_{i=1}^{5} h_i \Big/ \prod_{j=n-4}^{n} h_j\right)}{\ln\left(\prod_{i=1}^{5} y_i \Big/ \prod_{j=n-4}^{n} y_j\right)} + \frac{\ln\left(\prod_{i=1}^{5} (k_i/y_i)^{\frac{\alpha}{1-\alpha}} \Big/ \prod_{j=n-4}^{n} (k_j/y_j)^{\frac{\alpha}{1-\alpha}}\right)}{\ln\left(\prod_{i=1}^{5} y_i \Big/ \prod_{j=n-4}^{n} y_j\right)}
$$

$$
+ \frac{\ln\left(\prod_{i=1}^{5} A_i \Big/ \prod_{j=n-4}^{n} A_j\right)}{\ln\left(\prod_{i=1}^{5} y_i \Big/ \prod_{j=n-4}^{n} y_j\right)} = 1,
$$

where n is the sample size and countries i, ..., j, ..., n are ranked according to output per worker.

To calibrate the macroeconomic production function, I assume a production elasticity of physical capital of $\alpha = 1/3$, which is the standard figure used for parameterization in the literature. It broadly resembles the share of physical capital in factor income as reported in national income accounts of developed countries (Maddison 1987), and it also seems to apply for developing countries once the labor income of the self-employed and other proprietors is properly accounted for (Gollin 1998).

Data on output per worker y and physical capital per worker k are taken from Summers and Heston's (1991) Penn World Table, Version 5.6a of 1994. Output per worker y is measured in 1990 or the next available year. The 1990 value of the stock of physical capital K is constructed by the perpetual inventory method based on annual investment rates and an assumed depreciation rate of 6 percent. The initial value for K is estimated by $I_t / (\gamma_{I,t+10} + \delta)$, where I_t is the first year for which investment data are available, $\gamma_{I,t+10}$ is the average growth rate of investment in the subsequent decade, and δ is the depreciation rate (Hall and Jones 1999). The figures for labor L in 1990 are derived by multiplying per capita output with population and dividing by output per worker.

Global Evidence

Table 2.2a presents the covariance measure for the broadest sample of countries for which the relevant data is available. The sample size of 132 countries is determined by the availability of investment data in the Penn World Tables (PWT), which have been used to construct the physical capital stock. The first row begins with the first specification based on Mincerian human capital theory as used by Hall and Jones (1999), h^{HJ}, where 21 percent of the international variation in output per worker is accounted for by differences in human capital per worker. Since another 19 percent can be attributed to differences in the physical capital-output ratio, 60 percent remain as differences in residual total factor productivity. With the human capital specification h^M, which attributes rates of return to years of schooling through equation (2.13) instead of equation (2.16) and uses social rates of return estimated by the elaborate discounting method, 33 percent of development differences are accounted for by human capital differences. Using country-specific social rates of return in the specification h^r, the share attributed to human capital is only 18 percent.

Table 2.2a: Human Capital and Economic Development: World Evidence, Covariance Measure

X \ Z	h^X	$(k/y)^{\frac{\alpha}{1-\alpha}}$	A	Sample size
HJ	0.21	0.19	0.60	132
M	0.33	0.19	0.48	132
r	0.18	0.19	0.63	132
Q	0.45	0.19	0.36	132

Note: $\mathrm{cov}(\ln(y),\ln(Z))/\mathrm{var}(\ln(y))$ with Z given in each column. — For h^{HJ}, h^M, h^r, and h^Q, see equations (2.13) to (2.16).

Since cognitive skills are not well proxied by measures of mere school quantities or country-specific rates of return to education, results based on the quality-adjusted human capital specification, h^Q, are reported in the last row of Table 2.2a. The adjustment of the human capital specification for differences in the quality of schooling boosts the share of variation in development levels attributed to human capital differences to 45 percent. This evidence shows that the assumption implicit in all previous specifications, namely that differences in educational quality can be neglected in the specification of human capital stocks, can give rise to misleading results on the development effect of human capital in development accounting studies.

The results based on the five-country measure, reported in Table 2.2b, confirm the results based on the covariance method. The share attributed to human capital is slightly higher with the five-country measure for all the specifications reported, and it is higher with h^r than with h^{HJ}. With h^Q, the five-country measure attributes 47 percent of the variation in development levels to human capital differences.

Table 2.2b: Human Capital and Economic Development: World Evidence, Five-Country Measure

X \ Z	h^X	$(k/y)^{\frac{\alpha}{1-\alpha}}$	A	Sample size
HJ	0.24	0.19	0.57	132
M	0.39	0.19	0.42	132
r	0.26	0.19	0.56	132
Q	0.47	0.19	0.34	132

Note: $\ln\left(\prod\limits_{i=1}^{5} z_i \Big/ \prod\limits_{j=n-4}^{n} z_j\right) \Big/ \ln\left(\prod\limits_{i=1}^{5} y_i \Big/ \prod\limits_{j=n-4}^{n} y_j\right)$ with n = sample size, countries $i, ..., j,$ ..., n ranked according to y, and Z given in each column. — For h^{HJ}, h^M, h^r, and h^Q, see equations (2.13) to (2.16).

Table 2.3 shows the robustness of the calculated development impact of quality-adjusted human capital to further refinements and samples.[28] Using years of education in the population aged 25 and over (instead of 15 and over) leaves the human capital share unchanged. Recalculating the development accounting exercise for the year 1980 yields a development share attributed to differences in h^Q of 42 percent. Since these results may be affected by the oil-price shocks in the 1970s, an additional sample excludes countries dependent on primary resources by excluding all countries whose value added in the mining sector accounts for more than 10 percent of total value added. In this sample of 115 countries, the share attributed to quality-adjusted human capital is 47 percent in 1980 and 48 percent in 1990.

---

[28]   Results on the human capital share for the other specifications of the human capital measure and results of the five-country measure are reported in Table A2.2.

Table 2.3: Quality-Adjusted Human Capital and Economic Development: Further Evidence, Covariance Measure

	Z			Sample size
	h^Q	$(k/y)^{\frac{\alpha}{1-\alpha}}$	A	
1990 sample: Population 25 and over	0.45	0.19	0.36	132
1980 sample	0.42	0.19	0.39	132
1980 subsample: low mining share	0.47	0.22	0.31	115
1990 subsamples:				
Low mining share	0.48	0.20	0.33	115
Nonimputed s^{ATT}	0.51	0.19	0.30	104
Nonimputed Q	0.51	0.15	0.34	88
Nonimputed s^{ATT} and Q	0.52	0.15	0.33	85
PWT benchmark study (BS)	0.52	0.22	0.27	82
BS, nonimputed s^{ATT} and Q	0.60	0.13	0.27	64
Nonprojected Q	0.51	0.18	0.31	38
BS, nonimp. s^{ATT}, nonproj. Q	0.61	0.13	0.26	29

Note: $\text{cov}(\ln(y),\ln(Z))/\text{var}(\ln(y))$ with Z given in each column.

Further subsamples for the 1990 results reveal that the share attributed to human capital is understated through the use of nonoriginal data. When countries with imputed values on years of schooling, s^{ATT}, on the quality index, Q, or on either of them are excluded, the share of development variation accounted for by human capital exceeds 50 percent. The same is true when countries are excluded which never participated in one of the benchmark studies underlying the Penn World Tables. In the sample of PWT benchmark countries without imputed data, with a sample size of 64 countries, the share attributed to quality-adjusted human capital rises to 60 percent. Furthermore, of the 88 available values of the quality index, Q, more than half had been projected in Hanushek and Kimko (2000) on the basis of observed country and education-system characteristics. When confining the sample to the 38 countries with original data on educational quality, the calculated human capital share is 51 percent. And when combining all the restrictions discussed, yielding a sample of 29 countries which participated in a PWT benchmark study and which do not have any imputed or projected human capital data, 61 percent of the international variation in the level of economic development are accounted for by differences in quality-adjusted human capital. All this shows that the development impact of human capital seems to be severely understated by previous human capital specifications and by misreported human capital data.

2.3.3   Evidence on the Residual

Within the world sample of countries, differences in the residual still account for between 26 and 36 percent (depending on the inclusion of imputed human capital data) of the cross-country variance in economic development in 1990. This result may be due to three different causes. First, there may be sizable cross-country technological differences, so that the "technical-progress view" on the relation between human capital and economic development (Section 2.3.1) may have explanatory power. Second, cross-country differences in total factor productivity may arise from other factors, notably institutional differences across countries. Third, the residual may be caused by data recording errors, giving rise to attenuation bias in the shares attributed to the factor inputs, in which case the residual would not reflect real cross-country differences in total factor productivity.

Human Capital Stocks and Technical Differentiation

The results so far are solely based on the human-capital-augmented neoclassical model of growth and development. To test whether the focus on the "neoclassical view" and the neglect of the "technical-progress view" on the relationship between human capital and growth is warranted in an exploration of cross-country differences in levels of economic development, I estimated whether the recognition of the "technical-progress view" can add to an understanding of the residual by using a simple conclusion of this view. If a higher stock of human capital caused a country's rate of technological progress to be higher than that of other countries with lower stocks of human capital, then its level of total factor productivity should also be higher. It follows by integration from equation (2.19) that the level of total factor productivity, A, should be a positive exponential function of the stock of human capital per worker, h:

$$(2.22) \quad A_i = A_{i0} e^{\psi(h_i)t}.$$

Therefore, the stock of human capital and the natural logarithm of the level of total factor productivity of a country, i, should be positively correlated.

Calculating the level of total factor productivity as the residual in the neoclassical framework of equation (2.18), where $A_i = y_i / \left[(k_i / y_i)^{\alpha/(1-\alpha)} h_i \right]$ reflects what is left over of development differences after accounting for differences in factor inputs, in principle allows for a positive correlation between the log level of total factor productivity and the human capital input. This contrasts with the regression methodology used in Mankiw et al. (1992), where the level of total factor productivity and its growth rate are assumed to be constant across countries (and, hence, are part of the regression constant). By looking at the correlation between the logarithm of the residual A and the human capital stock, h, the underlying hypotheses of the neoclassical model that the level of technology is common to all countries can be tested and the potential addition of the "technical-progress view" to an understanding of the residual in the development-accounting framework can be estimated.

As can be seen in Table 2.4, there is indeed some correlation between the logarithm of the residual, A, and the human capital specifications which ignore quality differences, h^{HJ} and h^M. However, when differences in schooling quality are accounted for in the human capital stock, h^Q, there is basically no correlation between the log residual and the stock of human capital.[29] This evidence suggests that while the human-capital-augmented neoclassical growth model is able to explain a substantial amount of the cross-country dispersion in development levels, the effect of the stock of human capital on economic development working through technical differentiation, as stressed by "technical-progress view," does not seem to add to an explanation of international differences in development levels.

If the "technical-progress view" on the relationship between human capital and economic development was relevant for an understanding of cross-country differences in the level of economic development, international differences in the level of technology driven by differences in human capital stocks should add to an understanding of the residual. The fact that they do not, lends support to the hypothesis of the neoclassical model that the residual in cross-country productivity differences may not reflect differences in the technology used, corroborating the argumentation that, by the very nature of technological knowledge, all countries should in principle have access to the same technologies (Section 2.3.1). When neglecting potential attenuation bias in the results and assuming that the residual reflects real differences in the level of total factor productivity, these differences would then have to be caused by other cross-country differences which affect the productivity with which production factors are put to use. One causal factor which suggests itself is cross-country differences in the basic institutions which constitute the framework within which individuals produce and interact economically (Hall and Jones 1999).

---

[29] The same result is obtained when the linear relationship between A and h is explored: The correlation with A is 0.575 for h^{HJ}, 0.337 for h^M, 0.071 for h^r, and −0.043 for h^Q.

Table 2.4: Correlation between Residual and Human Capital

	$\ln(A)$
h^{HJ}	0.569
h^M	0.293
h^r	−0.020
h^Q	−0.139
Note: Correlation coefficient. — For h^{HJ}, h^M, h^r, and h^Q, see equations (2.13) to (2.16).

OECD-Sample Development Accounting Results

An indirect way to test whether international differences in residual total factor productivity reflect institutional differences is to look at a sample of countries in which institutional differences may not be large. One such sample is arguably the sample of OECD countries, which share common basic institutional features which allow markets to function properly. When evaluated relative to many developing countries, OECD countries all have comparatively reliable legal frameworks securing private property rights, freedom of contracting, agencies ensuring competitive markets, market-friendly policies, and internal monetary stability. They also exhibit a relatively high degree of openness to trade and capital mobility, which enables them to access similar technologies quickly. Because of these similar institutional frameworks, there should be no large differences in residual total factor productivity between OECD countries. Hence, all OECD countries may be assumed to produce on a common macroeconomic production function, so that differences in factor inputs should suffice to explain differences in development levels across these countries.[30]

I use the sample of all OECD countries in 1990, except Luxembourg, for which no schooling quantity data is available. With output per worker in Turkey at less than a quarter of the U.S. value and in Portugal and Greece at less than half the U.S. value, there is a sizable variation in development levels to be explained in this sample. One advantage of the OECD sample over the world sample is that data should be recorded more accurately, so that data quality problems should be relatively small.

As the results based on the covariance measure presented in Table 2.5a reveal, the share of development variation accounted for by differences in human capital stocks is larger in the OECD sample than in the world sample. With specification h^{HJ}, the share attributed to human capital is 39 percent, with h^M 70 percent, with

---

[30] Note that the sample of OECD countries may also be more likely to warrant the steady-state assumption.

h^r 50 percent, and with h^Q 100 percent. That is, the covariance between the quality-adjusted human capital specification and output per worker in the OECD sample is just as large as the variance of output per worker, so that the whole variation in development levels can be accounted for by differences in human capital when the human capital measure is adjusted for differences in the quality of schooling. This result is broadly confirmed by the five-country measure (Table 2.5b).

When the human capital specification accounts for differences in schooling quality, the development accounting evidence suggests that OECD countries are by and large producing on a common level of total factor productivity.[31] The

Table 2.5a: Human Capital and Economic Development: OECD Sample, Co-variance Measure

X \ Z	h^X	$(k/y)^{\frac{\alpha}{1-\alpha}}$	A	Sample size
HJ	0.39	0.15	0.47	23
M	0.70	0.15	0.15	23
r	0.50	0.15	0.35	23
Q	1.00	0.15	−0.14	23

Note: $\mathrm{cov}(\ln(y),\ln(Z))/\mathrm{var}(\ln(y))$ with Z given in each column. — For h^{HJ}, h^M, h^r, and h^Q, see equations (2.13) to (2.16).

Table 2.5b: Human Capital and Economic Development: OECD Sample, Five-Country Measure

X \ Z	h^X	$(k/y)^{\frac{\alpha}{1-\alpha}}$	A	Sample size
HJ	0.38	0.11	0.51	23
M	0.72	0.11	0.17	23
r	0.61	0.11	0.28	23
Q	0.94	0.11	−0.05	23

Note: $\ln\left(\prod_{i=1}^{5} Z_i \Big/ \prod_{j=n-4}^{n} Z_j\right) \Big/ \ln\left(\prod_{i=1}^{5} y_i \Big/ \prod_{j=n-4}^{n} y_j\right)$ with n = sample size, countries $i, \dots, j$, $\dots, n$ ranked according to y, and Z given in each column. — For h^{HJ}, h^M, h^r, and h^Q, see equations (2.13) to (2.16).

---

[31] This result is also confirmed by the fact that there is no correlation between total factor productivity, A, and output per worker, y, in the OECD sample when human capital is specified as h^Q (the correlation coefficient is −0.09).

evidence reveals that the "neoclassical view" on the relationship between human capital and economic development yields a model which fits the data well. As an explanation of the differences in output per worker between OECD countries, the human-capital-augmented neoclassical growth model suffices. The "technical-progress view" on growth effects of human capital does not seem to add to an understanding of the cross-country dispersion in development levels. The OECD results have an indication that the residual in the world evidence may be either due to poor data quality in many non-OECD countries or due to differences in basic institutions governing the market processes.

2.3.4   Data Recording Errors versus Specification Errors

Recent studies by Krueger and Lindahl (2001) and de la Fuente and Doménech (2000) have argued that there are serious data recording errors in the data on average years of schooling which lead to biased estimates of growth effects. As argued in Section 2.2.1.4, data quality should not be a major problem for cross-country level comparisons in 1990, because basically all observations at least in the OECD sample are direct census observations. To assess the importance of data quality problems in human capital measurement relative to the specification problems stressed in the present study, I compare development accounting results based on the three available data sets on average years of schooling in the population aged 15 and over which have been constructed on the basis of the attainment census method: the Barro and Lee (1996) data set, the Barro and Lee (2001) data set, and the de la Fuente and Doménech (2000) data set. Barro and Lee (2001) improve on the earlier data set by taking account of changes in the duration of schooling cycles and by using a refined fill-in procedure for missing observations. De la Fuente and Doménech (2000) thoroughly revise the Barro and Lee (1996) data set for the OECD sample by using additional national data sources and deleting data inconsistencies.

Comparing the covariance-measure results based on the Barro and Lee (1996) data set in Table 2.6a to the results in Table 2.2a, which are based on the revised Barro and Lee (2001) data set, shows that the improvement in data quality had only a minor impact on the development accounting results. The estimated share in output variation accounted for by differences in quality-adjusted human capital is half a percentage point higher in the case of the revised data set.

The more thorough revision of the OECD data set by de la Fuente and Doménech (2000) has a larger effect on the development accounting results when compared to the earlier OECD results in Table 2.5a, but the difference in the share attributed to quality-adjusted human capital is still only 4 percentage points (Table 2.6b).[32] The effect on development accounting results of having improved human capital data seems to be minor relative to specification effects of using superior rate of return estimates and adjusting for schooling quality. While improving on the recording of educational data is indeed a worthy issue, the recording issue of considering the quality of the *data* seems to be less important for development accounting studies than the specification issue of considering the quality of *human capital*.

Table 2.6a: Alternative Schooling Quantity Data Sets: Barro and Lee (1996), Covariance Measure

X \ Z	h^X	$(k/y)^{\frac{\alpha}{1-\alpha}}$	A	Sample size
HJ	0.20	0.19	0.61	132
M	0.33	0.19	0.48	132
r	0.19	0.19	0.62	132
Q	0.44	0.19	0.37	132

Note: $\mathrm{cov}(\ln(y),\ln(Z))/\mathrm{var}(\ln(y))$ with Z given in each column. — For h^{HJ}, h^M, h^r, and h^Q, see equations (2.13) to (2.16).

Table 2.6b: Alternative Schooling Quantity Data Sets: De la Fuente and Doménech (2000), OECD Sample, Covariance Measure

X \ Z	h^X	$(k/y)^{\frac{\alpha}{1-\alpha}}$	A	Sample size
HJ	0.46	0.15	0.40	21
M	0.86	0.15	−0.01	21
r	0.68	0.15	0.17	21
Q	1.04	0.15	−0.19	21

Note: $\mathrm{cov}(\ln(y),\ln(Z))/\mathrm{var}(\ln(y))$ with Z given in each column. — For h^{HJ}, h^M, h^r, and h^Q, see equations (2.13) to (2.16).

---

[32] The results for the two re-examinations based on the covariance measure are confirmed by the five-country measure.

2.4   The Benefits of High-Quality Education

The review of human capital specification has shown how the implementation of the concept of human capital has evolved in the empirical growth literature. In light of the differences between the different specifications, one should not wonder that different studies have found very different results on growth and development effects of human capital. The empirical results presented in this chapter reveal two crucial aspects in the construction of human capital measures, namely a differentiated weighting of schooling years by rates of return and the inclusion of the quality of education. International differences in quality-adjusted human capital can account for between 45 and 60 percent (depending on the inclusion of imputed human capital data) of the dispersion in development levels across a worldwide sample of countries in 1990 within the framework of a simple human-capital-augmented neoclassical model of economic growth and development. Furthermore, once cross-country differences in the quality of schooling are taken into consideration, differences in the accumulation of human capital across OECD countries can account for virtually the whole dispersion of their levels of economic development.

While this chapter has focused on education as a means to accumulate human capital, an encompassing specification of human capital should consider the whole range of investments that people make to improve their productivity. In addition to formal education, these investments also include informal education acquired parallel to schooling, skills acquired after schooling through training on the job, and experience gained through learning by doing. Furthermore, medical care, nutrition, and improvements in working conditions which avoid activities with high accident rates can be viewed as investments to improve health. While the variable age minus years in pre-schooling minus years in schooling has been used as a proxy for experience and the variables life expectancy and infant mortality rate have been used as proxies for health status, these are probably not very good measures of the productively available human capital accumulated through after-school skill acquisition and through health investments. A further complication lies in the fact that knowledge cannot only be gained, but also lost after it has been acquired in school. Nevertheless, the focus on the mere formal education component of human capital seems warranted because education also increases people's ability to learn later in live and to live healthier lives.

It can be mused that a high-quality education might lead to further potential benefits in areas of economic policy objectives other than long-run economic development, such as unemployment, inequality, and locational competition in an integrating world economy. Unemployment has risen sharply in Europe in recent decades, particularly among unskilled labor. This rise in unemployment can be mainly attributed to a shift in relative labor demand from unskilled to skilled labor (Schimmelpfennig 2000). This shift in favor of human capital to the detriment of workers with low levels of education is likely to accelerate in the "new economy," implying the threat of a "digital divide" (Siebert 2000b: 24). The most elegant way out of increasing unemployment would be to improve the productivity of unskilled workers (Siebert 1999b: 5–8). This can be achieved through the formation of human capital. Hence, a schooling system which ensures a high level of educational quality could help in lowering overall unemployment rates.

A second way out of the unemployment problem would be to allow wages to differ according to differences in qualification. Indeed, labor market institutions which restrict the necessary differentiation of wages in accordance with differential labor productivity are one of the rigidities which lie at the root of unemployment in Europe (Siebert 1997). Once the wage of each worker reflects his or her labor productivity, market forces will lead to a clearing of the labor market. However, the wage differentiation necessary to ensure a satisfactory level of employment may turn out to be unacceptable for other than purely economic reasons. Human capital formation might be a way to soften the problems of wage inequality arising from unregulated labor markets. While it cannot lead to a fully homogenous level of payments, human capital formation for all people in a country can bring about a more equal distribution of labor productivity in the work force, thereby lowering the necessary wage differentiation without causing unemployment (Siebert 1999b: 10). Such a strategy of increased education could also prevent a digital divide in the new economy.

Additionally, a schooling system which ensures high-quality education may have consequences in an integrating world economy which go beyond the benefits reaped in a closed economy. In the age of globalization, some factors of production such as mobile capital and mobile technological knowledge can move freely around the world and will settle at places which offer them the most productive opportunities. This leads to locational competition in which governments have to compete for these mobile factors of production. One of the policy instruments governments can use in order to attract mobile factors of production is the education system (Siebert 1999a: 278; 2000d: 147). Workers tend to be less mobile than other factors of production, and as such will compete for the mobile factors of production of the world. If a country succeeds in establishing an efficient schooling system which produces high-quality education for its people, this will make the country more attractive as a location for internationally mobile factors of production. Workers will be better educated than in other countries, and the best-educated work force will lure economic activity to the country. Thus, as globalization increases worldwide locational competition, a high-quality education system may lead to additional beneficial effects in an open economy by helping to keep and attract mobile factors of production into the country.

As a development accounting study, this chapter has taken a mainly descriptive approach in accounting for the "proximate" causes of international differences in levels of economic development—human capital, physical capital, and residual total factor productivity. To search for "ultimate" causes of economic development, one has to go beyond development accounting and look at what lies behind productivity and the accumulation of human and physical capital. Still, the development accounting results give an indication of where to look for these deeper causes. For example, the difference in the development accounting results between the world and OECD-sample results suggests that the analysis of institutions as an underlying cause of economic development may be promising (Olson 1996; Hall and Jones 1999).

More to the point of the findings in this chapter, research on the causes of differences in the quality of schooling seems to be a fertile path for growth research, since differences in schooling quality were shown to be a major factor in explaining international differences in the level of development. The remaining chapters of this study try to find out how schooling quality can be improved. Just as the institutions of an economy seem to be a central cause of economic development in general, differences in the institutions of the schooling systems will prove to be a central determinant of the cross-country differences in the quality of human capital. In his latest research on the relationship between education and growth, Temple (2001a: 917) suggests that rather than sticking to the analysis of growth effects of education, "[a] perhaps more interesting task for future research is to explore the fine detail of the institutional and incentive structure that best allocates a fixed amount of educational expenditure." This is the direction of research into which the current study tries to venture.

2.5   Appendix: Human Capital Data and Detailed Results

Table A2.1: Human Capital and Development Accounting Data for Various Countries[a] Relative to the United States

| | [1][b] | [2] | [3] | [4] | [5] | [6] | [7] | [8] | [9] | [10] | [11] | | |
	l	e	e^{MRW}	s^{PRO}	s^{PIM}	s^{ATT}	s^{DD}	h^{IU}	h^M	h'	h^Q	y	k
United States (abs.)[c]	–	*91.1*	*11.9*	*12.1*	*11.6*	*11.7*	*12.9*	*3.3*	*6.9*	*4.3*	*6.9*	*36 771*	*90 632*
Luxembourg	–	–	0.420	0.571	–	–	–	0.820	0.662	0.708	0.615	1.031	1.242
United States	–	1.000	1.000	1.000	1.000	1.000	1.000	1.000	1.000	1.000	1.000	1.000	1.000
Qatar	0.770	0.840	–	–	–	–	–	0.698	0.484	0.598	0.444	0.995	–
United Arab Emir.	0.770	0.776	–	–	–	–	–	0.698	0.484	0.598	0.444	0.995	–
Canada	–	1.093	0.891	0.826	0.862	0.936	0.991	0.950	0.898	0.864	1.216	0.935	0.993
Switzerland	–	0.783	0.403	–	0.599	0.864	0.971	0.897	0.804	0.819	1.370	0.892	1.256
Belgium	–	0.901	0.782	0.774	0.721	0.756	0.756	0.823	0.704	0.862	0.997	0.863	0.887
Netherlands	–	0.947	0.899	0.784	0.725	0.745	0.848	0.816	0.665	0.604	0.856	0.850	0.890
Italy	–	0.773	0.597	0.756	0.684	0.552	0.620	0.665	0.446	0.529	0.475	0.838	0.949
France	–	0.910	0.748	0.789	0.732	0.592	0.842	0.697	0.486	0.564	0.616	0.826	0.978
Australia	–	0.834	0.824	0.722	0.654	0.884	0.951	0.911	0.888	0.923	1.427	0.824	1.011
Germany, West	–	0.833	0.706	0.855	0.731	0.827	1.006	0.871	0.684	0.733	0.728	0.803	0.950
Bahamas	0.980	–	–	–	–	–	–	0.717	0.514	0.881	0.530	0.798	–
Norway	–	0.899	0.840	0.764	0.817	0.985	0.794	0.988	1.052	0.862	2.231	0.795	1.062
Sweden	–	0.813	0.664	0.797	0.848	0.810	0.807	0.859	0.735	0.776	1.062	0.772	0.832
Finland	–	0.980	0.966	0.896	0.844	0.799	0.765	0.852	0.734	0.763	1.141	0.744	1.052
Oman	–	0.600	0.227	–	–	–	–	0.617	0.402	0.506	0.341	0.732	0.540

Table A2.1 continued

	[1]b	[2]	[3]	[4]	[5]	[6]	[7]	[8]	[9]	[10]	[11]		
	l	e	e^{MRW}	s^{PRO}	s^{PIM}	s^{ATT}	s^{DD}	h^{HJ}	h^{M}	h^{r}	h^{Q}	y	k
United Kingdom	–	0.818	0.748	0.703	0.879	0.747	0.847	0.817	0.695	0.704	1.175	0.728	0.599
Austria	–	0.870	0.672	0.709	0.754	0.661	0.848	0.757	0.523	0.599	0.685	0.726	0.821
Spain	–	0.920	0.672	0.802	0.616	0.549	0.550	0.662	0.454	0.588	0.515	0.717	0.739
Puerto Rico	0.760	–	–	–	–	–	–	0.633	0.427	1.136	0.397	0.711	0.477
Kuwait	–	0.877	0.807	0.572	0.762	0.510	–	0.633	0.372	0.490	0.229	0.707	–
New Zealand	–	0.886	1.000	0.767	0.791	0.958	0.938	0.967	1.049	1.345	2.468	0.691	0.879
Iceland	–	0.894	0.857	0.708	0.787	0.691	–	0.781	0.609	0.664	0.697	0.679	0.760
Denmark	–	–	0.899	0.571	0.631	0.816	0.847	0.863	0.751	0.775	1.270	0.679	0.796
Singapore	0.890	0.673	0.756	0.570	1.083	0.507	–	0.631	0.420	0.428	0.746	0.663	0.664
Ireland	–	0.886	0.958	0.731	0.620	0.748	0.729	0.818	0.669	0.712	0.748	0.654	0.637
Israel	–	0.839	0.798	0.830	–	0.798	–	0.851	0.781	0.840	1.029	0.647	0.560
Saudi Arabia	0.590	0.542	0.261	0.244	–	–	–	0.617	0.402	0.506	0.341	0.640	0.422
Hong Kong	0.910	–	0.605	0.645	0.946	0.780	0.871	0.839	0.682	1.159	1.560	0.621	0.361
Japan	–	0.844	0.916	0.783	–	0.763	–	0.828	0.687	0.528	1.279	0.615	0.785
Bahrain	0.820	0.903	1.017	–	–	0.423	–	0.571	0.354	0.459	0.226	0.595	–
Trinidad & Tobago	0.970	0.761	0.739	0.489	–	0.610	–	0.713	0.517	0.661	0.512	0.541	0.420
Taiwan	–	–	–	0.386	–	0.679	–	0.774	0.581	1.301	0.771	0.501	0.335
Malta	–	0.827	0.597	0.565	–	–	–	0.737	0.567	0.655	0.766	0.495	0.378
Cyprus	–	0.796	0.689	–	0.660	0.742	0.613	0.814	0.662	0.445	0.651	0.491	0.440
Greece	0.900	0.845	0.664	0.695	0.753	0.681	–	0.775	0.605	0.654	0.686	0.482	0.481
Venezuela	0.880	0.772	0.588	0.571	0.569	0.422	–	0.570	0.357	0.615	0.308	0.474	0.446
Mexico	–	0.718	0.555	0.584	0.511	0.572	0.497	0.681	0.480	0.683	0.377	0.463	0.312
Portugal	–	0.785	0.487	0.539	0.493	0.418	–	0.567	0.342	0.436	0.327	0.452	0.352
Korea, Republic	0.970	0.866	0.857	0.657	0.665	0.847	–	0.885	0.789	0.908	1.207	0.436	0.331
Syria	0.660	0.752	0.739	0.548	–	0.435	–	0.579	0.361	0.510	0.262	0.432	0.261
USSR (Russia)	–	0.923	–	–	–	–	–	0.737	0.567	0.749	0.713	0.417	0.630

Table A2.1 continued

	[1]^b l	[2] e	[3] e^{MRW}	[4] s^{PRO}	[5] s^{PIM}	[6] s^{ATT}	[7] s^{DD}	[8] h^{HU}	[9] h^M	[10] h^r	[11] h^Q	y	k
Barbados	0.970	–	1.017	0.663	–	0.674	–	0.769	0.576	0.726	0.844	0.400	0.209
Argentina	0.960	–	0.420	0.664	0.652	0.693	–	0.782	0.638	0.450	0.674	0.365	0.359
Bulgaria	–	0.801	–	–	–	–	–	0.691	0.509	0.682	0.526	0.349	–
Jordan	0.820	0.598	0.908	0.618	0.424	0.506	–	0.630	0.407	0.568	0.369	0.344	0.228
Malaysia	0.800	0.645	0.613	0.474	0.534	0.514	–	0.636	0.430	0.661	0.512	0.341	0.276
Algeria	0.550	0.711	0.378	0.385	0.354	0.362	–	0.531	0.310	0.447	0.229	0.331	0.324
Iraq	0.520	–	0.622	0.377	0.360	0.278	–	0.469	0.262	0.365	0.206	0.323	0.314
Chile	0.940	–	0.647	0.576	0.618	0.593	–	0.698	0.515	0.438	0.284	0.322	0.272
Uruguay	0.970	0.847	0.588	0.634	0.679	0.604	–	0.707	0.507	0.775	0.587	0.322	0.253
Fiji	0.890	0.806	0.681	0.549	–	0.669	–	0.764	0.636	0.958	0.910	0.321	0.216
Iran	–	0.720	0.546	0.476	0.328	0.338	–	0.515	0.294	0.439	0.192	0.310	0.253
Belize	0.300	–	–	–	–	–	–	0.594	0.383	0.567	0.333	0.305	–
Brazil	0.810	0.739	0.395	0.458	0.380	0.342	–	0.519	0.305	0.761	0.260	0.300	0.239
Hungary	–	0.743	–	–	–	0.761	–	0.826	0.764	0.818	1.276	0.294	0.389
Mauritius	0.800	0.645	0.613	0.522	–	0.474	–	0.607	0.396	0.692	0.472	0.277	0.105
Colombia	0.900	0.622	0.513	0.540	0.436	0.400	–	0.556	0.333	0.520	0.284	0.275	0.174
Costa Rica	0.940	0.684	0.588	0.681	–	0.473	–	0.606	0.394	0.448	0.389	0.273	0.192
Yugoslavia	–	–	–	–	–	0.601	–	0.705	0.541	0.291	0.662	0.272	0.465
South Africa	0.800	0.874	0.252	–	–	0.460	–	0.596	0.399	0.730	0.440	0.261	0.216
Namibia	–	–	–	–	–	–	–	0.520	0.305	0.519	0.270	0.259	0.269
Seychelles	–	–	–	–	–	–	–	0.555	0.340	0.538	0.316	0.248	0.154
Ecuador	0.870	0.772	0.605	0.725	0.493	0.503	–	0.627	0.413	0.529	0.347	0.246	0.229
Tunisia	0.600	0.677	0.361	0.468	0.415	0.335	–	0.513	0.296	0.429	0.269	0.241	0.115
Turkey	0.790	0.606	0.462	0.523	0.387	0.353	–	0.525	0.309	0.434	0.276	0.235	0.186
Gabon	0.560	–	0.218	0.663	–	–	–	0.555	0.340	0.538	0.316	0.219	0.231
Yemen	–	–	0.050	–	–	0.126	–	0.370	0.191	0.266	0.179	0.219	0.077
Panama	0.890	0.739	0.975	0.661	0.644	0.688	–	0.779	0.619	0.885	0.619	0.218	0.192

Table A2.1 continued

	[1][b]	[2]	[3]	[4]	[5]	[6]	[7]	[8]	[9]	[10]	[11]		
	l	e	e^{MRW}	s^{PRO}	s^{PIM}	s^{ATT}	s^{DD}	h^{HJ}	h^{M}	h^{r}	h^{Q}	y	k
Czechoslovakia	–	0.787	–	–	–	–	–	0.737	0.567	0.655	0.654	0.210	0.277
Suriname	0.920	–	0.681	0.503	–	–	–	0.633	0.427	0.564	0.397	0.203	0.205
Poland	–	0.829	0.202	–	–	0.806	–	0.857	0.858	1.059	1.673	0.203	0.381
Guatemala	0.530	–	0.202	0.304	0.303	0.259	–	0.455	0.256	0.390	0.236	0.202	0.083
Reunion	–	–	–	–	–	–	–	0.555	0.340	0.538	0.316	0.198	0.158
Dominican Republic	0.800	–	0.487	0.471	0.412	0.378	–	0.541	0.320	0.483	0.283	0.188	0.145
Egypt	0.480	0.737	0.588	0.657	0.565	0.363	–	0.532	0.307	0.483	0.222	0.187	0.038
Peru	0.860	0.854	0.672	0.288	0.208	0.529	–	0.647	0.434	0.641	0.381	0.186	0.195
Morocco	0.930	–	0.303	–	–	–	–	0.553	0.336	1.387	0.276	0.184	0.072
Thailand	–	–	0.370	0.456	0.493	0.476	–	0.607	0.414	1.065	0.409	0.184	0.095
Solomon Islands	0.650	0.739	0.244	0.292	–	0.455	–	0.526	0.308	0.522	0.289	0.178	–
Botswana	–	–	–	–	–	–	–	0.593	0.396	2.135	0.287	0.178	0.108
Western Samoa	–	–	–	–	–	–	–	0.591	0.377	0.583	0.361	0.175	–
Grenada	–	–	–	–	–	–	–	0.594	0.383	0.567	0.333	0.174	–
Paraguay	0.910	0.615	0.370	0.510	0.500	0.523	–	0.642	0.442	0.709	0.376	0.174	0.111
Swaziland	0.720	0.720	0.311	0.447	–	0.450	–	0.590	0.398	0.685	0.346	0.171	0.094
Dominica	–	–	–	0.550	–	–	–	0.594	0.383	0.567	0.333	0.168	–
Tonga	–	–	–	–	–	–	–	0.591	0.377	0.583	0.361	0.164	–
St. Vincent & Grena.	–	–	–	–	–	–	–	0.594	0.383	0.567	0.333	0.158	–
Sri Lanka	0.890	3.728	0.697	0.499	0.540	0.517	–	0.638	0.421	0.728	0.382	0.156	0.071
El Salvador	0.690	0.620	0.328	0.349	0.428	0.362	–	0.531	0.324	0.454	0.228	0.149	0.062
St. Lucia	–	–	–	–	–	–	–	0.594	0.383	0.567	0.333	0.145	–
Bolivia	0.790	0.693	0.412	0.444	0.544	0.428	–	0.574	0.364	0.368	0.249	0.145	0.090
Vanuatu	–	–	–	–	–	–	–	0.591	0.377	0.583	0.361	0.143	–
Jamaica	0.830	0.697	0.941	0.488	0.693	0.404	–	0.558	0.336	0.457	0.347	0.140	0.139
Indonesia	0.820	0.673	0.345	0.370	0.381	0.341	–	0.518	0.302	0.494	0.285	0.137	0.099
Djibouti	0.410	0.215	–	–	–	–	–	0.520	0.305	0.519	0.270	0.133	0.069

Table A2.1 continued

	[1]b	[2]	[3]	[4]	[5]	[6]	[7]	[8]	[9]	[10]	[11]		
	l	e	e^{MRW}	s^{PRO}	s^{PIM}	s^{ATT}	s^{DD}	h^{HI}	h^{M}	h^{r}	h^{Q}	y	k
Bangladesh	0.350	0.381	0.269	0.288	0.269	0.187	–	0.407	0.217	0.358	0.210	0.130	0.018
Philippines	0.940	0.847	0.891	0.734	0.667	0.620	–	0.721	0.532	0.562	0.369	0.130	0.089
Pakistan	0.340	0.339	0.252	0.210	0.182	0.353	–	0.525	0.293	0.369	0.276	0.126	0.043
Congo	0.680	0.822	0.319	–	–	0.437	–	0.580	0.357	0.621	0.386	0.122	0.046
Honduras	0.690	–	0.311	0.467	0.383	0.358	–	0.528	0.317	0.508	0.235	0.121	0.069
Nicaragua	0.640	0.617	0.487	0.498	–	0.311	–	0.494	0.284	0.430	0.215	0.113	0.089
Romania	–	0.729	–	–	–	–	–	0.691	0.509	0.682	0.526	0.112	0.119
Mongolia	0.800	0.719	–	–	–	–	–	0.591	0.377	0.583	0.361	0.107	–
India	0.480	0.568	0.429	0.393	0.305	0.349	–	0.523	0.308	0.654	0.203	0.088	0.045
Cote d'Ivoire	0.340	–	0.193	0.340	0.181	–	–	0.520	0.305	0.519	0.270	0.084	0.047
Papua New Guinea	0.680	–	0.126	0.232	–	0.196	–	0.412	0.226	0.319	0.180	0.082	0.068
Guyana	0.970	–	0.983	0.514	–	0.484	–	0.614	0.416	0.689	0.462	0.081	0.149
Laos	0.520	–	–	–	–	–	–	0.526	0.308	0.522	0.289	0.078	–
Cape Verde Islands	0.630	0.605	–	–	–	–	–	0.520	0.305	0.519	0.270	0.075	0.070
Cameroon	0.570	0.577	0.286	0.449	0.269	0.262	–	0.457	0.258	0.432	0.244	0.068	0.031
Sierra Leone	0.270	0.314	0.143	0.164	0.190	0.182	–	0.403	0.215	0.360	0.199	0.068	0.005
Zimbabwe	0.820	0.754	0.370	0.402	0.389	0.429	–	0.575	0.356	0.726	0.311	0.066	0.047
Senegal	0.290	0.338	0.143	0.205	0.173	0.193	–	0.410	0.222	0.369	0.207	0.065	0.014
Sudan	0.400	0.341	0.168	0.173	0.160	0.140	–	0.378	0.197	0.322	0.185	0.063	0.041
Nepal	0.240	0.603	0.193	0.168	–	0.132	–	0.373	0.190	0.311	0.186	0.062	0.016
China	0.780	0.587	–	–	0.448	0.498	–	0.624	0.416	0.722	0.618	0.060	0.050
Liberia	0.340	–	0.210	0.267	–	0.183	–	0.404	0.215	0.487	0.199	0.058	0.033
Nigeria	0.490	–	0.210	0.166	0.210	–	–	0.447	0.249	0.426	0.228	0.057	0.034
Lesotho	0.670	0.665	0.168	0.404	–	0.334	–	0.512	0.312	0.366	0.339	0.057	0.033
Zambia	0.730	0.618	0.202	0.317	0.388	0.356	–	0.527	0.325	0.608	0.273	0.056	0.059
Haiti	0.410	–	0.160	0.220	0.226	0.248	–	0.447	0.249	0.406	0.226	0.054	0.018
Benin	–	0.333	0.151	0.193	–	0.166	–	0.393	0.209	0.358	0.194	0.052	0.019

Table A2.1 continued

	[1][b]	[2]	[3]	[4]	[5]	[6]	[7]	[8]	[9]	[10]	[11]		
	l	e	e^{MRW}	s^{PRO}	s^{PIM}	s^{ATT}	s^{DD}	h^{HU}	h^{M}	h^{r}	h^{Q}	y	k
Ghana	0.580	0.493	0.395	0.319	0.391	0.308	–	0.492	0.278	0.422	0.208	0.051	0.012
Kenya	0.720	0.637	0.202	0.285	0.356	0.311	–	0.494	0.292	0.518	0.227	0.051	0.028
Gambia	0.340	–	0.126	0.128	–	0.138	–	0.377	0.196	0.332	0.184	0.047	0.014
Mauritania	0.350	0.285	0.084	0.085	0.573	0.206	–	0.419	0.230	0.402	0.209	0.045	0.037
Somalia	–	–	0.092	0.068	–	–	–	0.447	0.249	0.398	0.224	0.045	0.022
Guinea	0.310	0.211	–	–	–	–	–	0.447	0.249	0.444	0.224	0.043	0.011
Togo	0.450	0.598	0.244	–	–	0.250	–	0.449	0.249	0.442	0.212	0.043	0.029
Madagascar	–	0.462	0.218	0.356	0.300	–	–	0.447	0.249	0.444	0.224	0.042	0.004
Mozambique	0.350	–	0.059	0.174	0.226	0.077	–	0.342	0.174	0.288	0.162	0.042	0.005
Rwanda	0.540	–	0.034	0.268	0.239	0.179	–	0.401	0.220	0.381	0.202	0.042	0.009
Bhutan	0.370	–	–	–	–	–	–	0.526	0.308	0.522	0.289	0.041	–
Guinea-Bissau	0.500	–	–	0.190	0.157	0.055	–	0.330	0.165	0.270	0.161	0.040	0.028
Angola	–	0.378	0.151	0.305	0.222	–	–	0.520	0.305	0.519	0.270	0.040	0.007
Myanmar (Burma)	0.810	0.494	0.294	0.409	0.222	0.211	–	0.422	0.228	0.377	0.220	0.037	0.012
Comoros	0.540	–	–	–	0.679	–	–	0.447	0.249	0.444	0.224	0.034	0.025
Central African Rep.	0.500	0.345	0.118	0.295	–	0.200	–	0.415	0.223	0.388	0.183	0.033	0.010
Malawi	0.520	0.436	0.050	0.163	0.293	0.231	–	0.436	0.248	0.348	0.222	0.033	0.013
Chad	0.430	–	0.034	0.151	–	–	–	0.447	0.249	0.444	0.224	0.031	0.004
Uganda	0.570	0.437	0.092	0.243	0.216	0.278	–	0.469	0.271	1.672	0.239	0.031	0.004
Tanzania	0.620	0.371	0.042	0.152	0.216	0.237	–	0.440	0.251	0.439	0.225	0.031	0.013
Zaire (Congo, D. R.)	0.720	–	0.303	0.358	0.344	0.239	–	0.441	0.246	0.436	0.212	0.030	0.008
Mali	0.250	0.151	0.084	0.119	0.097	0.057	–	0.331	0.165	0.271	0.161	0.030	0.008
Burundi	0.310	0.348	0.034	0.143	–	0.118	–	0.364	0.190	0.321	0.180	0.029	0.007
Burkina Faso	0.160	0.181	0.034	0.061	–	–	–	0.447	0.249	0.444	0.224	0.029	0.011
Niger	0.120	0.159	0.042	0.069	–	0.070	–	0.338	0.170	0.280	0.165	0.028	0.013
Ethiopia	0.310	0.206	0.092	0.094	0.049	–	–	0.447	0.249	0.415	0.224	0.019	0.004

[a] Countries are ranked according to output per worker, y. – [b] l (column [1]): Absolute value of the adult literacy rate. – [c] Absolute U.S. values reported in the first row. – See section 2.2.3 for further details.

Table A2.2a: Share of Human Capital: Further Samples, Covariance Measure

	h^{HJ}	h^M	h^r	h^Q
	Z			
1990 sample: Population 25 and over	0.22	0.34	0.20	0.45
1980 sample	0.21	0.33	0.19	0.42
1980 subsample: low mining share	0.23	0.36	0.22	0.47
1990 subsamples:				
Low mining share	0.22	0.35	0.19	0.48
Nonimputed s^{ATT}	0.23	0.37	0.19	0.51
Nonimputed Q	0.20	0.34	0.16	0.51
Nonimputed s^{ATT} and Q	0.20	0.33	0.16	0.52
PWT benchmark study (BS)	0.22	0.36	0.19	0.52
BS, nonimputed s^{ATT} and Q	0.20	0.35	0.13	0.60
Nonprojected Q	0.21	0.34	0.14	0.51
BS, nonimp. s^{ATT}, nonproj. Q	0.19	0.34	0.11	0.61

Note: $\operatorname{cov}(\ln(y),\ln(Z))/\operatorname{var}(\ln(y))$ with Z given in each column. — For h^{HJ}, h^M, h^r, and h^Q, see equations (2.13) to (2.16).

Table A2.2b: Share of Human Capital: Further Samples, Five-Country Measure

	h^{HJ}	h^M	h^r	h^Q
	Z			
1990 sample: Population 25 and over	0.24	0.39	0.26	0.47
1980 sample	0.19	0.30	0.18	0.36
1980 subsample: low mining share	0.23	0.36	0.22	0.44
1990 subsamples:				
Low mining share	0.24	0.39	0.26	0.47
Nonimputed s^{ATT}	0.25	0.40	0.18	0.51
Nonimputed Q	0.23	0.39	0.23	0.51
Nonimputed s^{ATT} and Q	0.24	0.39	0.22	0.54
PWT benchmark study (BS)	0.22	0.36	0.23	0.44
BS, nonimputed s^{ATT} and Q	0.19	0.35	0.15	0.47
Nonprojected Q	0.21	0.36	0.20	0.49
BS, nonimp. s^{ATT}, nonproj. Q	0.14	0.36	0.10	0.37

Note: $\ln\left(\prod_{i=1}^{5} Z_i \middle/ \prod_{j=n-4}^{n} Z_j\right) \middle/ \ln\left(\prod_{i=1}^{5} y_i \middle/ \prod_{j=n-4}^{n} y_j\right)$ with n = sample size, countries i, ..., j, ..., n ranked according to y, and Z given in each column. — For h^{HJ}, h^M, h^r, and h^Q, see equations (2.13) to (2.16).

3   The Missing Link between Expenditure and Schooling Quality

The preceding chapter has shown that the quality of schooling is crucial for economic development. It has become apparent that large differences in schooling quality exist across countries. Why is this so? How is the quality of schooling determined, and how can policy influence the quality of schooling? Higher expenditure on schooling resources are an obvious candidate to achieve this end. Given efficient use of available resources, differences in resource equipment of schools should lead to differences in schooling quality.

The question how educational inputs are transformed into educational output in the schooling system is, among other things, analyzed in the economics of education. The education production function is the concept used in the economics of education to explore the input-output relationship in education. Apart from the opportunity cost of students' time, teachers are the most important, and most costly, factor of production in schooling. Thus, much of the discussion of the impact of educational expenditure on students' performance goes under the heading of the "class-size debate," which deals with the effect of differences in teacher-student ratios on student performance. "At heart, questions of class size and student performance involve economics" (Krueger 1999b: 1).

A controversial discussion wages in the literature on what the vast evidence of within-country cross-section studies of education production functions tells us about the impact of educational expenditure on schooling quality, usually measured as students' performance on tests in central educational subjects (Section 3.1). While cases exist where increased resource endowment has led to superior student performance, the general empirical evidence seems to suggest that at given levels of expenditure, an increase in the amount of resources used in the schooling system does not lead to an increase in educational performance. This lack of a strong and systematic relationship between expenditure and performance has been shown both within the United States and within developing countries, although the developing country evidence suggests that there may be positive expenditure effects at very low levels of resource endowment. The missing link between expenditure and schooling quality extends to studies which account for the potential endogeneity of expenditure levels to students' performance, either through instrumental variable estimation or through data from controlled experiments. Still, the discussion in the literature has also shown that the within-country cross-section research faces methodological problems with respect to potential resource endogeneity, appropriate choice of instruments, and experimental test design.

In addition to the within-country cross-section evidence, two pieces of new evidence are presented in this chapter which are not plagued by the within-country cross-section problems and which strengthen the suggestion that increases in spending and better schooling quality do not necessarily go hand in hand. Section 3.2 reviews the international cross-section evidence and presents new cross-country evidence based on the Third International Mathematics and Science Study (TIMSS). The evidence shows that differences in the amount of inputs available in the schooling systems do not suffice as an explanation for the large international differences which exist in student performance levels in mathematics and science.

The missing positive resource-performance relationship is also evident in the second new piece of evidence, namely within-countries time series, presented in Section 3.3. The time-series evidence reveals that a vast expansion in educational expenditure per student over the past 15 to 25 years did not lead to an increase in schooling quality, neither within most OECD countries nor within several East Asian countries.

The main result which emerges from all three strands of evidence is that merely increasing the resources available to the schooling system does *not* increase the quality of schooling. Schools do not seem to be economically efficient. Within-country cross-section evidence, international cross-section evidence, and within-country time-series evidence all suggest that there is no clear positive relationship between educational expenditure and schooling quality.

3.1 Within-Country Cross-Section Evidence: A Survey of the Literature

3.1.1 The Concept of the Education Production Function

The production function approach views schools as locations where education is produced. Studies of the education production function link the output of the education process, i.e., the educational achievement of students, to the inputs available in schools (Hanushek 1986). Therefore, they are sometimes also called input-output analyses or cost-quality studies. Education production functions are usually estimated in the following form:

$$(3.1) \quad Q = B'\beta_1 + R'\beta_2 + \varepsilon.$$

Schooling quality, Q, as the output of educational production is usually measured by the performance of students on tests of cognitive skills.[33] Schooling inputs are encompassed in vectors of measures of students' family background characteristics, B, and of resource measures, R. The βs are vectors of parameters, and ε is an error term. The resource measures, R, can include variables such as expenditure per student, class size, teacher-student ratio, teacher characteristics, and endowment with teaching facilities. Note that class size is measured inversely to the teacher-student ratio. Thus, a positive effect of additional resources on student performance would be represented by an estimated *positive* coefficient on the teacher-student ratio, while being represented by an estimated *negative* coefficient on class size (or on the student-teacher ratio).

Given data on schooling output and schooling inputs, the education production function of equation (3.1) can be estimated, typically by single-equation regression, to yield evidence on the direction, magnitude, and significance of the input-output relationships. In this chapter, the main focus is on the relationship between schooling resources and schooling quality. In estimating this relationship, it is vital to control for the students' family background, such as income and education of the parents. Otherwise, the estimates of resource effects will be biased because family background and schools' resource endowment may usually be correlated. For example, in the United States, where most of the school funding comes from local property taxes, the resources available to a school district depend on the income of the local residents. The estimated resource effects would then not indicate a causal impact of resources but would instead just be a proxy for the impact of family background.[34]

The econometric estimation of education production functions began in earnest with the Coleman report (Coleman et al. 1966), a congressionally mandated study by the Office of Education in the United States. Since then, a large amount of research has focused on the estimation of education production functions, especially in the United States. During the three decades of analysis until 1994, more than a hundred individual publications in books or academic journals have been counted in literature surveys. In recent years, several journals have dedicated whole issues to the topic of the effectiveness of resource use in education, among them the *Journal of Economic Perspectives* (1996), the *Review of Economics and Statistics* (1996), and the *Economic Policy Review* of the Federal

---

[33] Section 5.2.2 discusses the use of test scores in cognitive achievement tests as measures of educational output in more detail in the context of the TIMSS data.

[34] As shown in Chapter 5, the concept of the education production function can also be extended to include institutional features of the schooling system as input factors.

Reserve Bank of New York (1998). The questions of how the econometric results in the literature can be summarized and what they tell us about policy implications have initiated a controversial discussion in the literature, with Eric Hanushek and Alan Krueger as the main antagonists in recent debates.

3.1.2   Conventional Within-Country Estimates from the United States

Hanushek's Summary of the U.S. Evidence

Hanushek (1997b, 1996b, 1999b), in updating his previous literature surveys (e.g., Hanushek 1981, 1986), summarizes the resource effects estimated by conventional within-country education production functions by tabulating them as statistically significantly positive, statistically significantly negative, and statistically insignificant.[35] He collects all the studies available through 1994 that meet three minimal publication, specification, and reporting criteria. First, they must be published in a book or journal to ensure minimal quality standards. Second, they must include some measure of family background in addition to at least one measure of schooling resources. And third, they must provide information about the statistical significance of the estimated resource effects. Most of the reported studies measure educational output by student performance on standardized tests, while some studies use other measures such as dropout behavior or subsequent earnings in the labor market.

From all the publications which meet the three criteria for analytical design and reporting of results to be included in the summary, Hanushek takes each separate estimate of a resource effect from an education production function as a single independent observation. A typical publication is likely to contain several sets of estimates, derived from different output measures, different grade levels, and different sampling designs. Hence, not all estimates can be considered as independent from each other. If several estimates in a publication are based on alternative specifications using the same sample and performance measure, only one of them was included.

Figure 3.1 reports the results of Hanushek's literature survey for the United States. The 90 individual publications with U.S. evidence included in the survey yielded 377 separate production function estimates.[36] While many of the inluded studies were produced in the direct aftermath of the Coleman Report of 1966, half of the available studies have been published since 1985. Without going into

---

[35]   The statistically insignificant estimates are sometimes subdivided into positive estiates, negative estimates, and estimates with unreported sign.

[36]   For a list of the included studies, see Hanushek (1997b).

Figure 3.1: Estimated Effects of Schooling Resources: United States[a]

Schooling inputs[b]	Insignificant	Negative	Positive

Classroom Resources

Teacher-student ratio (277) — 72 | 14 | 14

Teacher education (171) — 86 | 5 | 9

Teacher experience (207) — 66 | 5 | 29

Financial Aggregates

Expenditure per student (163) — 66 | 7 | 27

Teacher salary (119) — 73 | 7 | 20

Other School Resources

Facilities (91) — 86 | 5 | 9

Administrative inputs (75) — 83 | 5 | 12

Percent   Percent

100   80   60   40   20   0   20   40

[a]Summary of selected regression coefficients on various resource measures estimated by education production functions (dependent variable: student achievement). Percentage of statistically insignificant (white), statistically significant negative (grey), and statistically significant positive (black) regression coefficients. — [b]Number of estimates in parentheses.

Source: Adapted from Hanushek (1997b, 2000).

detail on the different estimates and their relative merits with respect to suitability and data quality, it is apparent that for most resource measures only a small fraction of the published estimates shows a statistically significant positive effect. For each of the resource categories, at least two-thirds of the estimates are statistically insignificant, and the statistically significant positive estimates are usually nearly balanced by statistically significant negative estimates. That is, without even looking at the size of the estimated effects, it is fair to say that there is not much confidence in getting noticeable effects of schooling resources on schooling quality. This leads Hanushek (1997b: 148) to conclude that "[t]here is no strong or consistent relationship between school resources and student performance." Furthermore, there seem to be large differences in the relationship across classrooms and schools, and the distribution of underlying resource parameters suggests that while resources are used effectively in some circumstances, in most circumstances they are not.

Krueger's Reinterpretation of the U.S. Evidence

A fierce political debate waged in the United States in the late 1990s about how to improve U.S. schools. In a Gallup poll, Americans even rated education as the most important issue in the 2000 presidential election campaign (Gallup 2000). The class-size debate usually takes central stage on this political agenda. In this political climate, Hanushek's (1997b) summary of the U.S. evidence has not gone without criticism.

Krueger (1999b) criticizes Hanushek's (1997b) method for summarizing the literature mainly on the basis of his weighting of estimates.[37] As described above, Hanushek's rule for weighting estimates is to give equal weight to any production function estimate, regardless of whether there was only one estimate or several estimates within the publications where it is taken from. Hence, more estimates would be taken from a publication which analyzes several subsamples of a larger data set than from a publication which uses only the complete sample of the larger data set. Therefore, Krueger argues that Hanushek's method gives larger weights to estimates based on smaller samples. Other things being equal, estimates based on smaller samples are likely to yield less significant results. Krueger (1999b) shows that publications included in Hanushek's summary with only one estimate tend to report far more statistically significant positive results than publications with many estimates. Thus, the prevalence of statistically insignificant estimates in Figure 3.1 may not be due to the lack of a systematic relationship between resources and student performance, but due to small sample sizes being overrepresented in Hanushek's averages.

In his reanalysis of Hanushek's results, Krueger (1999b) gives equal weight to each underlying publication, instead of each individual estimate extracted from the publications. His results, reported for the estimates of teacher-student ratios and expenditure per student, are replicated in Figure 3.2 ("Based on publications"). As expected, Krueger's method yields a larger proportion of statistically significant positive results and a smaller proportion of statistically insignificant results.

---

[37] A previous critique of Hanushek's method by Hedges et al. (1994) was based on issues in the method of meta-analysis. While illuminating, their study is not of central importance to the question of this chapter, because it is not based on the research question of whether resources *generally* have an impact on student performance. Instead, their study is based on the rejection of the null hypothesis that all resource estimates are simultaneously equal to zero, thereby asking the research question of whether there is *any* circumstance under which resources have a positive impact on student performance (Hanushek 1994, 1997b).

Figure 3.2: Krueger's Account of the U.S. Evidence[a]

Schooling inputs[b]	Insignificant	Negative	Positive

Teacher-Student Ratio

Based on estimates (277)	72	14	14
Based on publications (277)	64	10	26
Disaggregated data (266)	74	14	12
Value-added models (78)	80	8	12
Value-added disagg. (23)	83	13	4

Expenditure per Student

Based on estimates (163)	66	7	27
Based on publications (163)	56	6	38
Disaggregated data (135)	74	7	19

Percent   Percent

100   80   60   40   20   0   20   40

[a]Summary of selected regression coefficients on various resource measures estimated by education production functions (dependent variable: student achievement). Percentage of statistically insignificant (white), statistically significant negative (grey), and statistically significant positive (black) regression coefficients. — [b]Number of estimates in parentheses.

Source: Adapted from Krueger (1999b); Hanushek (2000); own calculations.

Based on a ratio of positive to negative results which gives equal weight to statistically significant estimates and statistically insignificant estimates, Krueger shows that the larger prevalence of positive results is unlikely to be caused by chance and therefore argues that class size is systematically related to student performance. However, the proportion of statistically significant positive results is still only 26 percent for teacher-student ratios and 38 percent for expenditure per student. Even in his reanalysis, the majority of results is either statistically insignificant or statistically significantly negative.[38]

---

[38]   Krueger (1999b) also reports results where publications are weighted by their number of citations in other works, which are quite similar to the results which give equal weight to each publication. Furthermore, he reports adjusted results based on re-

In direct response to Krueger's criticism, Hanushek (2000) shows that Krueger's assumption that publications with fewer individual estimates will tend to have larger sample sizes is incorrect. In the publications included in the survey, there is no clear relationship between the number of estimates per publication and the sample size. The median and the average of the sample size is about the same in publications with one estimate and in publications with more than seven estimates, while publications with two to three estimates have the largest median sample size and publications with four to seven estimates have the largest average sample size. The simple correlation between sample size and number of estimates in the underlying publications is insignificantly different from zero. Since the number of estimates per publication is not related to sample size, there is no obvious reason for Hanushek's weighting rule to be flawed. This fact basically erodes the foundation of Krueger's critique, since Hanushek's method does *not* give larger weights to estimates based on smaller samples. The prevalence of statistically insignificant resource estimates does not seem to stem from small sample size, but from a missing relationship between resources and student performance. Furthermore, the decision to include more than one estimate in a publication is generally based on sound econometric reasons, e.g., when the estimates come from different cities with differing standardized tests as measures of educational output.[39]

Hanushek (2000) argues that his general results may actually be biased in the direction of finding too many statistically significant positive effects rather than too few. First, there is considerable empirical evidence that a publication bias exists in the sense that studies with statistically significant estimates are more likely to be published.[40] Second, Hanushek et al. (1996) have shown that data aggregation to the state level leads to upward bias of estimated resource effects when differences in schooling policy across states are omitted in multiple state samples. When using only studies based on disaggregated data (at the classroom, school, district, or county level, but not at the state level), the proportion of

gressions of the percent of estimates being positive or negative, and significant or insignificant, on the number of estimates used from each study. This method seems rather dubious, since the assumption that these relationships are linear bears no theoretical foundation and can presumably be rejected empirically.

[39] Hanushek (2000) adds that Krueger's equal weighting of statistically significant estimates and statistically insignificant estimates in the calculation of his ratio of positive to negative results seems to violate the basic premise of his reweighting. He also questions the assumption that citation weights give a more accurate estimate of the quality of the underlying estimates, since studies are often cited because they are innovative, controversial, or just diverge from the rest of the literature, neither of which is necessarily a sign of quality.

[40] For example, in a recent review of estimates of the relationship between schooling and earnings, Ashenfelter et al. (1999) show that estimated rates of return to education suffer from considerable publication bias.

statistically significant positive estimates shrinks ("Disaggregated data" in Figure 3.2). This may actually be an explanation for the findings of Krueger's (1999b) reanalysis, since 40 percent of the publications which contain only a single estimate use state aggregate data, compared to only 4 percent of all estimates. Thus, weighting by publications rather than by separate estimates puts heavy weight on low-quality estimates. Third, when the research question is the effect of current resources on student performance, studies which do not control for initial performance may be misleading, since education is a cumulative process and builds on knowledge accumulated in earlier grades. Value-added models which control for students' performance at the beginning of a grade, usually by focusing on the growth in student performance over one grade, are conceptually superior for estimating resource effects. As reported in Figure 3.2 ("Value-added models"), only 12 percent of the estimates for teacher-student ratios from value-added models show a statistically significant positive effect, and only one of the available 24 estimates which come from value-added models with disaggregated data from within a single state shows a statistically significant positive sign.[41]

In sum, Krueger's (1999b) reanalysis seems to place much larger weight on low-quality and biased statistical estimates. And even then, still only 26 percent of the estimates for teacher-student ratios are statistically significant and positive. Based on conventional within-country education production functions, the econometric evidence for positive effects on schooling quality through increased resource expenditure across the whole range of schools remains weak.

3.1.3   Recent Research on Resource Endogeneity

3.1.3.1 The Unclear Direction of the Potential Bias

The data used to estimate resource effects usually originate from surveys conducted for other purposes. Ideally, experimental or randomized data should be used to estimate education production functions. Hence, conventional estimates of resource effects may be flawed because of endogeneity problems. That is, the resources devoted to the education process may not be exogenous to the performance of students. Instead, it is conceivable that the amount of resources depends on choices by politicians, administrators, teachers, and parents which may, among other things, be based on the level of performance achieved by the students. In this case, conventional ordinary least squares (OLS) estimates of resource effects in equation (3.1) will produce biased estimates of the causal effects of resources on schooling quality.

---

[41] No value-added models are available for expenditure per student.

The direction of the bias introduced by resource endogeneity is ambiguous (Hoxby 2000b). On the one hand, if resource choices are compensatory in that poor student performance induces an increase in available resources, this will cause estimated resource effects to be biased downwards. The within-school allocation of resources, usually decided upon by school administrators and teachers, may be one potential source of compensatory variation in school resources. For example, in his model of educational production, Lazear (2001: 778) argues that "class size is a choice variable and the optimal class size varies inversely with the attention span of the students." If available resources indeed vary primarily because schools are adjusting resources in response to the behavior and performance of the students in the sense that poor performance induces increased resource endowment, then the classes which are larger and endowed with fewer resources will have the better students and, therefore, higher measured schooling quality. The ensuing negative relationship between resources and schooling quality will not be an estimate of the causal effect of resources on student performance, but will mainly reflect the reverse causality running from student performance to allocated resources. Likewise, if policymakers design compensatory funding schemes which assign higher expenditure to weaker students, this will also bias the estimated resource effect downwards.

On the other hand, if resource choices are reinforcing in that better students receive more resources, this will cause estimated resource effects to be biased upwards. Both endogenous within-school resource allocations and between-school resource variations may actually be reinforcing. If schools respond more to the demands of parents who contribute more to their children's learning, and if these parental contributions are not sufficiently controlled for, the positive correlation between resource allocation and parental contributions will cause the estimated resource effects to be biased upwards. Likewise, policymakers may introduce reinforcing policies, e.g., by endowing better students with special facilities in order to support elite students.

In addition, residential choices by parents may be based on the amount of resources available in a school district and may thus also trigger compensatory or reinforcing resource variations. Indeed, Hoxby (2000b: 1245) suggests that school choice through parents' residential choice is "probably the single largest source of variation in school inputs" in the United States. If parents move to school districts with high schooling expenditure, the problem for empirical research is that their residential decision may be based on their children's ability or prior educational performance, either in a reinforcing or in a compensatory manner. Thus, residential choice is likely to generate resource endogeneity, and the resulting bias can go either way.

In sum, the direction of any potential bias introduced by resource endogeneity is unclear. Two possibilities exist to answer the questions of whether endogenous resource assignments indeed cause biased findings, and in which direction a potential bias may work. One possibility is to use instrumental variables to account for potential endogeneity of resource endowments (Section 3.1.3.2). The other possibility is to perform an experiment which randomly assigns different amounts of resources to different students (Section 3.1.3.3).

3.1.3.2 Instrumental Variable Estimates

The instrumental variable (IV) estimator is the most common econometric method used to solve a potential endogeneity problem. If there is resource endogeneity, the problem with conventional OLS estimates of equation (3.1) is that the resource measures, R, will not be independent of the error term, ε. With the IV estimator, an instrument which is correlated with the resource effect but uncorrelated with ε is used to extract information only from that part of the variation in the resource variable which is exogenous to the measure of educational output. In a first stage, the resource variables, R, are regressed on the instruments, I (γ is a vector of estimated parameters, and μ is an error term):

$$(3.2) \quad R = I'\gamma + \mu.$$

Given that the vector of instruments I is indeed independent of the error term ε of equation (3.1), the predicted values $\hat{R}$ of equation (3.2) will also be independent of ε, thus representing resource variations which are truly exogenous to conditional student performance. Therefore, in a second stage, the predicted values $\hat{R}$ are used instead of R in equation (3.1) to estimate the causal effect of resources on student performance. Quite often, the two-stage least squares (2SLS) approach of IV estimation is employed, where the list of instruments, I, in equation (3.2) entails not only the additional variable(s) chosen as special instrument(s) for the resource variable, but also all other exogenous variables of equation (3.1).

Several recent studies have used IV estimates to account for potential resource endogeneity. Akerhielm (1995) applies 2SLS estimation to account for the endogeneity of class size due to nonrandom allocation of students to different classes. She uses the average class size for a given subject in a student's school and total student enrollment in the school at the specific grade level as instruments for class size. The average class size in the school is meant to be exogenous to an individual student's performance while being strongly correlated with the student's actual class size, thereby bypassing the within-school nonrandom student allocation problem by excluding the within-school source of variation in class size. Total grade enrollment in the school is also meant to be exogenous to an individual student's performance but is meant to identify the fact that larger schools may be more able and therefore more likely to offer specialized small classes for lower ability students.

Akerhielm (1995) finds for a nationally representative sample of students from the United States that the OLS estimates show a positive relation between class size and student performance which is statistically significant in three out of four subjects. However, her IV estimates show a negative relation between class size and performance which is statistically significant in science and history while being statistically insignificant in mathematics and English. Hence, her findings seem to confirm positive resource effects, at least in some subjects. However, all the estimated effects are very small in size. Furthermore, it is unclear whether her IV approach yields truly exogenous variations in class size because the between-school variation in class size may be influenced by between-school sorting due to residential choice by parents, which is not instrumented for. Additionally, enrollment, which is used as an instrument, may arguably be associated with student performance, e.g., because better schools grow larger when parents choose to enroll their children there or because socio-economic status may be inversely related to population density, so that the IV estimate of the class-size effect may be contaminated by effects not caused by changes in class size.

Boozer and Rouse (2001) use state regulations on special education to instrument for class size. They argue that actual class size will be correlated with state regulations on maximum class sizes for several types of special needs classes to the extent that schools base the entire structure of their class sizes on such state policy. Using the same source of data used in Akerhielm's (1995) study, most of the IV estimates of their different specifications yield a negative effect of class size on student performance and are usually reported to be statistically significant.[42] The choice of the instruments may be flawed, however, since state regulations will probably reflect the preferences of the residents of the state towards education rather than maximum class sizes which are exogenously determined. That is, the instrument may be both endogenous and a proxy for parental preferences. Specification tests reject the null hypothesis of consistent IV estimates for most of their results.

Sander (1999) uses demographic characteristics of a school district, namely the percentage of the population of a school district which is of school age, to instrument for either expenditure per student or for teachers' salary in two specifications of an education production function. He argues that an increase in the school-aged part of a district's population reduces expenditure per student.

---

[42] However, the reported significance levels should be seriously biased upwards, since they do not take into account a school component of the error term due to the stratified sampling structure (Section 5.3.2.2).

No instrument is applied to the class-size variable. Sander (1999) estimates a 2SLS regression and finds that expenditure per student and average teachers' salary have modest positive effects on eighth-grade mathematics test scores of students in Illinois which are statistically significant at the 10 percent level, while neither has a statistically significant effect on mathematics performance in third grade. Class-size estimates are statistically insignificant in all cases. Sander's (1999) study suffers from the use of aggregated data, and doubts about the validity of the choice of instruments may be due.

Going beyond the United States, Angrist and Lavy (1999) exploit a potentially exogenous source of variation in the class size of Israeli primary schools which originates from an administrative rule. Maimonides, a twelfth century rabbinic scholar, proposed the rule of a maximum class size of 40. This rule on maximum class size establishes a nonlinear and nonmonotonic function between total grade enrollment in a school and class size in Israeli schools today which is presumably exogenous to student performance. Therefore, the class size predicted by enrollment through the nonlinear class-size function derived from Maimonides' rule can be used as an instrument for the actual class size. At the same time, any potential linear or monotonic effect of total enrollment on student performance can be controlled for in the estimation.

Angrist and Lavy (1999) find statistically significant positive IV estimates of effects of smaller classes for most of their specifications on mathematics and reading achievement in fifth grade and (albeit smaller) for reading in fourth grade, while the estimates for mathematics in fourth grade and for mathematics and reading in third grade are statistically insignificant and sometimes negative. While being superior to Akerhielm's (1995) study in controlling for smooth effects of total school enrollment on test scores, Angrist and Lavy's (1999) study may still suffer from endogeneity due to residential choice. Furthermore, Israel has relatively large class sizes and the range of class-size changes analyzed in this study is virtually restricted to between 20 and 40 students in a class, so that the relevance of the findings for general class-size reductions in developed countries is in doubt.

Hoxby (2000b) uses two identification strategies based on the natural longitudinal variation in the population of school-aged children to instrument for class-size effects. In the first strategy, exogenous variation in class size is generated by the fact that student cohorts vary in size due to the natural randomness in the timing of births. Using long panels of data on enrollment and kindergarten cohorts in each district, the random part of population changes can be isolated separately for each grade in each school and used as an instrument for class size. The second strategy is similar to the one pursued by Angrist and Lavy (1999) in that discontinuous changes in class size due to explicit class-size rules are exploited. Events are analyzed where a small change in enrollment triggers a maximum or minimum class-size rule in a specific school district and thereby changes the number of classes in a grade in a school. Based on a panel data set for Connecticut school districts, Hoxby (2000b) finds that there is no statistically significant relationship between class size and scores on mathematics, reading, and writing tests in fourth and sixth grade with any of the two identification strategies.

The lack of any statistically significant effect of class-size reductions on student achievement in Hoxby's (2000b) study is especially noteworthy, since the coefficients are very precisely estimated, that is, their estimated standard errors are very small. This virtually rules out the possibility that the statistical insignificance might be due to a problem of small sample sizes or other causes of imprecise estimates. Instead, it clearly points to the fact that there is no genuine link between resources and schooling quality.

Summing up, just like the conventional OLS estimates, the studies which try to account for possible resource endogeneity by IV estimation present no clear evidence that changes in resource endowments have positive effects on schooling quality. All those studies which find positive resource effects in some situations also report insignificant or even negative estimates for other situations. Furthermore, there is still some doubt with most of the studies whether truly exogenous resource variations are identified. The two most rigorous studies find some evidence of positive effects of large-scale class-size reductions in Israel (Angrist and Lavy 1999), but no evidence at all of effects of class-size reductions on schooling quality in the United States (Hoxby 2000b). That is, any potential biases introduced by resource endogeneity, which might hypothetically be directed either upwards or downwards (Section 3.1.3.1), seem to be canceling out at least in developed countries.

3.1.3.3 Experimental Estimates: Tennessee's Project STAR

While the studies summarized in the preceding sections rely on econometric methods to separate the different factors influencing the educational performance of students, an alternative and potentially superior method is to carry out a controlled experiment. In such an experiment, students are randomly assigned to classes with different resource endowments. Given the randomness of the assignment, the resource endowment of a student should be independent of his or her educational performance, so that an experiment opens the possibility of estimating the true relationship between resource expenditure and schooling quality.

The only large-scale random assignment experiment on educational resource endowment ever conducted in the United States is the Tennessee Student/ Teacher Achievement Ratio experiment, usually referred to as Project STAR. In the mid-1980s, Project STAR was pursued as a longitudinal study which randomly assigned students and teachers to classes of different size from kindergarten through third grade. Specifically, the design initially included three treatments: small classes of 13–17 students, regular classes of 22–25 students, and regular classes of this larger size with a full-time teacher's aide. Schools large enough to have at least one of each class-size treatment were solicited for participation, and random assignment took place within schools. After the initial assignment, the design called for students to remain in the same class-size treatment group for the full four years. Between 6,000 and 7,000 students in 79 schools were involved in the study each year.[43] After third grade, the experiment ended, with all students being assigned to regular classes.

The results of the Project STAR experiment can in principle be easily derived by comparing treatment and control groups. With random assignment, a simple comparison of the mean achievements between students in small and large classes should provide an unbiased estimate of the effect of class size on achievement. As publicized through an internal team of researchers and reviewed in Mosteller (1995), students in smaller classes in the first year of their education (kindergarten) scored statistically significantly higher on standardized tests in mathematics, reading, and word recognition than students in regular-size classes, but the achievement advantage of small classes increased only slightly and statistically insignificantly in the next three years of schooling. The class-size effects were larger for Black students and for students on free lunch. Students in regular classes with a teacher's aide did not perform significantly better than those in regular classes without a teacher's aide. Further findings on resource effects, seldom referred to in the discussion of Project STAR, is that teachers' experience and teachers' having a master's degree did not have a statistically significant effect on student achievement.

As is self-evident, the validity of experimental results depends crucially on the appropriate implementation of the test design of the experiment. In the actual implementation of Project STAR, considerable uncertainty about the results is introduced by several deviations from an ideal experimental design. While the initial examination of the Project STAR results by the internal researchers paid little attention to these potential threats to the validity of the experiment, Krueger (1999a) pursues a reanalysis of the Project STAR data in which he tries to address these issues. First, since randomization was done within schools and participating schools were self-selected, the exogeneity of the class-size assignment may only be valid within schools. Krueger adjusts for school effects by including separate dummy variables for each school. Still, the self-selection of schools may mean that schools with an efficient input-output relationship may be

---

43   The initial sample of 79 schools subsequently fell to 75 schools.

overrepresented in the Project STAR sample because these may show a higher willingness and motivation to participate in the experiment.

Second, students in regular-sized classes were rerandomized between classes with and without aides after kindergarten, thereby changing the classmates of students in regular-size classes. Third, many new students entered the program in first grade, mainly because kindergarten attendance was not mandatory in Tennessee at the time of the study. While their allocation to treatment groups was random, any difference in prior treatment is unknown and thus cannot be controlled for. Fourth, between each grade, about 10 percent of the students switched between small and regular classes. These nonrandom transitions seem to have been mainly triggered by behavioral problems and parental complaints. Fifth, actual class size varied more than intended—from 11 to 20 students in small classes and from 15 to 30 students in regular classes—presumably due to natural family relocation. To address the problems of class switching and class-size variability within a given type of assignment, Krueger uses the initial random assignment to a class type as an instrument for actual class size in a 2SLS approach. Thereby, only that part of class-size variation which is due to the initial assignment to the different class types is used in the estimation of test-score effects.

Sixth, less than half of the initial experimental group of students who entered the experiment in kindergarten remained in the experiment for all four grades. Some of these losses seem to have been caused by nonrandom switching to other schools after the class-type assignments had been made public. Krueger tries to adjust for nonrandom attrition in a crude way by imputing test scores for students who exited the sample by using the student's most recent test score. However, withdrawal rates prior to the start of kindergarten, which seem to have been larger for students assigned to regular-size classes, cannot be adjusted for.[44] All in all, Krueger (1999a) finds that none of the adjustments which he could make for deviations from an ideal experimental design overturn the main findings of Project STAR.

A seventh problem, which is imminent to any experiment, is that the actors in an experiment are aware of it (Hoxby 2000b). An experiment usually alters the prevailing incentive conditions, thereby potentially also altering the participants' behavior. Schools participating in an experiment such as Project STAR may realize that the experiment potentially affects the amount of resources available in the future and that if the experiment fails to show beneficial class-size effects, broad-based class-size reductions will never be enacted. Given that schools tend

---

[44] Krueger (1999a) presents an upper bound estimate of the possible effect of differential withdrawal before the start of kindergarten and shows that it seems to be relatively minor.

to have a self-interest in broad-based class-size reductions, they face incentives in the experiment which the fully enacted policy would not generate. Furthermore, teachers and students may respond to the fact that they are part of an experiment by temporarily increasing their productivity when they are being evaluated (so-called Hawthorne effects).[45]

An eighth limitation of the Project STAR experiment is that no pretest scores are available for participating students before they entered the experiment. As a consequence, it is impossible to assess the quality of student randomization for the initial experimental sample and for the subsequent additions to it (Hanushek 1999a). The estimated class-size effects would actually also be consistent with an initial assignment of somewhat better students to small kindergarten classes. Additionally, little information is available on the assignment of teachers.

Finally, it should be noted that the beneficial effect of being in a small class is largely restricted to the first year a student attends a small class. The interpretation of this finding depends on the underlying learning model with which one assesses it (Hanushek 1999b). Given that education is a cumulative process, one would expect the differences in performance to become wider through the grades as students in small classes continue to get more resources. But independent of the learning model employed, the empirical finding implies that additional resources in grades after kindergarten or possibly first grade do not yield significant achievement benefits. Even more, in their long-term follow-up of the students who participated in Project STAR, Krueger and Whitmore (2001) find that the benefit from being assigned to a small class from kindergarten through third grade appears to have declined to between one-half and one-quarter of the initial test-score advantage after students were returned to regular-size classes in fourth grade. While having been assigned to a small class increases the likelihood of taking a college entrance exam by the end of high school, students who attended small classes do not seem to have scored significantly better on these exams.

Most of the discussed flaws in the experimental design of Project STAR can only poorly be addressed, while others cannot be addressed at all, since they are imminent to explicit experiments. Thus, while explicit experiments have clear advantages over nonexperimental estimates, there are also a few disadvantages of explicit experiments. Furthermore, explicit experiments are rare, and up to now, there has been only one experiment, pursued in the U.S. state of Tennessee, to draw conclusions from.

However, it can be argued that "[o]ne well-designed experiment should trump a phalanx of poorly controlled, imprecise observational studies based on un-

---

[45]   Krueger (1999a) tries to partially check for Hawthorne effects by looking at just the effects of class-size variations among students assigned to regular-size classes.

certain statistical specifications" (Krueger 1999a: 528). It is a pity, then, that the design and the implementation of the Project STAR experiment carried so many uncertainties that there is considerable doubt whether Project STAR can produce unbiased results. In addition, the estimated effects appear relatively small, given the magnitude of the class-size reductions of about eight students (Hanushek 1999a). Project STAR provides no results for smaller reductions in class size than the one-third reductions it pursued or for reductions in later grades than the very first ones. Moreover, the addition of a teacher's aide as another kind of class-size reduction proved to be without any effect on student performance, as did the experience and education of the teacher as further resource variables.

Summarizing the within-country cross-section evidence on the effects of resource expenditure on schooling quality in developed countries, neither conventional estimates of education production functions nor studies which acknowledge the potential endogeneity of schooling resources show clear evidence that changes in resource endowments have sizable positive effects on schooling quality. Results based on the controlled experiment Project STAR point to relatively minor effects of class size on educational performance and suffer from methodological ambiguities. Hence, evidence based on IV estimation may actually provide the most reliable evidence up to now. But these studies are certainly not the last word on the issue.

In the class-size debate, there seem to be two sides which stand heavily opposed to each other, one arguing that there are positive resource effects, one arguing that if anything, estimated resource effects are negative. In a sense, each of the sides tries to show that the evidence presented by the other side is dubious. By being largely successful in this attempt, they might lead an independent observer of the debate to come to the conclusion that the evidence presented by both sides is indeed dubious. Put differently, it seems fair to conclude that there is no clear evidence that a broad-scale increase in resource expenditure has a significant impact on schooling quality.

3.1.4 Evidence from Developing Countries

Most of the available evidence on the link between resources and schooling quality within a country comes from the United States. Unfortunately, no such encompassing evidence is available for other developed countries. Actually, Psacharopoulos (2000) identifies a big gap between the United States and Europe in terms of applied research in the economics of education in general. He ventures the statement that "[d]ue to the active role of international organizations, ... more research has been done on the economics of education in developing countries relative to Europe" (Psacharopoulos 2000: 93).

While existent, educational research in developing countries tends to be much less extensive and less rigorous than that for the United States. Still, evidence from developing countries might be especially illuminating, since schools in developing countries on average work on much lower expenditure levels than schools in developed countries. If the education production function exhibits decreasing returns to resource use (see, e.g., Schettkat 2000), estimates of resource effects from countries further left on the production function (developing countries) should be more likely to yield positive resource effects than estimates from countries further right (such as the United States). As the Israeli evidence in Angrist and Lavy (1999) has shown, large-scale class-size reductions starting from a large class-size level may induce positive effects on student performance, while class-size variations at the small average class sizes as already reached in developed countries do not seem to show effects on student performance.

A Summary of Conventional Estimates from Developing Countries

Harbison and Hanushek (1992; see also Hanushek 1995) summarize 96 conventional estimates of education production functions from developing countries in a way similar to the U.S. evidence presented in Section 3.1.2.[46] As the findings depicted in Figure 3.3 show, there are obviously more statistically significant estimates of resource effects on student performance in developing countries than in the United States. While there are several potential explanations for this—e.g., there might be less rigorous controlling for family background—the differences in resource availability are large within developing countries, and most schools in developing countries work on much lower expenditure levels than schools in the United States. Therefore, the relatively more positive findings from developing countries lend support to the suggestion that schools in developed countries may be running into decreasing returns to the use of resources. That is, while there may be many circumstances in developing countries where resources lead to superior student performance, the marginal return to an increase in expenditure in developed countries seems to be close to zero.

Still, it should be noted that even in developing countries, only about one-quarter of the estimates of teacher-student ratios are statistically significantly positive, and these are matched by an equal number of estimates with a statistically significant negative sign. For none of the classroom resources, two-thirds of the estimates are statistically significantly positive. Therefore, a systematic relationship between resources and student performance is also in doubt in developing countries.

---

[46]   It should be noted that not all of the underlying studies on which the 96 estimates are based seem to satisfy the publication criteria mentioned in Section 3.1.2.

Figure 3.3: Estimated Effects of Schooling Resources: Developing Countries[a]

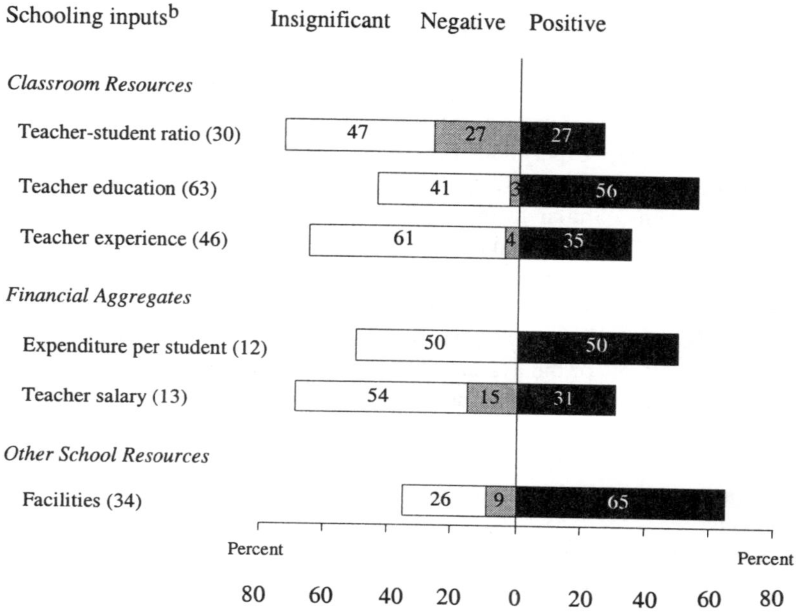

Schooling inputs[b]   Insignificant   Negative   Positive

Classroom Resources

Teacher-student ratio (30)   47   27   27

Teacher education (63)   41   6   56

Teacher experience (46)   61   4   35

Financial Aggregates

Expenditure per student (12)   50   50

Teacher salary (13)   54   15   31

Other School Resources

Facilities (34)   26   9   65

Percent   Percent

80   60   40   20   0   20   40   60   80

[a]Summary of selected regression coefficients on various resource measures estimated by education production functions (dependent variable: student achievement). Percentage of statistically insignificant (white), statistically significant negative (grey), and statistically significant positive (black) regression coefficients. — [b]Number of estimates in parentheses.

Source: Adapted from Harbison and Hanushek (1992).

Quasi-Experimental Evidence from a Developing Country

Just like the conventional within-country estimates for the United States, the developing-country studies summarized in Figure 3.3 might again be biased through resource endogeneity. A recent study from a developing country by Case and Deaton (1999) tries to address this problem by looking at a specific setting where variations in resource endowment can be presumed to be largely exogenous. They use data from South Africa immediately before the end of the apartheid regime. Under apartheid, resource decisions for most Black schools were made centrally by White-controlled entities over which Blacks had no control, and Black households were severely limited in their residential choice.[47] Therefore, there is presumably little endogeneity in the resource allocation in the sense that Black parents or administrators could deliberately change resource endowments. Furthermore, the system generated marked disparities in class sizes, with average class sizes varying across districts between 20 and more than 80 students per class. This setting specific to South Africa during apartheid can be viewed as a quasi-experiment where a substantial variation in resource endowments existed which could not endogenously be altered by parents or the administration. Thus, similar to the studies reported in Section 3.1.3, Case and Deaton's (1999) study focuses on exogenous resource variations.

They find statistically significant positive effects of smaller classes for Black students' achievement in numeracy tests, while the effects on literacy test scores are statistically insignificant, very small, and sometimes even negative. They also analyze the effects of the availability of specific facilities as further resource variables. For Black students, the presence of a secondary school library has a statistically significant positive effect on literacy scores, while the effect on numeracy scores is statistically insignificant. Likewise, the effects of primary school libraries and secondary school laboratories are statistically insignificant in both subjects.

For White students, no statistically significant effects of class size or other resource variables could be observed.[48] The fact that statistically significant effects are confined to Black students is consistent with the view that at the small class sizes which characterize schooling for non-Blacks in South Africa, reductions in class size had little or no effect on student performance. That is, Case and Deaton's (1999) findings point to potential positive resource effects at very low levels of resource endowment, which tend to disappear with rising levels of schooling expenditure.

---

[47] As is standard in the literature, the terms Black and White stand for the racial classification introduced under apartheid; following Case and Deaton (1999), I use capitals to register the specialized use.

[48] The statistical insignificance of the effects on Whites' test score achievements might be caused by the small sample size for the sample of White test score results. However, in addition to the effects of resources on test scores, Case and Deaton (1999) also analyze the effects of resources on educational attainment and enrollment, where the sample size is large also for White students. There, as well, they tend to find positive estimates for Black schools, while not for White schools.

3.2 International Cross-Section Evidence

While the within-country cross-section evidence on performance effects of resources might be flawed because of the endogeneity problem, the following two sections present new evidence based on different resource variations. This section looks at differences in schooling resources and schooling quality *across countries*, which are not plagued by the within-country cross-section endogeneity problem. This is because there is no mechanism which would move resources across countries in response to differences in the educational performance of students. While resources may vary due to adjustments made by policymakers, school administrators, and parents in response to students' performance within each country (Section 3.1.3.1), no country will transfer sizable amounts of its educational resources to another country because students there show inferior performance. Nor is there large-scale residential choice across countries due to international differences in educational spending.

3.2.1 Evidence from Previous Cross-Country Tests of Student Performance

Two studies by Hanushek and Kimko (2000) and Lee and Barro (2001) have examined international student achievement tests, albeit excluding the newest and most extensive one, namely the Third International Mathematics and Science Study which was conducted in 1994/95. Both studies estimate the effect of schooling resources on schooling quality in country-level education production functions which control for measures of family background. As their measure of schooling quality, Hanushek and Kimko (2000) use the normalized country test scores on six separate international tests.[49] They find that international variations in schooling resources do not have strong effects on international differences in test score performance. The estimated effects of expenditure measures on schooling quality are actually mostly significant with the wrong sign, and sometimes statistically insignificant. This finding holds regardless of the specific measure of schooling resources used, be it expenditure per student, teacher-student ratios, or a variety of other measures.

Lee and Barro (2001) pool evidence from thirteen subtests of international achievement tests, disaggregated by subject, year, and age of students. They find a statistically insignificant negative estimate for expenditure per student, while the effect of teacher-student ratios is statistically significantly positive. However,

---

[49] The single measure of schooling quality used in Section 2.2.2.3 is based on these tests.

Lee and Barro's (2001) results are based on data of limited quality, as they use the average teacher-student ratio in primary schools of a country as a resource variable, while their test scores mainly reflect performance in secondary education. They further report a positive effect of average teacher salary, which is statistically insignificant in their more stringent specification, and a statistically insignificant effect of the length of school days.

In sum, there is not much evidence in the cross-country data which would suggest that international differences in schooling quality are closely related to differences in the amount of schooling resources available. Additionally, it should be noted that the explanatory power of the models estimated in both of the mentioned studies is very low (Section 5.5.1 below). This suggests that cross-country differences in the performance levels of students are at best only weakly related to measures of family background and schooling resources.

3.2.2   International Variation in Expenditure and TIMSS Results

The previous studies did not consider the latest, largest, and most coherent cross-country student achievement study, the Third International Mathematics and Science Study (TIMSS). While I relegate a more extensive analysis of the TIMSS results to Chapter 5, Figures 3.4 and 3.5 illustrate the relationship between educational expenditure per student and TIMSS results at different grade levels. Again, cross-country differences in expenditure per student do not seem to help in understanding cross-country differences in educational performance. Schooling resources and student performance appear to vary independently from each other. The simple correlation between expenditure per student and average TIMSS test scores is 0.13 in the primary school years (third and fourth grade) and 0.16 in the middle school years (seventh and eighth grade), equivalent to R^2s of 0.02 and 0.03, respectively. By implication, the effectiveness of resource use as measured by the ratio of educational performance to resources seems to differ widely across countries.

In order to compare educational expenditure across countries, expenditure in local currencies (available from UNESCO *Statistical Yearbooks*) had to be converted to a common scale. For Figures 3.4 and 3.5, purchasing power parity (PPP) conversion factors (from World Bank 1999b) were used to transform local currency units into international dollars. This would only be a correct procedure if the deflator for educational spending was equal to the deflator for the broad basket of goods and services entering the PPP calculations. However, schooling is a labor-intensive service sector without substantial technological progress, while other sectors of the economy exhibit substantial capital deepening and technological advances during economic development. Therefore, the schooling sector faces the cost disease of services, i.e., increasing relative costs with rising levels of economic development, because in an efficient labor market teachers' salaries rise in line with increasing labor productivity in the other sectors of the economy (Baumol 1967; see Section 3.3.2.2 below for greater detail). As a consequence, the variation on the horizontal axis in the true picture of the relative resource endowments in different countries is probably smaller than in Figures 3.4 and 3.5, because rich countries' educational resources are overvalued with a PPP conversion factor relative to poor countries' educational resources. However, this does not change the finding that educational resources and student performance are unrelated across countries.

One possible way to account for this cost-disease effect is to deflate educational expenditure of each country by the respective economy-wide labor productivity, because the latter can serve as a proxy for the wage level in the economy and thus for the wage level in the education sector. When calculating real educational expenditure per student by dividing the nominal expenditure per student through the average labor productivity in the economy rather than using a PPP conversion factor, the conclusion that there is no relationship between expenditure per student and educational performance remains unchanged. The correlation between the measure of educational expenditure per student deflated by economy-wide labor productivity and average TIMSS test scores is 0.02 in primary schools and 0.17 in secondary schools, equivalent to R^2s of 0.00 and 0.03, respectively.

While educational expenditure has the advantage of being the most encompassing measure of resource availability, average class size has the advantage of being a resource measure which is directly comparable across countries. However, international variations in the quality of teachers are not captured by this measure, whereas they should be reflected in educational expenditure through differential spending on teachers. Relating TIMSS test results to average class size gives pictures very similar to Figures 3.4 and 3.5. The simple correlation between class size and TIMSS test scores is 0.06 in primary education (based on 23 countries) and –0.21 in secondary education (based on 34 countries), equivalent to R^2s of 0.00 and 0.04, respectively.[50] That is, there is again virtually no relationship between the resource measure and the measure of schooling quality across countries, with smaller classes being even slightly negatively related to student performance in primary schools.

---

[50] Some caution has to be given to the TIMSS measure of average class size, however, because the fraction of classes for which class size was not reported is fairly high in some countries. For a method of addressing this problem by data imputation, see Section 5.2.4. Using the imputed data from Chapter 5, the correlation between class size and TIMSS scores is small and positive also in secondary schools.

Figure 3.4: Expenditure and Educational Performance: The TIMSS Cross-Country Evidence in Primary Schools[a]

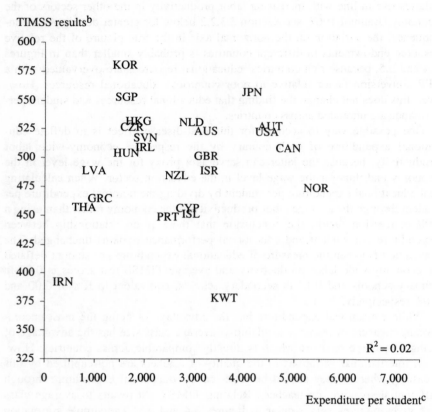

TIMSS results[b]

^aThe country abbreviations are: Australia (AUS), Austria (AUT), Canada (CAN), Cyprus (CYP), Czech Republic (CZR), Greece (GRC), Hong Kong (HKG), Hungary (HUN), Iceland (ISL), Iran (IRN), Ireland (IRL), Israel (ISR), Japan (JPN), Kuwait (KWT), Latvia (LVA), Netherlands (NLD), New Zealand (NZL), Norway (NOR), Portugal (PRT), Singapore (SGP), Slovenia (SVN), South Korea (KOR), Thailand (THA), United Kingdom (GBR), United States (USA). — [b]Average of TIMSS international mathematics and science scores in third and fourth grade. — [c]Expenditure per student at the primary level, in international dollars, 1994.

Source: IEA (1998); UNESCO, *Statistical Yearbook* (various issues); World Bank (1999b).

Figure 3.5: Expenditure and Educational Performance: The TIMSS Cross-Country Evidence in Secondary Schools[a]

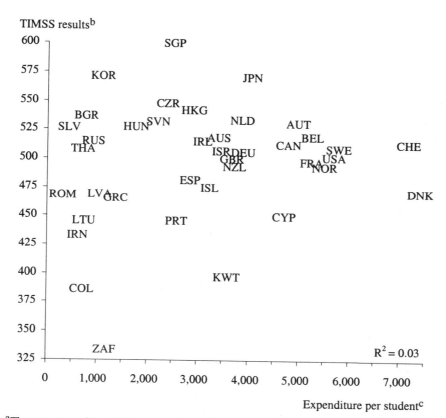

Expenditure per student[c]

[a]The country abbreviations are: Australia (AUS), Austria (AUT), Belgium (BEL), Bulgaria (BGR), Canada (CAN), Colombia (COL), Cyprus (CYP), Czech Republic (CZR), Denmark (DNK), France (FRA), Germany (DEU), Greece (GRC), Hong Kong (HKG), Hungary (HUN), Iceland (ISL), Iran (IRN), Ireland (IRL), Israel (ISR), Japan (JPN), Kuwait (KWT), Latvia (LVA), Lithuania (LTU), Netherlands (NLD), New Zealand (NZL), Norway (NOR), Portugal (PRT), Romania (ROM), Russian Federation (RUS), Singapore (SGP), Slovak Republic (SLV), Slovenia (SVN), South Africa (ZAF), South Korea (KOR), Spain (ESP), Sweden (SWE), Switzerland (CHE), Thailand (THA), United Kingdom (GBR), United States (USA). — [b]Average of TIMSS international mathematics and science scores in seventh and eighth grade. — [c]Expenditure per student at the secondary level, in international dollars, 1994.

Source: IEA (1998); UNESCO, *Statistical Yearbook* (various issues); World Bank (1999b).

In Section 5.5.2, the determination of the cross-country variation in TIMSS results is studied in greater detail through the estimation of a country-level education production function. The results for resource effects are that after controlling for international differences in family background and schooling policy variables, educational expenditure per student does not have a statistically significant effect on TIMSS mathematics or science results in secondary education. Average class size is statistically significantly positively related to both performance measures, suggesting that larger rather than smaller classes go hand in hand with better student performance.

In sum, the international evidence on resource effects based on TIMSS corroborates the finding that a strong and systematic relationship between increased educational expenditure and higher schooling quality is lacking across countries. Neither in the previous cross-country tests of student performance nor in TIMSS are better student test results related to higher expenditure levels on schooling. The large international differences in student performance levels in mathematics and science are a fact, and their occurrence cannot be explained by differences in the amounts of resources used.

3.3   Within-Country Time-Series Evidence

3.3.1   Changes in the Educational Input-Output Relationship over Time

A second new piece of evidence on the relationship between educational expenditure and the quality of schooling can be derived on the basis of within-country time-series data.[51] Actually, very little is known about changes in the educational input-output relationship over time. Thorough comparisons of schooling expenditure and schooling quality over time are available only for the United States (Hanushek 1997a), but not for other countries.

At least for OECD countries, the lack of knowledge about changes in the expenditure-performance relation in schooling over time is astonishing. Expenditure on schools accounted for 3.7 percent of gross domestic product (GDP) in the OECD in 1994, and teachers in primary and secondary education accounted for 2.9 percent of total employment in 1995 (OECD 1997: 63, 123). Thus, schooling accounts for larger fractions of GDP and employment in the OECD than many manufacturing industries.

---

[51]   Section 3.3 draws on Gundlach et al. (2001) and on Gundlach and Wößmann (2001).

Likewise, possible changes in the relationship between schooling inputs and the quality of schooling in East Asia have not been studied in detail. Most East Asian countries have achieved universal coverage of girls and boys in basic schooling. In addition, students from many East Asian countries have performed rather well in recent international comparisons of cognitive achievement (Figures 3.4 and 3.5). This impressive schooling record led some observers to conclude that formal education played an important role in explaining the "East Asian miracle" (World Bank 1993). Mingat (1998: 714) provides an optimistic assessment of the educational input-output relation by concluding that the high-performing Asian economies "have successfully obtained high educational outcomes ... while keeping the burden on public finance reasonable."[52]

In this section, I calculate changes both in schooling expenditure per student and in the quality of schooling over time for several OECD and East Asian countries. On the expenditure side (Section 3.3.2), one major obstacle to comparing schooling expenditure over time is that price deflators for the schooling sector are needed to separate changes in real resources from price changes. However, specific price deflators for the schooling sector are not readily available in the official statistics, and economy-wide price deflators may not be directly applicable to the schooling sector because of the "cost disease" of services. Based on Baumol's (1967) cost-disease model, I present two ways of deriving a price deflator for the schooling sector which in turn allow for the calculation of changes in real schooling expenditure per student over time. The results show that real schooling resources per student increased substantially in most OECD countries in 1970–1994 and in a number of East Asian countries in 1980–1994.

On the quality side (Section 3.3.3), the quality of schooling is measured by students' performance on standardized achievement tests, as in the preceding sections. Consistent time-series information on changes in the performance of students exists only for the United States, where the average cognitive achievement of students by and large did not change over the period 1970–1994. I use this constant performance of U.S. students as an intertemporal benchmark in the construction of an intertemporally comparable index of the quality of schooling

---

[52] Similarly, Rao (1998: 689) considers public schooling in four highly performing East Asian countries to be one of the sectors with an efficient allocation of resources and strict control over current expenditure. Quibria (1999: 441) provides a less optimistic assessment by pointing out that making appropriate investments in human resources is not a question of simply allocating more resources to the appropriate levels of education and that in many circumstances the quality of education which is delivered by schools leaves much to be desired. Behrman (1999: 186) notes that many studies on Asian countries overstate the gains from extending schooling years relative to the gains from improving schooling quality because they fail to control for the quality of schooling.

for other countries. By reformatting the level and the distribution of test scores in previous international cross-country tests, I derive a measure of the cognitive achievement of students in mathematics and natural science in OECD and East Asian countries which can be traced over time relative to the constant performance of U.S. students. This measure does not show substantial improvements in the quality of schooling for a sample of OECD countries in 1970–1994, with Sweden and the Netherlands as probable minor exceptions. Similarly, there were no sizable changes in the measure of schooling quality in most of the sampled East Asian countries in 1980–1994, while the quality of schooling deteriorated severely in the Philippines.

Taken together, substantial increases in real schooling expenditure per student did not lead to improvements in the quality of schooling in the form of student performance in most of the sampled OECD and East Asian countries. Thus, the time-series evidence from many countries suggests that a positive effect of increased educational expenditure on the quality of schooling is missing also over time.

3.3.2   Schooling Expenditure over Time

The measure of interest in this section is the change in the amount of schooling resources per student over time, i.e., the change in real expenditure devoted to schooling per student. On the basis of UNESCO data, the change in expenditure per student can only be calculated in nominal terms (Section 3.3.2.1). However, nominal changes in expenditure per student reflect both changes in real resources and changes in the price of schooling. Hence, one needs a price deflator for the schooling sector in order to evaluate changes in real schooling resources. Since official statistics do not report a price deflator for schooling, I derive two kinds of price deflators suitable for the schooling sector, which should render equivalent results given perfect data (Section 3.3.2.2). These are then used to calculate changes in real educational expenditure per student over time for samples of OECD and East Asian countries (Section 3.3.2.3).

3.3.2.1 Nominal Changes in Schooling Expenditure

Using data on schooling expenditure and students from various issues of the UNESCO *Statistical Yearbook*, schooling expenditure per student, x_S, in primary and secondary education can be calculated according to

$$(3.3) \quad x_{S,t}^i = \frac{CUREXP_t^i \cdot \left(PERFIR_t^i + PERSEC_t^i\right)}{\left(STUFIR_t^i + STUSEC_t^i\right)},$$

where $x_{S,t}^i$ is educational expenditure per student, $CUREXP_t^i$ is current educational expenditure, $PERFIR_t^i$ is the percentage of current expenditure spent at the first level of education, $PERSEC_t^i$ is the percentage of current expenditure spent at the second level of education, $STUPFIR_t^i$ is the number of students enrolled at the first level of education, and $STUPSEC_t^i$ is the number of students enrolled at the second level of education, everything for country i at time t.[53] For several countries, the UNESCO data had to be adjusted to ensure comparability over time. Section 3.5.1 presents all the data used for the calculations and lists the data adjustments made.

Based on equation (3.3), the average annual nominal growth rate of schooling expenditure per student, Δx_S, is calculated for a sample of OECD countries in 1970–1994. While the necessary data for the time span 1970–1994 are not available for non-OECD countries, both expenditure and schooling quality data are available for a sample of East Asian countries for the period 1980–1994.[54] Column (1) of Table 3.1 shows the average annual nominal growth rate of schooling expenditure per student for OECD countries in 1970–1994 and for East Asian countries in 1980–1994.

These growth rates of schooling expenditure are measured in nominal terms. The question is how much of the nominal increases is due to changes in the price of schooling, and how much is due to real changes in resources. In order to get a measure of changes in real schooling resources, the nominal changes have to be deflated by suitable price deflators for the schooling sector. Thus, the following derivation of price deflators for schooling is a means in order to achieve the end of measuring real changes in schooling resources.

---

[53] In the UNESCO data, the identification of primary and secondary educational institutions is based on the International Standard Classification of Education (ISCED). According to ISCED, education at the first level (ISCED level 1) is education whose main function is to provide the basic elements of education (e.g., elementary schools, primary schools). Education at the second level (ISCED levels 2 and 3) provides general and/or specialized instruction as provided by middle schools, secondary schools, high schools, and vocational or technical institutions and is based on at least four years of previous instruction at the first level. In this study, pre-primary education and education at the third level (e.g., universities) are not considered.

[54] The sample periods for the two samples of countries were chosen so as to cover the longest time span for which all the necessary data are available.

Table 3.1: Nominal Changes in Schooling Expenditure per Student[a]

| | Δx_S | | |
| | (1) | (2) | (3) |
OECD	1970–1994	1970–1990	1970–1994 constant structure[b]
Australia	13.5	15.3	13.5
Austria	8.6	9.1	8.6
Belgium	8.4	9.2	8.1
Canada	9.2	10.4	–
Denmark	10.4	11.2	–
Finland	10.7	12.0	10.7
France	12.1	12.7	11.8
Germany	8.1	8.5	–
Greece	20.9	21.5	20.9
Ireland	13.5	14.5	13.0
Italy	16.3	17.2	16.1
Japan	9.3	9.9	9.3
Mexico	41.4	40.5	40.8
Netherlands	6.2	6.8	6.0
New Zealand	14.3	15.6	14.1
Norway	11.5	12.7	11.7
Portugal	24.8	26.9	24.7
Spain	19.7	20.6	19.5
Sweden	9.5	12.0	9.4
Switzerland	7.3	7.7	7.1
United Kingdom	12.5	14.8	12.4
United States	7.8	9.1	–
East Asia	1980–1994		1980–1994 constant structure[b]
Hong Kong[c]	15.4	–	15.3
Philippines	13.8	–	–
Singapore	9.2	–	9.0
South Korea[c]	18.0	–	18.1
Thailand	13.3	–	13.5

[a]Average annual rate of change, in percent. — [b]Calculated by assuming that the shares of primary and secondary students in total schooling enrollment remained constant at the 1970 level for the OECD countries and at the 1980 level for the East Asian countries. — [c]Hong Kong: 1980–1995. South Korea: 1980–1993.

Source: Based on Table A3.1.

3.3.2.2 Baumol's Cost-Disease Effect and Price Deflators for Schooling

In the derivation of a price deflator for the schooling sector, it is important to note that differences in productivity growth across the sectors of an economy will result in changes in relative prices. Thus, differential productivity growth across sectors poses a special problem for time-series research on schooling resources. The consequence for the price of schooling can be shown on the basis of Baumol's (1967) famous cost-disease model, which I use to derive a price deflator for the schooling sector in two different ways which should yield equivalent results when perfect data is available.

Baumol's Cost-Disease Model

From a technological point of view, schooling is most likely a sector with stagnant productivity, just as many other service sectors. Similar to performing a symphony or a haircut, schooling is labor intensive, and the applied technology may not have changed much over the past quarter century, which is in stark contrast to technological developments in manufacturing industries. The labor input required to produce an automobile has declined significantly, but performing a symphony or a haircut requires the same amount of labor input as ever. Schooling may not be very different.

These sectoral differences in productivity growth have consequences for the relative price of schooling. Suppose that a constant amount of labor, L, is the only factor of production in the economy. The economy has two sectors. One sector is called S (schooling), with productivity growth r_S. The other sector, O, exhibits productivity growth r_O. Sectoral productivity growth differs, with r_O larger than r_S. Output of the two sectors can be described by two production functions as

(3.4) $\quad Y_S = aL_S e^{r_S t}$ and

(3.5) $\quad Y_O = bL_O e^{r_O t}$,

where Y_i is the level of output of sector i at time t (t subscripts are omitted), a and b are constants, and L_i is the quantity of labor employed in sector i.[55]

---

[55] Note that the simplifying assumption that labor is the only factor of production seems sensible for the labor-intensive schooling sector, which is the sector we are interested in. As long as r_O is taken to represent anything which increases labor productivity in the other sector, i.e., both technical progress and capital deepening, the model seems readily applicable to issues concerning the schooling sector.

Wages per unit of labor, w, in the economy are determined by labor supply and labor demand in a competitive labor market. Profit-maximizing firms will demand labor until the value of the marginal product of a unit of labor equals the wage. The marginal products of labor in the two sectors are given by the derivation of the two production functions as

(3.6) $\dfrac{\delta Y_S}{\delta L_S} = ae^{r_St}$ and

(3.7) $\dfrac{\delta Y_O}{\delta L_O} = be^{r_Ot}.$

Equating the value of the marginal products to the common wage gives

(3.8) $w = p_S ae^{r_St} = p_O be^{r_Ot},$

where p_i is the price of output in sector i. Hence, the relative price of schooling follows as

(3.9) $\dfrac{p_S}{p_O} = \dfrac{b}{a}e^{(r_O - r_S)t}.$

Applying the differentiation rule for exponential functions, this equation implies that the percentage change over time in the relative price of schooling equals the sectoral difference in productivity growth:

(3.10) $\dfrac{\delta(p_S/p_O)/\delta t}{p_S/p_O} = r_O - r_S.$

Thus, the price of schooling grows faster than the price of the other sector, and the difference is equal to the differential advantage in productivity growth of the other sector. Put differently, the price deflator for the schooling sector is given by

(3.11) $\Delta p_S = \Delta p_O + r_O - r_S,$

where Δ indicates an annual rate of change.

Deriving Price Deflators for the Schooling Sector

Unfortunately, even making the assumption that $r_S = 0$, we cannot directly apply equation (3.11) to the whole economy in order to calculate the price deflator for schooling, Δp_S, in an empirical application because we do not know changes in the price and productivity of the rest of the economy, Δp_O and r_O. But we can derive two kinds of price deflators for the schooling sector based on this model which can be calculated with available data. The first one is based on price and productivity increases in the whole economy, and the second one is based on price increases in other stagnant-productivity service sectors.

To derive the first deflator with which nominal increases in school spending have to be confronted, the Baumol model can be applied to the whole economy, where we do have data on changes in prices and productivity. To focus on the GDP deflator, Δp_{GDP}, and productivity growth in the whole economy, r_{GDP}, to enable an empirical application, the model can be reformulated by using two additional equations. One additional equation is that the price level of GDP may be written as

$$(3.12) \quad p_{GDP} = p_S^{(Y_S/Y)} p_O^{(Y_O/Y)},$$

with Y_S/Y as the output share of schooling and Y_O/Y as the output share of the other sectors of the economy. It follows that

$$(3.13) \quad \Delta p_S - \Delta p_{GDP} = \Delta p_S - \left(\frac{Y_S}{Y}\right)\Delta p_S - \left(\frac{Y_O}{Y}\right)\Delta p_O,$$

and, hence, in combination with equation (3.11) that

$$(3.14) \quad \Delta p_S - \Delta p_O = \frac{\Delta p_S - \Delta p_{GDP}}{Y_O/Y} = r_O - r_S.$$

The other additional equation is that the economy-wide growth rate of labor productivity is given by

$$(3.15) \quad r_{GDP} = r_S \frac{Y_S}{Y} + r_O \frac{Y_O}{Y},$$

which can be rearranged to

$$(3.16) \quad r_O - r_S = \frac{r_{GDP} - r_S}{Y_O/Y}.$$

Inserting (3.16) into (3.14) yields

$$(3.17) \quad \Delta p_S = \Delta p_{GDP} + r_{GDP} - r_S,$$

which shows that if we assume that productivity is constant in the schooling sector ($r_S = 0$), a price deflator for the schooling sector can be calculated as the sum of the GDP deflator and the growth rate of labor productivity in the whole economy. If there were productivity increases in the schooling sector ($r_S > 0$), calculating the price deflator based on the assumption that $r_S = 0$ would over-state the price deflator, i.e., it would understate the real increases in educational resources when nominal expenditure increases were deflated by this deflator.

A second deflator for the schooling sector can be derived by applying the Baumol model only to the service sector. In this interpretation, S indicates schooling as before and O indicates other service industries, Ser, which are known to exhibit stagnant or near-stagnant productivity.[56] Otherwise, equations (3.4)–(3.11) could be used as before, with r_O now expected to be close to zero. In this setting, equation (3.11) for the price deflator of schooling changes to

$$(3.18)\quad \Delta p_S = \Delta p_O^{Ser} + r_O^{Ser} - r_S.$$

That is, assuming constant productivity both in schooling and in other service industries—or at least equal productivity growth in the two sectors ($r_S = r_O^{Ser}$)—price increases in schooling and the other services should be identical:

$$(3.18)'\quad \Delta p_S = \Delta p_O^{Ser}.$$

Hence, price increases in other service industries which are presumed to exhibit constant productivity can be used as a second price deflator for the schooling sector. The advantage of this second approach is that the model assumption that labor is the only factor of production seems readily warranted for the service sector. The disadvantage is that only relative changes in the prices of the different services can be identified as long as r_O^{Ser} is presumed rather than observed to be close to zero.

The two kinds of estimates of the price deflator for the schooling sector based on equations (3.17) and (3.18) are identical if

$$(3.19)\quad \Delta p_{GDP} + r_{GDP} = \Delta p_O^{Ser} + r_O^{Ser}.$$

If services other than schooling actually exhibit stagnant productivity ($r_O^{Ser} = 0$), it follows from an application of the model to these service sectors and the rest of the economy that according to equation (3.10) their relative price should grow with r_O, so that similar to equation (3.17), it also follows that

$$(3.20)\quad \Delta p_O^{Ser} = \Delta p_{GDP} + r_{GDP},$$

---

[56]   Rothstein with Miles (1995) first suggested adjusting rising expenditure on education for the increase in a service-sector price index.

which reproduces equation (3.19) for $r_O^{Ser} = 0$. Hence, with perfect data, choosing a reference service sector with stagnant productivity should result in identical empirical estimates of the price deflator of the schooling sector based on equations (3.17) and (3.18).

Data for Calculating Price Deflators for Schooling

In order to calculate a price deflator for the schooling sector according to equation (3.17), we need data on the price deflator for the GDP and on changes in economy-wide labor productivity. Both measures are calculated on the basis of World Bank (2000) data. The GDP deflator is taken to calculate the average annual increase in the economy-wide price level, Δp_{GDP}, in OECD countries in 1970–1994 and in the sample of East Asian countries in 1980–1994 (column (1) of Table 3.2). The average annual rate of change in economy-wide labor productivity, r_{GDP}, is calculated on the basis of GDP data in constant local currency units and of data on the total labor force for the relevant countries and time periods (column (4)).

To derive a price deflator for schooling based on equation (3.18), price deflators for service sectors with presumably constant productivity, Δp_O^{Ser}, have to be calculated. I calculated price deflators for two such service sectors on the basis of national accounts statistics as provided by the United Nations *National Accounts Statistics* (various issues). The deflator for producers of government services (PGS, column (2)) measures the increase in the price of services in the public sector, which includes schooling. The deflator for community, social and personal services (CSPS, column (3)) measures the increase in the price of privately provided services,[57] which may be similar to schooling in terms of their labor intensity and their expected low rate of productivity growth.[58] Except for

---

[57] In the System of National Accounts (SNA), "Community, social and personal services" (CSPS) equal that part of category 9 of the International Standard Industrial Classification of All Economic Activities (ISIC) which is privately provided in a profit-oriented way. That is, economic activities of producers of government services, private nonprofit services to households, and domestic services are subtracted from ISIC 9 to obtain only those services which are supplied by establishments whose activities are intended to be self-sustaining, whether through production for the market or for own use. ISIC category 9 does not include services such as wholesale and retail trade, communications and transportation, and financing, insurance, and real estate and business services, which all may be considered to experience at least modest productivity gains.

[58] Both Rothstein and Mishel (1997) and Hanushek (1997a) use a Consumer Price Index for Services (CPI-S) and a "Net Service Index" (calculated by removing expenditure on medical care and housing from the CPI-S) as deflators for the schooling sector. However, production-side deflators like PGS and CSPS appear to be preferable according to the underlying model.

Table 3.2: Changes in Various Deflators and in Labor Productivity[a]

	Deflators[b]			Productivity[c]
	Δp_{GDP}	Δp_{PGS}	Δp_{CSPS}	$r_{GDP} = \Delta \frac{Y}{L}$
	(1)	(2)	(3)	(4)
OECD	1970–1994			
Australia	7.6	8.1	7.7	1.0
Austria	4.6	6.2	5.9	2.0
Belgium	5.2	6.3	6.3	1.7
Canada	5.8	8.2	7.0	0.7
Denmark	6.5	7.4	7.7	1.2
Finland	7.7	9.3	8.0	1.7
France	6.8	9.5	4.9	1.8
Germany	3.9	4.7	5.2	1.7
Greece	14.7	16.9	17.3	1.7
Ireland	8.6	–	–	3.3
Italy	10.8	13.4	12.4	1.8
Japan	4.1	6.4	6.3	2.8
Mexico	29.6	36.4	38.3	0.5
Netherlands	4.3	4.5	5.3	0.8
New Zealand	9.2	–	–	0.1
Norway	5.9	–	–	2.1
Portugal	14.3	–	–	2.1
Spain	10.5	11.3	–	1.8
Sweden	7.5	8.5	8.5	0.6
Switzerland	4.2	–	–	0.4
United Kingdom	8.6	–	–	1.5
United States	5.4	6.6	6.6	0.8
East Asia	1980–1994			
Hong Kong[d]	7.9	–	–	4.5
Philippines	12.2	14.6	13.6	−1.2
Singapore	2.8	4.7	5.3	5.0
South Korea[d]	7.1	12.8	8.8	5.9
Thailand	4.4	6.0	5.3	5.2

[a]Average annual rate of change, in percent. — [b]PGS: Producers of government services. CSPS: Community, social and personal services. — [c]Real GDP per worker. — [d]Service-sector deflators: Hong Kong: 1980–1995. South Korea: 1980–1993.

Source: Based on Table A3.2.

differences in the two service-sector price deflators for France and South Korea, the two service deflators tend to be broadly similar.

On average, the two service-sector deflators exceed the GDP deflator by 1.7 percentage points in the sample of 15 OECD countries for which all three deflators are available in 1970–1994. For every country in the East Asian sample in 1980–1994, the two service deflators exceed the GDP deflator by more than one percentage point, and in some cases the difference exceeds two percentage points. These empirical facts are in line with the basic assumption of the cost-disease model, namely that productivity growth in services is below the economy-wide average.

3.3.2.3 Real Changes in Schooling Expenditure

Basic Results

Table 3.3 presents the central results on real changes in schooling expenditure per student over time in the samples of OECD and East Asian countries. To measure the change in real schooling resources, the results in column (1) use the price deflator calculated according to equation (3.17) under the assumption of a constant productivity in the schooling sector ($r_S = 0$) for all the countries in the two samples. According to this measure, real schooling expenditure per student rose by more than 1 percentage point per annum in very single OECD country in the sample. That is, real resources per student available in the schooling sector expanded substantially. Likewise, in the sampled East Asian countries real expenditure on schooling per student also increased by an order of magnitude, with an increase of 1.4 percentage points per annum in Singapore being the minimum.

Columns (2) and (3) report the increase in real schooling expenditure per student when the price deflator for the schooling sector is calculated on the basis of price increases in comparable service sectors as suggested in equation (3.18). The estimates of the change in real schooling expenditure per student based on the PGS deflator and on the CSPS deflator support the finding that real schooling expenditure per student increased substantially in many OECD and East Asian countries. These service-sector-based estimates broadly confirm the direction of the whole-economy-based estimates in column (1). The estimated increase in real schooling resources per student based on the price deflators of the two other labor-intensive service sectors in the East Asian countries is also comparable in size to the estimate based on the first measure of a schooling-sector price deflator.

Table 3.3: Real Changes in Schooling Expenditure per Student[a]

	$\Delta x_S - (\Delta p_{GDP} + r_{GDP})$ (1)	$\Delta x_S - \Delta p_{PGS}$ (2)	$\Delta x_S - \Delta p_{CSPS}$ (3)
OECD	1970–1994		
Australia	4.9	5.4	5.8
Austria	2.1	2.5	2.7
Belgium	1.5	2.1	2.1
Canada	2.7	1.0	2.2
Denmark	2.6	3.0	2.7
Finland	1.3	1.4	2.6
France	3.4	2.5	7.2
Germany	2.4	3.4	2.8
Greece	4.4	4.0	3.7
Ireland	1.6	–	–
Italy	3.8	2.9	4.0
Japan	2.4	2.9	3.1
Mexico	11.3	5.0	3.1
Netherlands	1.2	1.7	0.9
New Zealand	5.0	–	–
Norway	3.4	–	–
Portugal	8.4	–	–
Spain	7.4	8.4	–
Sweden	1.4	1.1	1.0
Switzerland	2.8	–	–
United Kingdom	2.4	–	–
United States	1.6	1.2	1.2
East Asia	1980–1994		
Hong Kong[b]	3.0	–	–
Philippines	2.8	–0.8	0.1
Singapore	1.4	4.6	4.0
South Korea[b]	5.0	5.2	9.2
Thailand	3.7	7.3	8.0

[a]Average annual rate of change, in percent. — [b]Hong Kong: 1980–1995. South Korea: 1980–1993.

Source: Based on Tables 3.1 and 3.2.

Taken together, the three measures of changes in real schooling expenditure per student indicate that the amount of resources per student available in the schooling sectors of many OECD and East Asian countries increased substantially, and that there seem to be large differences in the change in schooling resources per student across countries. For example, the average of the three measures of the average annual increase in real schooling expenditure per student in Australia of 5.4 percent means that real resources per student rose by 250 percent in Australia over the 24 years from 1970–1994. Real schooling expenditure per student increased by about 200 percent in France, by about 100 percent in Germany and Japan, and by about 40 percent in the United States. Four of the five sampled East Asian countries experienced similar increases in real resources per student over a time span of only 14 years. Real schooling expenditure per student increased by about 150 percent in South Korea and Thailand from 1980–1994, and by more than 50 percent in Hong Kong and Singapore. Notably, the results suggest that most OECD and East Asian countries display a higher increase in real expenditure on schooling per student than the United States.[59] Exceptions are the Netherlands, Sweden, and the Philippines, where the increase in real educational expenditure per student was relatively small.

Robustness of Results

The general results for many OECD countries for the 1970–1994 period may suffer from structural breaks in the education data series which are due to certain reclassifications after 1990 in countries participating in a survey jointly conducted by UNESCO, OECD, and Eurostat. Comparisons of educational time-series data for the 1990s are potentially unreliable because of variations in the schooling programs covered by secondary education and because of conceptual changes which distribute expenditure previously reported as a residual category among the different levels of education. Overall, it seems that for the OECD countries in the UNESCO statistics, a large increase in students reported to be enrolled in secondary education is not accompanied by an equivalent increase in total expenditure. For example, the number of students enrolled in secondary education in the United Kingdom was 46.4 percent higher in 1993 than in 1991, while expenditure at the secondary level was only 28.5 percent higher.[60] The structural break in the education data series may cause a downward bias in the estimated increase in real schooling expenditure because the increase in total expenditure seems to be underreported relative to the increase in students for a number of countries between 1990 and 1994.

---

[59] For a comparison of the findings for the United States with Hanushek's (1997a) results, see Section 3.5.2.

[60] This increase in expenditure in the United Kingdom is even overstated, since expenditure in 1993 includes capital expenditure, which is excluded in 1991.

To control for this possibility, the average annual nominal change in schooling expenditure can be calculated for the period 1970–1990, where no structural break biases the findings. As expected, column (2) of Table 3.1 shows that schooling expenditure increased faster in every country except Mexico in 1970–1990 than in 1970–1994. For many OECD countries, the annualized difference is larger than one percentage point. This finding suggests that the estimates of the increase in schooling expenditure in 1970–1994 probably underestimate the true increase in real resources in the schooling systems.

In contrast, the findings might overstate the true increase in schooling resources if spending on more expensive secondary education increased relative to spending on primary education. To take account of such possible shifts in the structure of spending, changes in schooling expenditure for the OECD countries in 1970–1994 can be calculated as if the shares of students in primary and in secondary education had remained constant at their 1970 levels. Column (3) of Table 3.1 provides the results. The largest difference relative to column (1) is 0.6 percentage points in the case of Mexico.[61] Similarly, when calculating changes in schooling expenditure for the East Asian countries in 1980–1994 as if the shares of students in primary and in secondary education had remained constant at their 1980 levels, the largest difference relative to column (1) is 0.2 percentage points.[62] Therefore, a shift in the structure of expenditure towards secondary education cannot account for the large increases in schooling expenditure per student which occurred in most OECD and East Asian countries.

---

[61]   In Canada, Denmark, and the United States, no breakdown of schooling expenditure between the first and second level is available for 1970 data. However, the shift between first-level and second-level students was small in these countries. In the United States, the share of first-level students in first-and-second-level students changed from 59 percent in 1970 to 53 percent in 1994. In Germany, the 1994 expenditure breakdown between the first and second level is not available. However, the fact that the calculation assuming a constant 1970 student share gives an average annual increase in schooling expenditure of 7.6 percent for the period 1970–1990 as compared to the previous estimate of 8.5 percent suggests that up to one percentage point of the increase in schooling expenditure in Germany may be due to the large shift in the German student population from primary to secondary education.

[62]   In the Philippines, no breakdown of schooling expenditure between the first and second level is available for 1994 data. However, the shift from first-level to second-level students was smaller in the Philippines than in any other East Asian country for which results are reported here. Hence, it is unlikely that the small shift towards secondary education had a major impact on the change in schooling expenditure in the case of the Philippines.

3.3.3 Schooling Quality over Time

Real schooling expenditure per student increased substantially in most of the sampled OECD and East Asian countries. The question of interest is now whether this vast expansion of schooling resources per student led to an improved quality of schooling. To answer this question, a measure of the change in schooling quality over the sampled time periods has to be calculated. The problem with measuring the quality of schooling over time is that consistent time-series data on the cognitive achievement of students are not available from within-country sources for nearly all of the countries.

Only in the United States, the National Assessment of Educational Progress (NAEP) began to monitor the performance of U.S. students aged 9, 13, and 17 years in mathematics and science in the early 1970s. The NAEP has used the same assessment content and administration procedures over time, so the reported average test scores of U.S. students are intertemporally comparable. The test scores show that the average performance of U.S. students did not change significantly in 1970–1994 (Figure 3.6). While mathematics and science test scores for 9 and 13 year old students have slightly increased, the performance of 17 year old students, representing the quality of schooling at the end of secondary education, has slightly decreased. As a benchmark for the further calculations, the cognitive achievement of U.S. students can be taken to be constant over the period 1970–1994.

Figure 3.6: U.S. Student Achievement by Age-group, 1970 and 1994

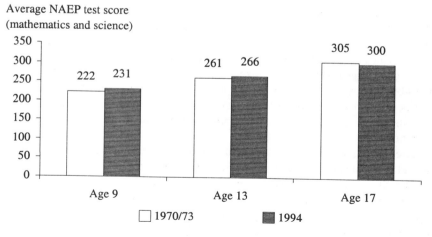

Source: U.S. Department of Education (1997: 86–88).

In addition to the intertemporal U.S. evidence, there is cross-country evidence on student performance for selected years. The International Association for the Evaluation of Educational Achievement (IEA) has conducted cross-country science studies in 1970/71 and in 1983/84, and cross-country mathematics studies in 1964 and in 1980–82. The IEA's Third International Mathematics and Science Study (TIMSS), which integrates the two subjects, was conducted in 1994/95. These studies include achievement tests for students at different ages. All studies include tests conducted for students in the middle and final school years, and except for the two studies which covered only mathematics, students were also tested in the primary school years.

To match my results for changes in expenditure on schooling with results for changes in the quality of schooling, the time periods of interests for an intertemporal comparison of the cognitive achievement of students are 1970–1994 for the OECD countries and 1980–1994 for the East Asian countries. Two measures are constructed to compare the performance of students over time. One measure focuses on the results of the science studies only, which are available for 1970, the early 1980s, and 1994. The other measure is an equally weighted average of the results of the science and the mathematics studies, where the latter are only available for 1964 instead of 1970. The samples are limited to countries which have participated in studies at both relevant points in time. This leaves a sample of eleven OECD countries in 1970–1994 and a sample of five East Asian countries in 1980–1994. Background information on achievement data is provided in Section 3.5.1, which also lists the original results of the international achievement tests in Table A3.3.

A direct comparison of the results of the 1970, 1980, and 1994 international tests is impossible because the design of test questions, the distribution of difficult and easy questions within a test, and the format in which test results are reported was not held constant. Nevertheless, one can calculate changes in the performance of students for each country over time subject to specific assumptions about the level and the distribution of the reported test results. This is possible because independent of the specific test actually conducted, in each case the performance of students from other countries relative to the constant performance of U.S. students is known, and the latter can serve as an intertemporal benchmark.

Even after normalizing the test results to a common level, a direct comparison would be misleading. The reason is that the standard deviation of the reported test results varies substantially between 1970, 1980, and 1994, e.g., from 0.239 in 1970 to 0.037 in 1994 within the sample of eleven OECD countries in the science test for the middle school years. These figures imply that constant performance of students in country A at one standard deviation above the sample mean would translate into a test score of 23.9 percent above the mean in 1970 but only of 3.7 percent above the mean in 1994. That is, one would falsely infer a relative decline in performance when not considering the differences in the standard deviations of the test results, which reflect the different test designs in 1970 and 1994.

Three hypotheses are used to adjust the reported results of the separate subtests for differing means and standard deviations. The first hypothesis is

H1:   *The mean and the standard deviation are constant across all subtests within the sample of OECD countries.*

Under H1, the original international test scores of Table A3.3 are transformed according to

$$(3.21) \quad T_{H1,b}^{i} = \left(\frac{S_b^i}{\overline{S}_b^O} - 1 \right) \cdot \frac{\left(\sigma / \overline{S} \right)_{TIMSS}^{O}}{\left(\sigma / \overline{S} \right)_b^{O}} + 1,$$

where $T_{H1,b}^i$ is the transformed test score for country i in subtest b under H1, S_b^i is the original test score for country i in subtest b, $\overline{S}_b^O$ is the mean of test scores of the OECD sample in subtest b, $\left(\sigma / \overline{S} \right)_{TIMSS}^{O}$ is the average coefficient of variation (ratio of the standard deviation to the mean) of the OECD sample in the TIMSS subtests, and $\left(\sigma / \overline{S} \right)_b^{O}$ is the actual coefficient of variation of the OECD sample in subtest b.[63]

The hypothesis of a constant mean and standard deviation in the OECD sample is justified if the distribution of test scores across OECD countries did not change substantially over time.[64] That is, H1 implies that the average standard deviation in the OECD countries reported under the TIMSS test design also prevails in all subtests conducted in the early 1970s and 1980s. Note that for the intertemporal comparison of the test results of the East Asian countries between 1980 and 1994, the hypothesis is also that mean and standard deviation are constant within the sample of participating OECD countries. That is, the distribution of results among the relatively homogenous group of OECD countries is

---

[63] The results derived on the basis of equation (3.21) are independent from the level of the mean, which is chosen to be the same in all subtests. The average coefficient of variation in the TIMSS subtests was chosen as the coefficient of variation common to all transformed test scores.

[64] Hanushek and Kimko (2000) assume in one of their calculations that the mean and the standard deviation of international achievement tests remained constant *for the sample of countries participating in the respective subtest.* This is a problematic assumption since different groups of countries participate in different subtests. For instance, only developed countries participated in the first IEA mathematics test, while many developing countries participated in the TIMSS tests.

assumed not to have changed substantially between the early 1980s and the mid-1990s.

Given H1, a measure of the change in the cognitive achievement of students in country i relative to the performance of US students is derived as

$$(3.22) \quad Q^i = \frac{\dfrac{1}{s}\sum_s \dfrac{1}{a}\sum_a \dfrac{T^i_{1994,s,a}}{T^{US}_{1994,s,a}}}{\dfrac{1}{s}\sum_s \dfrac{1}{a}\sum_a \dfrac{T^i_{t_0,s,a}}{T^{US}_{t_0,s,a}}} \cdot 100 \,,$$

where Q^i is an index of the quality of schooling in country i in 1994 with quality in the base year t_0 (1970 in OECD countries and 1980 in East Asian countries) set to 100, $T^i_{t,s,a}$ is the transformed test score of country i at time t in subject s and age-group a. Subject s is either equal to 1 (science only) or to 2 (mathematics and science), and age-group a is equal to 3 (with 1 = primary school years, 2 = middle school years, and 3 = final school years) except for the first two mathematics studies, where it is equal to 2 (given that there were no tests in the primary school years).[65]

Column (1) of Table 3.4 shows the results under H1 for the science tests, and column (2) for the combined mathematics and science tests. The finding is that the performance of students in natural science and mathematics did not change much within the sample of OECD countries in 1970–1994 under H1. For the East Asian countries in 1980–1994, the performance of South Korean and Singaporean students (in science) slightly increased, while the performance of students in Hong Kong and Thailand slightly decreased. The average performance of students from the Philippines in science seems to have deteriorated substantially.

Applying a different common coefficient of variation than the one which prevailed under the TIMSS subtests would result in what might be called a concertina effect. A higher coefficient of variation would move the figures on the quality index, Q, further away from 100, while a lower coefficient of variation would move the Q figures closer to 100. Therefore, all results derived for different hypotheses regarding mean and standard deviation can only be interpreted in qualitative terms. A Q figure smaller than 100 means a decrease in the performance of students over the sampled period. This figure can be compared across countries, but not in quantitative terms. For example, it is estimated that New Zealand's decrease in science performance in 1970–1994 under H1 (87.9)

---

[65]   Missing data for subtest scores, as evident from Tables A3.3 and A3.4, are replaced by assuming that the test score of a country relative to the United States in a specific subtest is equal to the average score of that country relative to the United States in the other subtests for the given subject and year.

Table 3.4: Changes in the Quality of Schooling[a]

	H1		H2		H3	
	Science	Math. & science	Science	Math. & science	Science	Math. & science
	(1)	(2)	(3)	(4)	(5)	(6)
OECD	1970–1994					
Australia	94.3	97.7	94.4	97.8	94.9	98.1
Belgium	95.8	95.3	95.7	95.4	95.5	96.7
France	88.2	93.4	87.9	93.4	86.6	93.6
Germany	96.0	95.2	96.2	95.4	97.8	97.1
Italy	99.7	101.3	99.7	101.3	100.1	101.4
Japan	97.2	98.1	97.3	98.3	97.5	99.3
Netherlands	103.5	101.7	103.7	101.9	105.7	103.5
New Zealand	87.9	90.3	87.8	90.3	87.7	90.5
Sweden	104.3	104.3	104.5	104.5	105.9	105.6
United Kingdom	94.3	91.8	94.4	92.1	95.1	93.6
United States	100.0	100.0	100.0	100.0	100.0	100.0
East Asia	1980–1994					
Hong Kong	92.6	94.4	92.6	94.8	94.6	98.2
Philippines	78.6	–	76.8	–	78.3	–
Singapore	101.7	–	101.9	–	104.5	–
South Korea	101.9	–	102.4	–	102.2	–
Thailand	88.6	95.7	88.1	95.3	90.5	95.7

[a]Base year = 100 (1970 for OECD and 1980 for East Asia). Index of the quality of schooling based on the performance of students on standardized international achievement tests relative to the constant performance of U.S. students in 1970 (1964 in mathematics) and 1994 for OECD countries and in 1980 (1983 in science) and 1994 for East Asian countries.

Source: Based on Table A3.3.

was larger than Japan's decrease (97.2), but the measure does not tell by how much it actually changed because any other common coefficient of variation might be used in equation (3.21).

Hence, assuming alternative standard deviations of test results across countries could have a large impact on the absolute value of the measure of change in the quality of schooling. To check for the robustness of the results derived under H1, two further assumptions are considered regarding mean and standard deviation of test results.

The next assumption is

H2:   *The U.S. test score and the standard deviation of the OECD sample are constant across all subtests.*

This hypothesis takes directly into account that the performance of U.S. students did not change significantly over the period from 1970 to 1994, while it allows the OECD sample mean to change. The transformed test scores under H2 are calculated as

$$(3.23) \quad T^i_{H2,b} = \left(\frac{S^i_b}{S^{US}_b} - 1 \right) \cdot \frac{(\sigma^O/S^{US})_{TIMSS}}{(\sigma^O/S^{US})_b} + 1,$$

where $T^i_{H2,b}$ is the transformed test score for country i in subtest b under H2, S^{US}_b is the original U.S. test score in subtest b, $(\sigma^O/S^{US})_{TIMSS}$ is the average ratio of the standard deviation of the OECD sample to the U.S. test score in the TIMSS subtests, and $(\sigma^O/S^{US})_b$ is the actual ratio of the standard deviation of the OECD sample to the U.S. test score in subtest b. Using the U.S. test score instead of the sample mean to normalize the test results to a common level, transformed test data are received under the hypothesis that each subtest has the same U.S. test score and the same standard deviation of the OECD sample (but different means).[66] Columns (3) and (4) of Table 3.4 show the results under H2, which are almost identical to the results derived under H1. For most OECD countries, the quality of schooling appears to have remained unchanged in 1970–1994, if not declined. In the East Asian countries, the quality of schooling also did not change by much in 1980–1994, with the exception of the Philippines, where it deteriorated substantially.

Finally, it can be assumed

H3:   *The U.S. test score and the deviation of the test scores of the OECD sample from the U.S. test score (as opposed to the standard deviation of the OECD sample) are constant across all subtests.*

The deviation of the OECD sample test scores from the U.S. test score is calculated as

$$(3.24) \quad d^{US}_b = \sqrt{\frac{1}{n}\sum_n (U^i_b - U^{US}_b)^2},$$

---

[66]   Results derived under H2 (and H3) are independent from the chosen level of the U.S. test score applied to all subtests.

where d_b^{US} is the deviation from the U.S. test score in subtest b, n is the size of the OECD sample excluding the United States ($n = 10$ in both sampled periods), and $U_b^i = S_b^i / S_b^{US}$.

Using equation (3.24), the original test scores can be transformed according to

$$(3.25) \quad T_{H3,b}^i = \left(\frac{S_b^i}{S_b^{US}} - 1 \right) \cdot \frac{d_{TIMSS}^{US}}{d_b^{US}} + 1,$$

where $T_{H3,b}^i$ is the transformed test score for country i in subtest b under H3, d_{TIMSS}^{US} is the average deviation of the OECD sample test scores from the U.S. test score in the TIMSS subtests, and d_b^{US} is the actual deviation of the OECD sample test scores from the U.S. test score in subtest b. In this case, each subtest has the same U.S. test score and the same deviation of the test scores of the OECD sample from the U.S. score. Columns (5) and (6) of Table 3.4 show the results under H3, which do not differ substantially from the results for changes in the quality of schooling derived under H1 and H2.

The findings under H1–H3 can be interpreted as suggesting that no OECD country has achieved a sizable increase in the quality of schooling in 1970–1994. While there may have been a slight increase in the average cognitive achievement of students in the Netherlands and in Sweden, and probably constant performance in Italy, all other countries in the OECD sample seem to have faced a decline in student achievement in mathematics and science. On average, the performance of students appears to be flat in OECD countries in 1970–1994. Similarly, no East Asian country has achieved a major increase in the quality of schooling in 1980–1994. While there might have been slight increases in Singapore and South Korea, the quality of schooling seems to have declined slightly in Hong Kong and Thailand, and it seems to have deteriorated sharply in the Philippines. Hence, on average, the performance of East Asian students seems to have been as flat as that of OECD countries' students.

3.3.4 The Time-Series Evidence on Expenditure and Quality in Schooling

Figure 3.7 summarizes the empirical findings for the OECD countries in 1970–1994. For each country, the average change in the performance of students in mathematics and science is plotted against the average increase in real expenditure per student on schooling. Only in Sweden and the Netherlands, the moderate increase in real per-student expenditure on schooling was accompanied by an increase in the measure of student performance. Other OECD countries in the sample experienced substantial increases in real resources per student available

Figure 3.7: Changes in Schooling Expenditure and Quality in OECD Countries, 1970–1994[a]

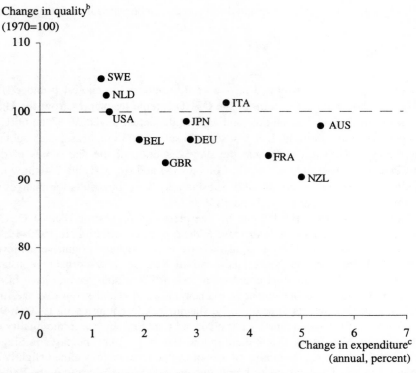

[a]The country abbreviations are: Australia (AUS), Belgium (BEL), France (FRA), Germany (DEU), Italy (ITA), Japan (JPN), Netherlands (NLD), Sweden (SWE), United Kingdom (GBR), United States (USA). — [b]Average of the estimated changes in performance in mathematics and science under H1–H3. — [c]Average of the estimated real changes in schooling expenditure per student.

Source: Tables 3.3 and 3.4.

in their schooling sectors, but with the exception of Italy, the average performance of their students in cognitive achievement tests declined. That is, in the vast majority of countries, the large increases in educational expenditure per student did not trigger an increase in the quality of schooling. The relation between changes in real schooling expenditure per student and changes in the quality of schooling across OECD countries is actually negative (the Pearson rank correlation coefficient is –0.57). That is, those OECD countries with a large

Figure 3.8: Changes in Schooling Expenditure and Quality in East Asian Countries, 1980–1994[a]

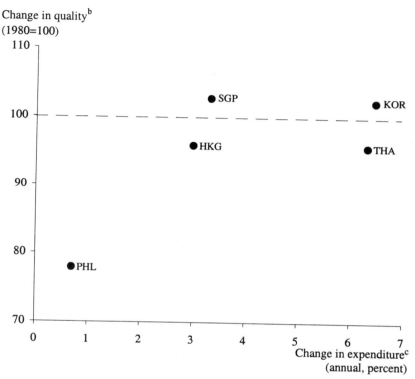

[a]The country abbreviations are: Hong Kong (HKG), Philippines (PHL), Singapore (SGP), South Korea (KOR), Thailand (THA). Average of the estimated changes in performance in mathematics and science under H1–H3. — [b]Average of the estimated changes in performance in mathematics and science under H1–H3. — [c]Average of the estimated real changes in schooling expenditure per student.

Source: Tables 3.3 and 3.4.

increase in real schooling expenditure per student experienced a dismal change in their students' average educational performance.

Figure 3.8 presents the same summary picture of the empirical findings for the sample of East Asian countries in 1980–1994. Taken together, the findings suggest that there is no positive resource-performance relation over time in the five East Asian countries, either. While real resources per student available to the schooling systems in Hong Kong, Singapore, South Korea, and Thailand expanded substantially, the average performance of students remained largely constant. As shown in Gundlach and Wößmann (2001), the resource expansion in these countries seems to result from a government decision to increase the amount of schooling inputs by raising the number of teachers per student without controlling for improved quality of schooling. The exception among the East Asian countries is the Philippines, where the teacher-student ratio actually decreased. But the effectiveness of resource use in schooling also declined in the Philippines because the performance of students deteriorated substantially while the overall per-student resource level increased slightly.

One potential explanation for the findings might be that—in equivalence to the cross-section discussion in Section 3.1.1—the family background of the students might have worsened. Students coming to school today may lack many of the basic capabilities required for a successful education and may, therefore, be increasingly expensive to educate. Such effects may play a significant role in countries with a large inflow of immigrant families with school-aged children or in countries with rising levels of poverty. But there are also counterbalancing effects. On average, parents in the sampled countries enjoy higher incomes and are better educated than 25 or 15 years ago, and the number of children per family has declined. Hence, children may actually start schooling with better basic capabilities than ever before. Indeed, Grissmer et al. (1994) present evidence that in the United States, the net effect of the trends in the different family background influences have worked in the direction of making students better prepared for learning.[67] This evidence makes the lack of positive performance effects of increased educational spending even more severe.

Another explanation for the findings could be that the measure of changes in the cognitive achievement of students is misleading because there are other dimensions of the quality of schooling than mathematics and science—e.g., reading and writing capabilities—and these could have improved. While such possibilities should be addressed in further research, the magnitude of the estimated increase in real schooling expenditure per student seems to point to different explanations. For most OECD countries in Table 3.3, one would have to assume that the performance of students has increased by more than 60 percent (by more than 2 percent per year) in 1970–1994 to reconcile the actual rise in schooling expenditure, and similar magnitudes apply to the East Asian countries. I am unaware of any evidence supporting such dramatic improvements in the performance of students over the last 25 years.

I conclude that the within-country time-series evidence shows no relationship between changes in schooling expenditure and changes in the quality of school-

---

67   See also the discussion on the aggregate time-series evidence for the United States in Hanushek (1999b).

ing. The schooling sectors in most OECD and East Asian countries have seen a substantial increase in available resources over the last 15 to 25 years, while sizable improvements in the educational performance level of students can hardly be detected.

With productivity generally defined as units of output per unit of input, productivity in the schooling sector may be defined as educational performance per expenditure unit, both measured in per-student terms. Therefore, rising schooling expenditure per student in combination with constant average schooling quality in many OECD and East Asian countries means that the productivity of schooling declined in these countries. Even more, the results reveal that what has been called a "productivity collapse" in U.S. schools by Hanushek (1997a) is dwarfed by the decline of schooling productivity in many other OECD countries, with Sweden and the Netherlands as probable exceptions. In all other OECD countries in the sample, real expenditure per student on schooling increased faster than in the United States and, with the exception of Italy, the educational performance of students declined relative to the United States. Likewise, the results for several East Asian countries also point to a decline of schooling productivity. All in all, they cast doubts concerning an efficient allocation of schooling resources.

3.4   The Missing Resource-Performance Relation in Schooling

The general conclusion which emerges from the different strands of evidence on schooling expenditure and the quality of schooling is that there is no clear relationship between the two. There may still be some controversy in the literature on within-country cross-section evidence about whether the absence of any statistically significant positive input-output relation can be taken at face value, and there certainly are circumstances where expenditure does matter for schooling quality, especially in developing countries where schools have to work at very low levels of resource endowment. However, a uniform across-the-board expansion of the amount of resources available to the schooling system does not seem to render significant positive effects at the expenditure levels currently prevailing in developed countries.[68] Furthermore, it is obvious and generally ac-

---

[68] Some studies in the economics of education also focused on other measures of output than cognitive achievement, like future labor market performance (Card and Krueger 1992; Heckman et al. 1996; Case and Yogo 1999), again with inconclusive results on resource effects.

cepted that international differences in the amount of resources used do not suffice as an explanation for the large international differences which exist in student performance levels in mathematics and science. And the aggregate within-country time-series evidence shows that large-scale increases in real expenditure per student over the last 15 to 25 years did not trigger advancements in the quality of schooling in most OECD countries and in selected East Asian countries.

This range of evidence implies that in order to improve the quality of schooling, the structure of decision making and the incentives within the schooling sector may have to be changed rather than the level of expenditure. Just providing more resources is unlikely to improve student performance if future actions of schools follow their past behavior. While some schools seem to make good use of additional resources, others do not. In total, schools do not seem to be economically efficient in transforming resources into schooling quality.

Since variations in schooling resources do not seem to lead to variations in the quality of schooling in the real world, the central question of the main determinants of schooling quality remains unanswered so far. Put differently, the question can be posed in terms of why there are differences in the effectiveness of resource use between schools. To answer this question, one has to look more closely at the institutional set-up of the schooling system. This set-up generates the incentives which drive the behavior of the different groups of agents involved in educational production. This is the topic to be addressed theoretically and empirically in the following two chapters.

3.5   Appendix

3.5.1   Data on Schooling Expenditure, Deflators, and Student Achievement

This appendix reports definitions, sources, and data for the variables used in the calculations of Section 3.3. Adjustments and intrapolations of the data used for individual countries are explained in detail where appropriate.

Education Data

- The basic education data for OECD and East Asian countries are reported in Table A3.1.
- Source: Various issues of the UNESCO *Statistical Yearbook*.

- The 1970 and 1990 education data for Germany refer to West Germany only, while the 1994 data refer to unified Germany. The inclusion of East German data in 1994 may understate the schooling price increase in West Germany since teacher wages and other costs were lower in East Germany in 1994.
- For Hong Kong, the ending year of the education data sample period is 1995 instead of 1994, so that the figures reported are average annual growth rates over a 15 year period. For South Korea, the ending year of the education data sample period is 1993 instead of 1994 because of a structural break in the South Korean data in 1994, so that the figures reported are average annual growth rates over a 13 year period.

CUREXP: Current public expenditure on education (Table 4.1 of the 1998 UNESCO *Yearbook*)

- For Greece, Japan, Sweden, the United Kingdom, and the United States the 1994 figure is total expenditure on education in 1994 times current expenditure as percent of total expenditure (in the most recent year available). For Austria, the 1994 figure is the average of 1993 and 1995. For Denmark, the 1990 figure is the average of 1989 and 1991. For Japan, the 1990 figure is the average of 1988 and 1992, where the 1992 figure is total expenditure on education in 1992 times current expenditure as percent of total expenditure (in the most recent year available).
- For the Philippines, the 1994 figure is taken from 1995. For Japan, the 1994 figure is total expenditure on education in 1994 times current expenditure as percent of total expenditure (in the most recent year available).

PERFIR: Percentage of current educational expenditure spent at the first level of education (Table 4.2 of the 1998 UNESCO *Yearbook*)

- For the United Kingdom, the 1994 figure is the average of 1993 and 1995. For Japan, the 1990 figure is the average of 1988 and 1992. For Denmark, the 1990 figure is the average of 1989 and 1991. For Portugal, the 1970 figure is the average of 1965 and 1975. For Austria, Denmark, Greece, and Ireland the 1994 percentage figure is taken from 1995. For Austria, the 1970 percentage figure is taken from 1968.
- For several countries, published expenditure on primary education include expenditure on pre-primary education for selected years. In these cases, the pre-primary expenditure share was extracted in the following way: Data on students enrolled at the pre-primary level (Table 3.3 in the 1998 UNESCO *Yearbook*), which is available for all years of the samples, is used to calculate the share of pre-primary students in the sum of pre-primary and primary students for the year in which the spending breakdown between primary and

pre-primary level is given and for the year in which it is not given. The share of pre-primary spending in the sum of pre-primary and primary spending is then calculated for the year in which the breakdown is given. Assuming that the share of pre-primary spending moved parallel to the share of pre-primary students, the pre-primary spending figure can be extrapolated to the year in which the breakdown is not given. This makes it possible to subtract the pre-primary share of educational expenditure from the published joint expenditure on primary and pre-primary education. Since pre-primary spending and students always represent a minor share relative to primary or secondary spending and students, this adjustment does not significantly influence the results.

- The following adjustments were made. For Canada, Denmark, Ireland, Spain, the United Kingdom, and Australia, data on educational expenditure in 1994 were used to subtract pre-primary educational expenditure in 1970. For Belgium, Canada, and the United States, 1994 data were used to adjust the 1990 figure. For Greece, 1970 data were used to adjust the 1994 figure. For Germany, 1990 data were used to adjust the 1970 and 1994 figures. For New Zealand, the 1970 figure was adjusted by using the average of the pre-primary percentages reported for 1965 and 1975.

- For the Philippines, the 1994 percentage figure is the figure in the most recent year available. For Singapore, the 1994 percentage figure is taken from 1995. For Thailand, the 1980 percentage figure is taken from 1981.

PERSEC: Percentage of current educational expenditure spent at the second level of education (Table 4.2 of the 1998 UNESCO *Yearbook*)

- For the United Kingdom, the 1994 figure is the average of 1993 and 1995. For Japan, the 1990 figure is the average of 1988 and 1992. For Denmark, the 1990 figure is the average of 1989 and 1991. For Portugal, the 1970 figure is the average of 1965 and 1975. For Austria, Denmark, Greece, and Ireland, the 1994 percentage figure is taken from 1995. For Austria, the 1970 percentage figure is taken from 1968.

- For the Philippines, the 1994 percentage figure is the figure in the most recent year available. For Singapore, the 1994 percentage figure is taken from 1995. For Thailand, the 1980 percentage figure is taken from 1981.

STUFIR: Total number of students enrolled at the first level of education (Table 3.4 of the 1998 UNESCO *Yearbook*)

- The 1994 figure for the United Kingdom includes students enrolled in infant classes in primary schools, previously considered as pre-primary education, as well as students below compulsory school age in independent and special pre-primary schools.

STUSEC: Total number of students enrolled at the second level of education (Table 3.7 of the 1998 UNESCO *Yearbook*)

- For New Zealand, the 1970 figure on students in total secondary education is students enrolled in general secondary education in 1970 times the 1975 relation of students enrolled in total secondary education to students enrolled in general secondary education.
- For Singapore, the vocational part of the 1994 figure is full-time enrollment only.

Table A3.1: Education Data for OECD and East Asian Countries in various years

	CUREXP[a]			PERFIR[b]			PERSEC[b,c]		
OECD	1970	1990	1994	1970	1990	1994	1970	1990	1994
Australia	1,139	17,889	22,823	30.6	57.4	29.9	23.2	inc.	39.6
Austria	13,503	89,858	111,112	29.6	17.7	21.1	47.8	46.6	47.7
Belgium	54,166	321,427	435,593	24.7	20.8	21.1	51.7	42.9	46.9
Canada	6,428	40,288	46,123	62.8	59.0	61.5	inc.	inc.	inc.
Denmark	6,294	53,583	69,787	69.8	10.9	21.5	inc.	54.2	39.7
Finland	2,405	26,757	34,978	35.8	27.9	25.3	49.5	39.4	37.7
France	24,599	327,427	397,868	23.8	17.6	20.4	43.9	40.7	50.0
Germany	16,927	88,499	140,600	35.0	13.4	67.9	31.5	47.5	inc.
Greece	5,091	306,303	550,698	48.8	28.2	32.9	28.3	45.1	40.9
Ireland	69.0	1,303	1,880	41.7	29.0	25.2	40.9	40.1	41.6
Italy	2,429	40,400	75,370	28.4	26.6	22.8	38.1	63.2	48.5
Japan	2,098	17,038	17,200	37.6	31.0	37.0	37.3	37.7	41.8
Mexico	7.1	16,617	61,672	47.7	26.7	39.8	27.2	29.6	32.1
Netherlands	7,069	29,200	31,113	20.8	16.3	23.1	38.6	37.7	39.0
New Zealand	213	4,252	5,270	36.6	26.9	23.7	25.5	25.3	40.7
Norway	3,696	44,109	65,407	47.5	39.5	31.2	23.4	24.7	23.0
Portugal	2,743	378,252	724,138	47.3	42.3	34.5	27.5	32.5	38.8
Spain	35.4	1,936	2,941	45.3	23.3	22.3	23.4	45.0	53.2
Sweden	10,785	93,083	106,680	42.7	47.6	26.2	17.7	19.6	40.2
Switzerland	2,766	14,395	18,116	33.2	46.3	27.0	40.2	25.1	47.0
United Kingdom	2,334	25,318	34,223	22.2	26.1	30.0	32.0	43.8	44.2
United States	56,000	265,074	326,853	70.5	36.0	31.7	inc.	37.0	36.1
East Asia	1980	1994		1980	1994		1980	1994	
Hong Kong	3,036	29,852		33.7	21.4		35.7	35.0	
Philippines	4,023	36,834		61.4	73.1		15.7	inc.	
Singapore	587	2,486		35.8	25.7		41.1	34.6	
South Korea	1,158,967	9,344,751		49.9	40.9		33.2	39.0	
Thailand	15,867	108,485		55.1	51.0		28.3	21.5	

Table A3.1 continued

	STUFIR			STUSEC		
OECD	1970	1990	1994	1970	1990	1994
Australia	1,812,000	1,583,024	1,639,577	1,136,960	1,278,163	2,003,504
Austria	531,934	370,210	381,363	630,254	746,272	786,156
Belgium	1,021,511	719,372	738,768	723,703	769,438	1,061,790
Canada	3,736,450	2,375,704	2,413,126	1,978,564	2,292,497	2,469,552
Denmark	443,031	340,267	328,875	407,103	464,555	444,682
Finland	386,230	390,587	387,306	509,691	426,864	454,707
France	4,939,683	4,149,143	4,071,599	4,281,446	5,521,862	6,003,797
Germany	6,344,774	2,561,267	3,727,157	2,704,796	5,972,607	8,152,297
Greece	907,446	813,353	710,774	520,323	851,353	842,633
Ireland	520,122	416,747	380,983	208,705	345,941	390,680
Italy	4,856,953	3,055,883	2,815,631	3,823,556	5,117,897	4,825,719
Japan	9,558,139	9,373,295	8,612,106	8,666,937	11,025,720	9,878,568
Mexico	9,248,290	14,401,588	14,574,202	1,584,342	6,704,297	7,264,619
Netherlands	1,462,376	1,082,022	1,189,112	1,006,327	1,401,739	1,508,772
New Zealand	400,445	318,568	331,666	305,897	340,915	404,563
Norway	385,628	309,432	314,062	302,792	370,779	370,925
Portugal	992,446	1,019,794	896,681	445,574	670,035	945,077
Spain	3,929,569	2,820,497	2,364,910	1,950,496	4,755,322	4,744,829
Sweden	615,331	578,359	643,768	554,480	588,474	791,848
Switzerland	500,492	404,154	461,805	345,786	567,396	561,716
United Kingdom	5,806,349	4,532,500	5,208,961	4,149,067	4,335,600	6,677,836
United States	28,700,000	22,429,000	23,823,662	19,910,000	19,270,000	21,122,633
East Asia	1980		1994	1980		1994
Hong Kong	540,260		467,718	468,975		473,817
Philippines	8,033,642		10,903,529	2,928,525		4,762,877
Singapore	291,722		251,097	187,532		210,473
South Korea	5,658,002		4,347,317	4,285,889		4,580,040
Thailand	7,392,563		6,291,945	1,919,967		3,382,755

[a]In million local currency units; in billion local currency units in Italy, Japan, Mexico, and Spain. — [b]In percent. — [c]inc.: indicates that the figure is included in *PERFIR*.

Source: UNESCO *Statistical Yearbook* (various issues).

Deflator Data

- The basic data for the calculation of deflators for OECD and East Asian countries are reported in Table A3.2.
- Source: The World Bank's (2000) World Development Indicators; various issues of the United Nations *National Accounts Statistics*.
- The GDP deflator is taken from World Bank (2000).
- Because of the structural break in the German data series in 1990/1991, the reported GDP deflator figure for Germany is calculated on the basis of data from IMF (2000) as the average annual increase in the GDP deflator in 1970–

1994 with the exclusion of the increase in 1990/1991, i.e., as a 23-year average (the German GDP deflator figure for 1991 is 0.878).

- The PGS and CSPS deflators are calculated on the basis of UN *National Accounts Statistics*. For any given year, they are calculated by dividing expenditure in current prices by expenditure in constant prices, after adjusting the constant-price data so as to reflect the most recent base year as a common base year. PGS and CSPS are the categories of the SNA kind-of-activity classification called "Producers of government services" and "Community, social and personal services", respectively, taken from Tables 1.10 and 1.11 of the UN *National Accounts Statistics*.
- The reported PGS and CSPS figures for Mexico and the United States and the CSPS figure for Germany are average annual growth rates in 1970–1993 instead of 1970–1994. The PGS and CSPS figures of Canada are average annual growth rates in 1970–1992.
- PGS and CSPS data were not available for the sample period for Ireland, New Zealand, Norway, Portugal, Switzerland, the United Kingdom, and Hong Kong. CSPS data were not available for Spain.
- For France, the PGS data include "Other producers" (private nonprofit services to households and domestic services). For Italy, the CSPS data include Finance, insurance, real estate and business services. The constant-price CSPS figures for the Netherlands encompass ISIC codes 6 to 9 until 1986.
- The reported PGS and CSPS figures for South Korea are average annual growth rates in 1980–1993 instead of 1980–1994.
- The GDP figure is gross domestic product at market prices in constant local currency units, taken from World Bank (2000).
- Because of the structural break in the German data series in 1990/1991, the reported GDP figure for Germany is calculated on the basis of data from IMF (2000) as the average annual increase in the GDP deflator in 1970–1994 with the exclusion of the increase in 1990/1991, i.e., as a 23-year average (the German GDP figure is 3,346 billion DM for 1991 and 3,463 billion DM for 1994, both in 1995 prices).
- The labor force figure is the total labor force, represented by the economically active population as defined by the International Labour Organization and taken from World Bank (2000).

Table A3.2: Deflator Data for OECD and East Asian Countries in various years

	Base year	GDP deflator[a]		
OECD		1970	1990	1994
Australia	1989	0.176	1.033	1.094
Austria	1983	0.465	1.221	1.397
Belgium	1990	0.323	1.000	1.137
Canada	1992	0.257	0.962	1.025
Denmark	1990	0.223	1.000	1.069
Finland	1990	0.169	1.000	1.070
France	1980	0.391	1.836	2.015
Germany	1995	0.373	0.823	0.980
Greece	1990	0.051	1.000	1.751
Ireland	1990	0.139	1.000	1.100
Italy	1990	0.091	1.000	1.217
Japan	1990	0.391	1.000	1.053
Mexico	1993	0.001	0.648	1.083
Netherlands	1990	0.394	1.000	1.096
New Zealand	1990	0.116	1.000	1.070
Norway	1990	0.250	1.000	1.040
Portugal	1990	0.045	1.000	1.399
Spain	1986	0.128	1.285	1.596
Sweden	1990	0.190	1.000	1.143
Switzerland	1990	0.419	1.000	1.137
United Kingdom	1990	0.148	1.000	1.169
United States	1992	0.291	0.938	1.050
East Asia		1980		1994
Hong Kong	1990	0.459		1.390
Philippines	1985	0.400		2.209
Singapore	1990	0.764		1.124
South Korea	1995	0.343		0.933
Thailand	1988	0.725		1.347

Table A3.2 continued

OECD	Base year	PGS deflator[a]			CSPS deflator[a]		
		1970	1990	1994	1970	1990	1994
Australia	1989	0.176	1.044	1.142	0.194	1.055	1.149
Austria	1983	0.376	1.312	1.579	0.412	1.323	1.642
Belgium	1985	0.307	1.131	1.343	0.323	1.171	1.408
Canada	1986	0.239	1.238	1.355	0.309	1.249	1.355
Denmark	1980	0.367	1.824	2.038	0.401	2.071	2.358
Finland	1990	0.133	1.000	1.122	0.187	1.000	1.193
France	1980	0.240	1.883	2.133	0.665	1.852	2.087
Germany	1991	0.364	0.949	1.086	0.337	0.954	1.091
Greece	1970	1.000	25.830	42.420	1.000	26.100	45.580
Ireland	1990	–	–	–	–	–	–
Italy	1985	0.095	1.660	1.963	0.116	1.502	1.905
Japan	1990	0.251	1.000	1.121	0.255	1.000	1.093
Mexico	1980	0.144	89.270	181.700	0.175	155.200	305.000
Netherlands	1990	0.391	1.000	1.126	0.336	1.000	1.152
New Zealand	1990	–	–	–	–	–	–
Norway	1990	–	–	–	–	–	–
Portugal	1985	–	–	–	–	–	–
Spain	1986	0.123	1.290	1.619	–	–	–
Sweden	1991	0.153	0.947	1.071	0.164	0.929	1.165
Switzerland	1980	–	–	–	–	–	–
United Kingdom	1990	–	–	–	–	–	–
United States	1985	0.330	1.254	1.436	0.366	1.364	1.602
East Asia		1980		1994	1980		1994
Hong Kong	1990	–		–	–		–
Philippines	1985	0.473		3.171	0.456		2.731
Singapore	1990	0.611		1.155	0.576		1.182
South Korea	1990	0.305		1.461	0.452		1.357
Thailand	1988	0.814		1.829	0.765		1.569

Table A3.2 continued

OECD	GDP[b] 1970	GDP[b] 1990	GDP[b] 1994	Labor force[c] 1970	Labor force[c] 1990	Labor force[c] 1994
Australia	200	369	421	5.38	8.53	8.92
Austria	828	1,485	1,602	3.12	3.55	3.77
Belgium	3,910	6,554	6,831	3.57	3.99	4.15
Canada	347	694	732	8.74	14.73	15.43
Denmark	544	825	904	2.37	2.93	2.91
Finland	270	515	477	2.21	2.59	2.60
France	2,029	3,545	3,667	21.83	24.96	25.49
Germany	1,543	2,520	–	35.75	39.72	40.76
Greece	7,075	13,143	13,696	3.43	4.17	4.38
Ireland	12	28	33	1.12	1.30	1.39
Italy	738	1,311	1,346	20.99	24.39	25.13
Japan	188	430	455	53.22	64.24	66.23
Mexico	499	1,141	1,312	15.18	30.79	34.93
Netherlands	312	517	561	4.82	6.88	7.23
New Zealand	49	72	81	1.10	1.65	1.77
Norway	359	723	834	1.59	2.12	2.21
Portugal	4,541	9,855	10,454	3.53	4.85	4.95
Spain	20,512	39,018	40,604	12.84	15.92	16.44
Sweden	918	1,360	1,339	3.78	4.62	4.74
Switzerland	229	317	315	2.95	3.56	3.71
United Kingdom	348	549	570	25.59	28.78	29.20
United States	3,470	5,922	6,402	88.17	124.72	132.75

East Asia	1980	1994	1980	1994
Hong Kong	308.8	727.5	2.47	3.12
Philippines	609.8	766.4	18.84	28.15
Singapore	32.9	94.8	1.05	1.49
South Korea	110.7	346.4	15.63	21.34
Thailand	913.7	2,695.1	24.29	34.64

[a]Base year = 1. — [b]In billion constant local currency units; in trillion constant local currency units in Italy and Japan. The respective base year is the one reported for the GDP deflator, except for Germany, where it is 1991. — [c]In million.

Source: World Bank (2000): GDP deflator, GDP, labor force; UN *National Accounts Statistics* (various issues): PGS and CSPS deflators.

Student Achievement Data

- The basic data on student achievement for OECD countries are reported in Table A3.3a, and for East Asian countries in Table A3.3b.
- Source: Lee and Barro (2001); IEA (1998).
- The first IEA mathematics study was conducted in 11 countries in 1964, and the first IEA science study in 17 countries in 1970–71. The second IEA mathematics study (1980–82) and the second IEA science study (1983–84) were conducted in 17 countries. The different TIMSS subtests were conducted for different sample sizes ranging from 21 countries to 39 countries in 1994–1995.
- Almost all studies include three subtests for students in the primary, middle, and final school years, except for the first two IEA mathematics studies which were not conducted for students in the primary school years. In the first and second IEA mathematics studies, students in the middle school years were aged 13. In the first and second IEA science study, students in the primary school years were aged 10, while students in the middle school years were aged 14 in the first IEA science study and 13 in the second IEA science study. In the TIMSS study, students in the primary school years are selected from the two grades with the largest proportions of 9-year-olds (third and fourth grades) and students in the middle school years are selected from the two grades with the largest proportions of 13-year-olds (seventh and eighth grades). Final school years always refers to students in their last year of secondary education. No East Asian country took part in the final-years TIMSS tests.
- The data for the first and second IEA mathematics study and for the first and second IEA science study are taken from Lee and Barro (2001). They are reported in percent-correct format.
- The TIMSS data are taken from several publications by the IEA (1998). They are reported in proficiency scale, which is constructed to generate an international mean of 500 and a standard deviation of 100 over the range of 0 to 1,000 for the countries participating in a test.
- The characteristics of the Philippine school sample are not completely known.

Table A3.3a: Scores in International Student Achievement Tests for OECD Countries

Year:	1964		1970/71			1994/95									
	IEA I[a]					TIMSS[b]									
Subject:	Mathematics		Science			Mathematics		Science		Mathematics		Science		Math.	Scien.
Age/grade:	13	Final	10	14	Final	4th	3rd	4th	3rd	8th	7th	8th	7th	Final	Final
Australia	27.0	31.3	–	30.8	41.2	546	483	562	510	530	498	545	504	522	527
Belgium	43.4	50.1	39.8	22.9	27.3	–	–	–	–	545.5	532.5	510.5	485.5	–	–
France	30.0	48.4	–	–	30.5	–	–	–	–	538	492	498	451	523	487
Germany	36.3	41.7	37.3	29.6	44.8	–	–	–	–	509	484	531	499	495	497
Italy	–	–	41.3	23.1	26.5	–	–	–	–	–	–	–	–	476	475
Japan	46.0	45.5	54.3	39.0	–	597	538	574	522	605	571	571	531	560	558
Netherlands	30.6	46.2	38.3	22.3	38.8	577	493	557	499	541	516	560	517	522	529
New Zealand	–	–	–	30.3	48.3	499	440	531	473	508	472	525	481	552	559
Sweden	21.9	39.6	45.8	27.1	32.0	–	–	–	–	519	477	535	488	–	–
United Kingdom	32.9	43.6	37.1	26.7	38.5	516.5	457	543.5	491.5	502	469.5	534.5	490	–	–
United States	25.4	20.0	44.3	27.0	22.8	545	480	565	511	500	476	534	508	461	480

[a]Results reported in percent-correct format. — [b]Results reported in proficiency scale.

Source: Lee and Barro (2001): IEA I; IEA (1998): TIMSS.

Table A3.3b: Scores in International Student Achievement Tests for East Asian Countries

	IEA II[a]					TIMSS[b]							
	1980–82		1983/84			1994/95							
	Mathematics		Science			Mathematics		Science		Mathematics		Science	
Age/grade:	13	Final	10	13	Final	4th	3rd	4th	3rd	8th	7th	8th	7th
Hong Kong	49.9	73	46.7	54.7	62.9	587	524	533	482	588	564	522	495
Philippines	–	–	39.6	38.3	–	–	–	–	–	399	386	395	382
Singapore	–	–	46.7	55	62.6	625	552	547	488	643	601	607	545
South Korea	–	–	64.2	60.3	–	611	561	597	553	607	577	565	535
Thailand	42.7	31.3	–	55	–	490	444	473	433	522	495	525	493
Note: OECD													
Australia	–	–	53.8	59.3	47.8	546	483	562	510	530	498	545	504
Belgium	52.8	47	–	–	–	–	–	–	–	545.5	532.5	510.5	485.5
Canada	50.9	41.6	57.1	62	40.8	532	469	549	490	527	494	531	499
France	53.5	–	–	–	–	–	–	–	–	538	492	498	451
Japan	63.5	68	64.2	67.3	51.4	597	538	574	522	605	571	571	531
Netherlands	58.1	–	–	66	–	577	493	557	499	541	516	560	517
New Zealand	46.4	49.8	–	–	–	499	440	531	473	508	472	525	481
Norway	–	–	52.9	59.7	49.8	502	421	530	450	503	461	527	483
Sweden	43.5	55.8	61.3	61.3	44.4	–	–	–	–	519	477	535	488
United Kingdom	48.8	49.4	48.8	55.7	63.7	516.5	457	543.5	491.5	502	469.5	534.5	490
United States	46	35.8	55	55	40.4	545	480	565	511	500	476	534	508

[a]Results reported in percent-correct format. — [b]Results reported in proficiency scale.

Source: Lee and Barro (2001): IEA II; IEA (1998): TIMSS.

3.5.2   Differences to Previous Time-Series Results for the United States

For the United States, this study finds that schooling expenditure per student increased by 1.2 percent per year relative to other service sectors (Table 3.3), which contrasts with Hanushek's (1997a: 192) result that "educational productivity is falling at 3.5 percent relative to low productivity sectors of the economy." Differences between national and UNESCO data, differences in the deflators employed, differences in the time periods considered, or a combination of all these factors could explain the different results for the United States.

Hanushek (1997a) uses education data from the Digest of Education Statistics of the U.S. Department of Education. The reported annual nominal increase in school expenditure per student is 7.6 percent in 1982–1991 and 9.5 percent in 1967–1991.[69] Using the same source (U.S. Department of Education 1998) to calculate the figures for my sample periods 1970–1994 and 1970–1990, I get 8.2 percent and 9.2 percent, respectively, which is close to my U.S. figures calculated on the basis of UNESCO data (see columns (1) and (2) of Table 3.1).[70]

Furthermore, Hanushek (1997a) uses a consumer price index for services (CPI-S) to deflate nominal expenditure per student. The entry in his Table 2 incorrectly reports the CPI deflator and not the CPI-S deflator in 1982–1991. Recalculating the CPI-S deflator on the basis of the original data (Council of Economic Advisors 1999) reveals that the actual increase in the CPI-S is 4.8 percent in 1982–1991 and 7.0 percent in 1967–1991. Therefore, the decline in schooling productivity estimated by Hanushek is 2.8 percent in 1982–1991 and 2.5 percent in 1967–1991, rather than 3.5 percent. For my sample period 1970–1994, the average annual rate of change in the CPI-S deflator is 6.6 percent. That is, it is exactly equal to the PGS deflator and the CSPS deflator calculated on the basis of UN data (Table 3.2).

The difference between the annual rate of change in educational expenditure per student based on U.S. national data and the annual rate of change in the CPI-S deflator equals 1.5 percent in 1970–1994. My estimate of 1.2 percent reported in Table 3.3 reflects that my 1994 figure most likely underestimates educational expenditure because of a structural break in the UNESCO data series (Section

---

69   Since education data are reported by school year, e.g., 1990/91, it is arbitrary whether the data are allocated to the beginning (1990) or to the end (1991) of the school year. While Hanushek (1997a) uses the end of the school year, I use the beginning of the school year because decisions on educational spending and numbers of students enrolled are for the most part fixed at the beginning of the school year. Therefore, what Hanushek calls 1967–1991 would be called 1966–1990 in my classification.

70   The difference between the U.S. Department of Education figure of 8.2 percent and the UNESCO figure of 7.8 percent for the 1970–1994 period confirms that my 1994 figure may underestimate the increase in schooling expenditure because of the structural break in the UNESCO data between 1990 and 1994 (Section 3.3.2.3).

3.3.2.3). Otherwise, the differences between my results and Hanushek's results are neither related to different data sources nor to different deflators and can be completely ascribed to differences in the sample period. In the United States, expenditure on schooling has increased at a similar pace to the increase in the prices of other services since the early 1990s, which is the sole reason for my lower estimate of the increase in schooling expenditure in the United States in 1970–1994 compared to the (corrected) estimates for 1967–1991 and 1982–1991 by Hanushek (1997a).

4   Modeling the Production of Schooling Quality

4.1   Incentives in the Public Schooling System: A Principal-Agent Problem

Everywhere in the world, public schools dominate the production of the basic education of students. As *The Economist* (1999: 21) put it, "[i]n most countries the business of running schools is as firmly in the grip of the state as was the economy of Brezhnev's Russia." Like other command and control systems, public schooling systems arguably may not set suitable incentives for improving students' educational performance or for containing costs. It is usually assumed that a performance-maximizing behavior ensues in private sectors because market competition imposes penalties on firms that fail to use their resources effectively. Inefficiency leads to higher costs and higher prices—practically an invitation for competitors to lure away customers. Such a loss of customers has a negative effect on firms' profits, the objective which firms usually strive to maximize, so that they have an incentive to make an efficient use of their resources.

But in the education market, "[i]t is not obvious that schools have stringent achievement maximization objectives imposed on them" (Hoxby 2000b: 1240). The relative lack of competition in the schooling sector tends to dull the incentives to improve quality while holding down costs. Moreover, in the public system, the ability of parents and students to ensure that they receive a high-quality education is constrained by a large number of obstacles to "opting out by feet," that is, to leaving a bad school. They have to rely almost exclusively on the government, school administrators, and school personnel to monitor one another's behavior and to create appropriate quality-control measures.

Hence, it is crucial for the quality of schooling that the institutions and policies established in a society create incentives for all the actors in the education process to use resources in ways that maximize educational performance. Within a country's schooling system, the relevant institutions and policies include the ways in which a society manages and finances its schools, how student performance is assessed, and who is empowered to make basic educational decisions, such as which curricula to follow, which teachers to hire, and which teaching methods to follow. The challenge of all these institutions is to create a set of incentives which induces students, teachers, and the school administration to behave in ways which do not necessarily further vested interests but instead further students' educational performance. For instance, without the right incentives, teachers may avoid using the most promising teaching techniques, preferring to selfishly use the techniques which are most convenient to themselves. In terms of policy, one might speculate that if a country assesses the performance of students with some sort of national exam and uses this information to monitor teachers, teachers will focus more on raising student achievement than would otherwise be the case.

This chapter develops an economic model of the production of education in schools which is capable of depicting the impact of different institutional features of the schooling system on the quality of schooling. It starts with an application of the theory of institutional economics to the schooling sector in general terms (Section 4.2). Institutions allocate the rights of decision-making in a system and determine the incentives faced by the actors. In the education process, a network of principal-agent relationships exists, relationships which entail conflicts between the interests of different groups and serious problems of monitoring due to informational advantages of self-interested agents. This can create adverse incentives and leeway for the agents to act opportunistically, leading to an inefficient use of given resources and to misallocations of resources across different uses. By determining decision-making rules and incentives, the institutional structure of the schooling system can, thus, influence the quality of the education which is ultimately produced.

The few economic models of the schooling system available in the literature which deal with the influence of institutions on the production of education are scattered among several approaches which are restricted to specific effects. Among those models which do include institutional effects, Costrell (1994) and Betts (1998) model education as a principal-agent problem where a policymaker sets educational standards and students choose their effort in response to these standards. They restrain the model to the optimal setting of educational standards and come to conflicting conclusions for an egalitarian policymaker. Hoxby (1999) analyzes the effects of central versus local school financing on schooling productivity in an agency model where schools are producers of local public goods facing decentralized Tiebout choices by households. She finds favorable effects of local financing on the productivity of schooling producers. Bishop (1998) presents a simple model of schooling in which the behavior of students and the community depends on incentives which are in turn influenced by the informational content of signals which the schooling system produces.[71] He confines his analysis to the effect of external examinations, which are shown to render positive effects on the community's schooling priorities, students' motiva-

---

[71] The model is sketched out in an appendix to the working-paper version of the work published in Bishop (1999).

tion, and students' educational performance by rewarding learning and by changing peer incentives.

Epple and Romano (1998) restrict their schooling model to the analysis of the sorting of students into public and private schools by ability and income. Lazear (2001) presents a model of educational production where classroom learning is a public good which can be disrupted by individual students and where schools choose class sizes according to students' behavior. He shows that private schools may produce higher student achievement by setting higher disciplinary incentives for students. In essence, the few existing models of schooling which deal with institutional features limit themselves to special issues. They fall short of being capable of producing hypotheses on the effects which a broad range of potential institutional features might have on the quality of the education produced by schools.

Thus, Section 4.3 builds on the only model which is directly constructed to reflect the impact of an institutional feature on students' educational performance, namely Bishop's (1998) model of the effect of external examinations. Bishop's basic framework is extended to depict the influence of further institutions. The network of principal-agent relationships in schooling as described in Section 4.2 is stripped down to only two actors in this model: The government chooses the level of educational spending which maximizes its net benefits, given students' efforts, and the students choose the level of their effort which maximizes their net benefits, given the government's spending choice. In the jointly determined equilibrium, the quality of the education produced in schools is shown to depend on several external parameters which are given by the institutional structure of the schooling system. While this model is quite parsimonious, it contains the essential features necessary to understand the influence of institutions in the educational process.

The model is applied to assess the impact of different institutional features of the schooling system on the quality of schooling output (Section 4.4). It is argued that central examinations favor students' educational performance by increasing the rewards for learning, decreasing peer pressure against learning, and improving the monitoring of the education process. School autonomy on standard setting and performance control is detrimental to educational performance because it increases the scope for diverting resources from teaching, whereas school autonomy in process operations and personnel-management decisions is conducive to educational performance because it increases the informational content and effectiveness of teaching. As regards the level of administrative decision-making, both local and central administrative levels render negative effects on schooling quality. Teachers' influence on teaching methods, teachers scrutinizing the performance of their students, parents' influence in the education process, and competition from private schools increase the quality of schooling, because they favor schooling effectiveness, increase the rewards for learning and the political priority given to schooling quality, and limit the scope for resource diversion. By contrast, teachers' influence on their salary levels and work load, and a high degree of political leverage of teacher unions decrease the quality of schooling, because they favor resource diversion to the furthering of vested interests and lower the priority given to schooling quality in the political process.

4.2   Institutional Economics Applied to the Schooling Sector

4.2.1   The Role of Institutions in the Schooling System

In studying the economic forces at work in the schooling sector, one is easily led to the simple production-function argumentation that more inputs such as smaller classes, higher teacher salaries, or more teaching material should lead to higher schooling output in the form of improved educational performance of students. However, this would require the efficient use of resources in the sense that inputs are used in a performance-maximizing way. Because the incentives elicited by competition and the price system which tend to create the efficient input-output link in other sectors of the economy are usually not at work in the public schooling sector, we cannot simply presuppose that the educational input-output relation in schools is efficient.

Instead, we have to look at the institutional structures which prevail in the schooling system and at the monetary and intrinsic incentives they create for the different groups involved in educational production. As Landsburg (1993: 3) put it, "[m]ost of economics can be summarized in four words: 'People respond to incentives.'" Therefore, to understand the economic forces at work in the schooling sector, I analyze the incentives influencing the different actors involved in the production of education and the different institutional structures which create these incentives.

Generally speaking, institutions are constraints devised by human beings. They constitute the rules of the game in a society, thereby structuring human interactions (North 1994). Institutions enclose formal and informal rules and their enforcement instruments. Within the schooling system, relevant institutions govern the distribution of decision-making powers between the different actors involved. The set of given institutions creates a system of property rights, i.e., rights of actors to use resources and to limit competition for resources as well as entitlement rights. That is, institutions determine who is eligible to make decisions on the use of resources in different areas. Furthermore, institutions determine the provision of information in the system and the rewards and penalties which the actors get in response to their actions (Furubotn and Richter 1997). Thereby, institutions define and limit the set of possible choices of all actors involved and thereby form the prevailing incentive structure.

While institutions are the rules of the game, the people who are the players in this game act within this system of rules. Assuming that individual actors behave rationally, they maximize their objective functions subject to the constraints set by the institutions. Therefore, they respond to the incentives created by the set of given institutions. The behavior of the people involved in educational production is reflected in their decisions on the allocation of resources across different functional categories (e.g., number of teachers, teachers' salaries, instructional material) and on the effectiveness of the use of these resources. This, in turn, affects the outcome of the education process, namely the performance of the students.

Consequently, institutions influence student performance by creating a system of rights to decide on resource allocation which establishes the incentives which steer actors' behavior in a particular direction. In North's (1994: 359) explanation of economic performance, "[i]nstitutions form the incentive structure of a society, and the political and economic institutions, in consequence, are the underlying determinants of economic performance." In the same consequence, political and educational institutions are the underlying determinants of educational performance.

4.2.2   Agency Problems and Inefficiencies in Schooling

Institutions are not per se created in ways which ensure efficiency. Quite to the contrary, in the schooling system, there are a lot of problems of agency, incomplete contracts, and adverse incentives which work against an efficient use of resources. The institutions governing the education process can be viewed as a network of principal-agent relationships. Within these relationships, a principal has an (explicit or implicit) contract with an agent to act on his behalf. The agent is self-interested, and he enjoys some informational advantage over the principal (asymmetric information). The self-interest of the agent might conflict with the principal's interest, and the informational advantage will make it costly (or even impossible) for the principal to monitor the actions of the agent completely. This leads to adverse incentives, giving the agent some leeway to act opportunistically—i.e., selfishly in his own interest instead of the principal's interest—without being penalized. While it might be in the interest of the "ultimate" principal in the education process to maximize student performance with given resources— parents are probably the actors which come nearest to something like an "ultimate" principal in schooling—the vested interests of the different agents will lead to a misallocation across different inputs and an inefficient use of the inputs.

A (still hugely simplifying) picture of the network of principal-agent relationships in educational production looks as follows: Voters (including parents) entrust the government with the task of ensuring schooling for the children. The government hands the implementation over to the administration. The administration transfers the task of schooling provision to school management (usually exercised by heads of school or school governing boards). School management employs teachers and teaching aides for tuition of the children. And ultimately it is the students who have to do the learning. Each of these contracts is laden with problems of monitoring. There is no clear-cut property right of students or parents to decide how the money for their schooling is spent. Instead, all the agents involved respond to the incentives set by the institutions: They can use the room created by imperfectly monitored contracts to advance their own interests. They can divert resources from the use of maximizing the educational performance of the students to the use of advancing their own objectives.

It would be a vast simplification of reality to assume that the different groups of agents maximize a single objective each. In reality, each group of agents faces multifarious interests, and the institutional structure can change the relative costs and benefits of advancing one objective or the other. While teachers have a genuine interest in increasing their income at a given work load or decreasing their work load at a given income, no one will deny that most teachers also get satisfaction from seeing their students progressing, thereby raising their welfare level. Furthermore, teachers might face negative consequences from their heads of school or from parents when they are doing a bad job. Thus, teachers often face conflicting interests, and their relative advancement may be easier or harder in different institutional surroundings. If the performance of students is observed, the achievement of higher student performance will have a higher pay-off for teachers than if it is not. Likewise, if teachers have a lot of leeway to decrease their work load without facing negative consequences, this will have adverse effects on student performance relative to a situation where they have less leeway.

Parents are probably the actors with the clearest unidimensional interest in a high level of their children's educational performance. While the students themselves certainly have an interest in their own performance, they will weigh this objective against other objectives such as the amount of leisure time and the possibility of making or losing friends through studying less or more. In the same way as with teachers and students, the school management and the administration will face a trade-off between advancing the educational performance of students' and reducing their own work load, while they also care for their own monetary pay-off and for their school's or district's reputation. Finally, in the public-choice view, the government's interest lies in its reelection, so that it will do whatever it has to do to increase the likelihood of being reelected. This, in turn, will be influenced by the ability of the different interest groups to lobby for their objectives.

The advancement of their own interests by the different groups of agents may lead to two kinds of inefficiencies in the allocation and use of schooling resources. First, it may be in the interest of some agents to make inefficient use of given resources (although resources may be allocated efficiently across different inputs). For example, a teacher may be inclined to use part of a lesson for more pleasant things than stressful teaching of mathematics, as long as this lack of mathematical tuition is not monitored. Second, the agents' interest may lead to a misallocation of resources across functional categories (causing inefficiency even if these resources were then used effectively). If it is in the interest of a group of agents with decision power over resource allocation to overspend on one input relative to others, the marginal productivity of this input would be lower than that of the other inputs (given decreasing returns to each individual input), leading to a student performance level inferior to a situation of efficient spending. For example, if teachers have a say in budgetary matters, they may want to increase spending on teachers at the expense of spending on instructional material, so that the marginal product of material inputs is higher than the marginal product of teacher inputs and schooling output could be higher at the given expenditure level.

Therefore, "there is an enormous gap between children sitting in a classroom and an increase in human capital" (Pritchett and Filmer 1999: 223). An increase in expenditure per student does not necessarily have to lead to increased student performance—as shown empirically in Chapter 3. Likewise, lower class sizes do not necessarily have to go hand in hand with better schooling quality. The classes may already be so small that the marginal productivity of a reduction in class size (an increase in teachers per student) is negligible. Even more, the input "teacher per student" may not be used with the same effectiveness everywhere. If a more productive way of using resources in bigger classes outweighs any potential positive effect of smaller classes, class size could even be positively related to student performance.

Section 4.4 gives a more detailed analysis of the different kinds of educational institutions, the incentives they create for different educational actors, and probable consequences for students' educational performance. That analysis of the impact of different institutional features of the schooling system on the quality of schooling is based on the model of educational production presented in the following section. Among the institutional features analyzed, institutions such as external examinations and a competitive environment set by a large private schooling sector should focus agents' interests on students' learning and should be best suited to face monitoring problems, thereby being conducive to student performance. In a similar way, the distribution of decision-making powers and responsibilities between schools and the educational administration, as well as between different administrative levels, should impact on the prevailing incentive structure and on the quality of schooling. Institutions determining the influence, freedom of action, and accountability of teachers and parents should also matter for the actors' incentives and for the educational performance of the students.

4.3 A Basic Model of Educational Production in Schools

In the following, the arguments of the economics of institutions as applied to the schooling sector are crystallized into a model of the production of educational quality in the schooling system. This model is very parsimonious, stripped down to the bare necessities to be able to demonstrate the point of focus, namely the effects of institutions on actors' incentives and thus on the quality of educational production. It contains only one principal-agent relationship. The principal is represented by the government, which reflects the public interest and decides on the level of school spending. The only agent in the model is the student, whose effort is an input into the educational production process and who has interests which diverge from those of the public. The incentives faced by both, the government and the students, are influenced by the prevailing institutional structure of the schooling system. The choices of other actors in the schooling system—such as teachers, parents, heads of school, and the administration—are exogenous to the model. They come in as determinants of the effectiveness of resource use in the education production function and of the priority given to a high-quality education in the political process.

The structure of the model builds on Bishop's (1998) sketch of an economic model of the schooling sector. Its basic idea is that rational actors maximize the difference between their individual benefits and their individual costs, i.e., their net benefits. Schooling quality is a function of educational spending and the effort of the student. The government chooses the level of educational spending which maximizes its net benefits given the level of student effort. The student acts to maximize his own net benefits given the level of educational spending. All choices are made for given institutions of the schooling system, and they respond to changes in the institutional structure. In effect, rational choices of students and the government determine the level of schooling quality, and institutions influence these choices by altering the incentives for the actors.

4.3.1   The Education Production Function

For ease of presentation, the education production function which depicts what is happening in schools is taken to be of the Cobb–Douglas form. While this functional choice is more specific than would be necessary to reach the conclusions of the model, the main intuition and results of the model can readily be followed in this specific functional form.[72] Thus, schooling quality, Q, as reflected in students' educational performance, is produced in the schooling system according to

$$(4.1) \quad Q = AE^{\alpha}(IR)^{\beta}, \qquad \alpha + \beta < 1.$$

Students are assumed to be perfectly homogenous, so that student subscripts are omitted in all equations. In effect, all student-related variables may be viewed as aggregations for a whole population of students. Three inputs go into the production process: learning ability, A, student effort, E, and effectively employed resources, combined into the term IR.

The student's learning ability, A, is exogenous to the model. It combines all effects which determine the readiness of students to learn when they are in school. This is not only the students' innate ability, but also his family background and prior learning experience. By contrast, student effort, E, is controlled by the student himself. It reflects the student's motivation, time, and engagement devoted to learning. Student effort is probably the most important input in the education process, given that with student-teacher ratios of, e.g., 20 to 1, students spend about 20 times as many hours learning as teachers spend teaching.

The term IR combines the amount of resources going into teaching, given by R, with the effectiveness with which these resources are used, given by I. The effectiveness, I, of resource use in the education process is determined by the amount of information necessary for an efficient education which is available to those who make the educational decisions. I is the information on how to teach effectively at the local level. It reflects whether allocation choices, hiring decisions, teaching methods, and similar decisions are made in the most effective way to further the learning of the specific students in a given school at a given time. Hence, it measures how knowledgeable the educational choices are, standing for the effectiveness with which educational spending is used to produce schooling quality. It combines the effectiveness of the allocation of resources across different functional categories of inputs and the effectiveness of the use of

---

[72] The main necessary features of a more general model are that there is complementarity between student effort and resource input in educational production and that certain institutional features enhance the productivity of resource usage.

these resources. In effect, I is a school effectiveness index, exogenous to the model. It is given by the institutional decision-making structure of the schooling system which lays down who is allowed to decide on educational tasks. Hence, it is a technical parameter imposed on teachers and schools, not something chosen by teachers or schools.

R is the amount of educational resources employed in teaching. This is not necessarily the same as the total amount of educational expenditure, X, spent in the schooling system, which is chosen by the government. R and X may differ from one another because part of the original government spending may be diverted to further objectives different from schooling quality, Q, before being used in the schooling process at all:

$$(4.2) \quad R = (1-d)X,$$

where d is the share of original spending diverted to other objectives, which is exogenous to the model. The government can directly control X. Thus, the total amount of expenditure spent on schooling in the model is based on governmental choices endogenous to the schooling process, as argued in Section 3.1.3. However, the government cannot directly determine R. Note that if $d = 1$ at the margin, any additional educational expenditure by the government will have no effect at all on students' educational performance.

The parameter d is a measure of how much the institutional setting of the schooling system allows self-interested producers of schooling to divert resources from teaching students. It thus reflects how much actors in the administration, in school management, and in the teaching force are allowed to or prevented from using administrative funds, school funds, and teacher time for objectives which do not increase schooling quality. In contrast to the parameter I, the parameter d may be thought of as being influenced by the intentional behavior of local schools and teachers. In the model, the parameters d and I are thought of as being independent from each other.

The parameters α and β are the elasticities of schooling quality, Q, with respect to student effort, E, and effective spending, IR, respectively. The Cobb–Douglas form of the education production function ensures that student effort and educational spending interact positively. An improvement in resource endowment enhances the effect of greater student effort, and vice versa. Furthermore, the function has decreasing returns to scale as $\alpha + \beta < 1$.[73] A proportionate increase in both student effort and effective spending causes a less than proportionate increase in schooling quality, which should be a realistic feature

---

[73] Note again that this is a sufficient assumption but not a necessary one because it is more specific than necessary. Even in the given functional setting, the assumption that $\alpha < (1 - \beta)\mu$ would suffice to reach all the qualitative conclusions of the model.

because additions to students' educational achievement are increasingly hard to produce.

4.3.2   Student Maximization

As indicated before, the two actors in the model—the government and the student—have one choice variable each which they use to maximize their respective net benefits. The student, S, chooses his level of effort, E, given the government's spending decision and given the exogenous institutional parameters. That is, he chooses how hard to study in order to maximize his expected benefits relative to his expected costs. The student's benefits, B_S, are given by

$$(4.3) \quad B_S = wQ = wAE^\alpha (IR)^\beta,$$

where w combines the extrinsic rewards for learning, l, and the intrinsic rewards, j: $w = l + j$. The extrinsic rewards, l, reflect the impact of the absolute level of the student's educational performance, Q, on the present discounted value of lifetime earnings in the labor market, including any effects operating through admission to and completion of colleges and graduate programs. The intrinsic rewards, j, stand for the present discounted value of the nonpecuniary benefits of learning, including the joy of learning for its own sake and the honor and respect which parents, teachers, and others may give for educational performance.

The costs of student's effort, C_S, are given by

$$(4.4) \quad C_S = cE^\mu, \qquad \mu > 1,$$

where c is a cost parameter. These costs combine the loss of control over one's in-class time, the additional time spent learning, the psychic energy of learning, and the money for tuition and books. In addition, the costs to the individual student may include the peer pressure against learning, e.g., of being called a "nerd" or "teacher's pet." Most of the costs will usually be the opportunity costs of the students' time, i.e., the cost of giving up other more pleasant activities. The elasticity, μ, of cost with respect to effort is assumed to be greater than one because the marginal cost of effort rises as effort increases. Given that the total amount of time available per day is fixed, taking additional time of the day away from leisure activities to learning creates increasing costs.

The student chooses the effort level, E, which maximizes his net benefits, i.e., his benefits minus his costs:

(4.5) $\quad S : \max_{E} (B_S - C_S) \Rightarrow \dfrac{\partial (B_S - C_S)}{\partial E} = \alpha w A E^{\alpha-1}(IR)^{\beta} - \mu c E^{\mu-1} = 0.$

This yields the optimal level of student effort, E, for any given level of spending, X, chosen by the government:

(4.6) $\quad E = \left[\dfrac{\alpha}{\mu c} w A (I(1-d)X)^{\beta} \right]^{\frac{1}{\mu-\alpha}}.$

4.3.3 Government Maximization

To determine the government's choice of the level of spending, X, we have to look at the benefits and costs of the government, G. The government's benefits, B_G, are given by

(4.7) $\quad B_G = PwQ = PwAE^{\alpha}(IR)^{\beta}.$

Assuming for simplicity that there are no external benefits of education, the rewards for learning, w, again including both extrinsic and intrinsic rewards, are equivalent for the individual student and for the general public. In addition to the benefits wQ which are thus equivalent to the student's benefits in equation (4.3), the benefits of the government are weighted by the parameter P which reflects the priority which the government gives to schooling quality. P characterizes the political power of supporters of high academic standards in the governance of schools, such as parents, relative to the political power of those whose objectives lie elsewhere. The latter may include voters whose main concern is keeping taxes down or teachers who place higher priority on decreasing their work load by decreasing educational standards.

The cost of school inputs to the government, C_G, is equal to the government's overall educational expenditure:

(4.8) $\quad C_G = X.$

Note that it is total spending, X, which determines the government's cost, not effective resource use R.

Likewise, overall spending X—not R—is the choice variable under the control of the government. It chooses X in order to maximize its net benefits, given students' effort and given the institutional setting:

(4.9) $G : \max_{X}(B_G - C_G)$

$$\Rightarrow \frac{\partial(B_G - C_G)}{\partial X} = \beta P w A E^{\alpha}(I(1-d))^{\beta} X^{\beta-1} - 1 = 0.$$

This determines the level of total educational spending, X, which is optimal to the government, given the level of effort, E, chosen by the students:

(4.10) $X = \left[\beta P w A E^{\alpha}(I(1-d))^{\beta}\right]^{\frac{1}{1-\beta}}.$

4.3.4   Equilibrium

Equations (4.6) and (4.10), which determine the optimal levels of student effort, E, and government spending, X, both contain the two endogenous variables E and X. This system of equations can be solved to yield the levels of student effort, E, government spending, X, and schooling quality, Q, in equilibrium, where both the government's and the student's net benefits are maximized. Student effort, E, results as

(4.11) $E = \left[\left(\frac{\alpha}{\mu c}\right)^{1-\beta} Aw(\beta PI(1-d))^{\beta}\right]^{\frac{1}{\Delta}},$

where

(4.12) $\begin{aligned} \Delta &\equiv \mu - \beta\mu - \alpha \\ &= (1-\beta)\mu - \alpha > \alpha\mu - \alpha = \alpha(\mu-1) > 0. \end{aligned}$

Hence, the student's effort is positively affected by his learning ability, A, by the rewards, w, for learning, by the political priority, P, for high-quality schooling, and by school effectiveness, I, while it is negatively affected by the cost factor, c, of effort to the student and by the share of diverted spending, d, in overall spending.

Overall educational spending, X, in equilibrium is given by

(4.13) $X = \left[\left(\frac{\alpha}{\mu c}\right)^{\alpha} (Aw)^{\mu}(\beta P)^{\mu-\alpha}(I(1-d))^{\beta\mu}\right]^{\frac{1}{\Delta}}.$

Note that government spending, X, is determined by the same exogenous parameters as student effort, E, and in the same directions, only with different elasticities. Combining equations (4.11) and (4.13) into the educational production function (4.1) yields the equilibrium level of schooling quality, Q:

$$(4.14) \quad Q = \left[\left(\frac{\alpha}{\mu c} \right)^{\alpha} A^{\mu} w^{\alpha + \beta \mu} (\beta P I (1 - d))^{\beta \mu} \right]^{\frac{1}{\Delta}}.$$

Again, ability, A, rewards, w, political priority, P, and school effectiveness, I, yield positive effects on schooling quality, Q, while cost of effort, c, and diverted spending, d, have negative impacts.

The elasticities of the response of student effort, E, government spending, X, and schooling quality, Q, with respect to each of the exogenous variables, derived from equations (4.11) to (4.14), are summarized in Table 4.1. The elasticities of student effort, E, and of government spending, X, with respect to

Table 4.1: Elasticities of Endogenous Variables with Respect to Exogenous Variables

	Student effort, E	Government spending, X	Educational quality, Q
Ability, A	$\eta_{EA} = \dfrac{1}{\Delta}$	$\eta_{XA} = \dfrac{\mu}{\Delta}$	$\eta_{QA} = \dfrac{\mu}{\Delta}$
Cost of effort, c	$\eta_{Ec} = -\dfrac{1-\beta}{\Delta}$	$\eta_{Xc} = -\dfrac{\alpha}{\Delta}$	$\eta_{Qc} = -\dfrac{\alpha}{\Delta}$
Rewards, w	$\eta_{Ew} = \dfrac{1}{\Delta}$	$\eta_{Xw} = \dfrac{\mu}{\Delta}$	$\eta_{Qw} = \dfrac{\alpha + \beta \mu}{\Delta}$
Priority, P	$\eta_{EP} = \dfrac{\beta}{\Delta}$	$\eta_{XP} = \dfrac{\mu - \alpha}{\Delta}$	$\eta_{QP} = \dfrac{\beta \mu}{\Delta}$
Effectiveness, I	$\eta_{EI} = \dfrac{\beta}{\Delta}$	$\eta_{XI} = \dfrac{\beta \mu}{\Delta}$	$\eta_{QI} = \dfrac{\beta \mu}{\Delta}$
Limit to diversion, $(1-d)$	$\eta_{E(1-d)} = \dfrac{\beta}{\Delta}$	$\eta_{X(1-d)} = \dfrac{\beta \mu}{\Delta}$	$\eta_{Q(1-d)} = \dfrac{\beta \mu}{\Delta}$

Source: Equations (4.11) to (4.14).

the different parameters combine through the education production function to yield the elasticities of schooling quality, Q, which is the ultimate focus in this study. All the elasticities depend solely on the parameters α, β, and μ. The elasticity of schooling quality, Q, with respect to ability, A, is relatively large given that $\mu < 1$, whereas the elasticity of Q with respect to cost of effort, c, is relatively small since $\alpha < 1 - \beta$. The elasticity of Q with respect to rewards, w, is larger than that with respect to political priority, P, school effectiveness, I, and share of nondiverted spending, $(1-d)$.

4.4   Institutions, Incentives, and Schooling Quality

The parameters which influence the level of schooling quality achieved in the model of educational production are mainly driven by the institutional setting in the schooling system. The institutional setting determines the school effectiveness, I, the scope for spending diversion, d, the size of the rewards for learning, w, the cost of effort, c, and the political priority for high-quality schooling, P. These parameters shape the incentive structure with which the actors in the schooling process are faced. They thus influence the behavior of the actors, i.e., student effort and government spending in the model. And these actions, in turn, determine the quality of schooling produced in the system. In short, institutions influence the educational performance of the students.

Hence, the model of educational production allows us to analyze the impact of educational institutions on schooling quality. Bishop (1998) restricted his analysis to the influence of external examinations on the incentive structure of the students (Section 4.4.1). I have extended the model to cover additional educational institutions in order to derive hypotheses on the incentives they create and on their probable consequences for the quality of schooling. Six main institutional features of the schooling system are considered: centralized examinations, the distribution of decision-making power between schools and administration, the distribution of decision-making power between different levels of administration, teachers' influence in the schooling system, parents' influence, and the extent of competition from private educational institutions in the system. As some of the institutions affect different parameters of the model in a different direction and as the relative size of these effects seems rather speculative from a theoretical perspective, the model presented here should be understood as a reasoning tool to depict the different potential effects of institutions in the schooling system, while the ultimate determination of the sign and size of the net effects has to be left to the empirical investigation of Chapter 5.

4.4.1 Central Examinations

The institution of centrally and thus externally set examinations profoundly alters the incentive structure within the schooling system compared to school-based or teacher-based examinations. Central exams signal the achievement of a student relative to an external standard, thereby making students' performance comparable to the performance of students in other classes and schools.[74] As students get marks relative to the country mean, their level of educational quality is made observable and transparent, which simplifies the monitoring of the performance of students, teachers, and schools. Thereby, the incentives of all educational actors to further schooling quality differ between schooling systems which have central examinations and systems which do not have them. The influence of central examinations on the quality of schooling may run through three basic channels: increased external rewards for learning, decreased peer pressure against learning, and increased monitoring of teachers and schools.

First of all, central examinations change the students' incentive structure relative to autonomous local examinations. By creating comparability to an external standard, central examinations improve the signaling of academic performance to advanced educational institutions and to potential employers. These institutions will thus give greater weight to schooling quality when they make admissions and hiring decisions. In consequence, their decisions become less sensitive to other factors such as family connections, racial and religious stereotypes, the chemistry of a twenty-minute job interview, performance relative to the class mean, or aptitude tests which lean more to measuring innate ability than to measuring overall educational performance.

Hence, transition to the institution of central examinations, *CenExa*, should have a positive effect on the rewards for learning, w, especially on the extrinsic part:

$$(4.15) \quad \frac{\partial w}{\partial CenExa} > 0.$$

As students' rewards for learning grow, anything which increases the quality of schooling becomes more worthwhile. Students respond to an increase in rewards, w, by increasing their learning effort, E, and governments respond by increasing educational spending, X (Table 4.1). The result is an increase in schooling quality, Q. The elasticities in Table 4.1 show that the effect of an increase in w

---

[74] For a more detailed description of the characteristics of "curriculum-based external exit examination systems," see Bishop (1997, 1999).

on schooling quality, Q, is relatively large compared to the effects of other institutional parameters.

The impact of rising rewards for learning, w, on schooling quality, Q, is largest when the elasticities of schooling quality with respect to student effort, α, and government spending, β, are substantial and when the marginal cost curve for student effort is flat (μ close to 1):

$$(4.16) \quad \frac{\partial \eta_{Qw}}{\partial \alpha} = \frac{\mu}{\Delta^2} > 0, \qquad \frac{\partial \eta_{Qw}}{\partial \beta} = \frac{\mu^2}{\Delta^2} > 0, \qquad \frac{\partial \eta_{Qw}}{\partial \mu} = -\frac{\alpha}{\Delta^2} < 0.$$

That is, central examinations should have the strongest impact on schooling quality when student effort and government spending have a strong impact on schooling quality and when the marginal cost of effort to the student is small.

A second channel through which central examinations may impact on educational production is through their impact on peer behavior. Grading relative to class performance gives students an incentive to lower average class performance because this allows the students to receive the same grades at less effort. The cooperative solution of students to maximize their joint welfare is for everybody not to study very hard. Thus, with grades relative to the class level, students have an incentive to apply peer pressure on other students in the class not to be too studious and to distract teachers from teaching a high standard (Bishop 1999). With centralized external examinations, in contrast, these incentives are no longer given because inferior class work will only harm the students.

The peer denigration of studiousness is reflected in the cost of student effort, c. By making the negative impact of a student's effort on his classmates' grades vanish, central examinations should lower peer pressure against learning and thus have a negative impact on c:

$$(4.17) \quad \frac{\partial c}{\partial CenExa} < 0.$$

A smaller cost of effort, c, increases student effort, E, government spending, X, and schooling quality, Q (Table 4.1). The impact of central examinations on schooling quality Q through reducing students' cost of effort will again be higher the higher the elasticities of production, α and β, and the smaller the elasticity of students cost, μ, with respect to effort, since

$$(4.18) \quad \frac{\partial \eta_{Qc}}{\partial \alpha} = \frac{(\beta - 1)\mu}{\Delta^2} < 0, \qquad \frac{\partial \eta_{Qc}}{\partial \beta} = -\frac{\alpha\mu}{\Delta^2} < 0, \qquad \frac{\partial \eta_{Qc}}{\partial \mu} = \frac{\alpha(1-\beta)}{\Delta^2} > 0.$$

The negative effect of c on Q is more negative, i.e., larger in absolute terms, the larger α, etc.

The distraction of teachers from teaching a high standard is reflected in the teaching effectiveness index, I. By lowering the peer incentive to distract teachers relative to decentralized examinations, central examinations should increase I:

$$(4.19) \quad \frac{\partial I}{\partial CenExa} > 0.$$

As shown by the elasticities depicted in Table 4.1, an increase in teaching effectiveness, I, has a positive effect on student effort, E, government spending, X, and schooling quality, Q. Thus, increased teaching effectiveness, I, is a further channel through which central examinations positively impact on the quality of schooling. Again, this effect will be the stronger the larger are the elasticities of schooling quality with respect to student effort and government spending and the smaller is the elasticity of the cost of learning with respect to student effort:

$$(4.20) \quad \frac{\partial \eta_{QI}}{\partial \alpha} = \frac{\beta\mu}{\Delta^2} > 0, \quad \frac{\partial \eta_{QI}}{\partial \beta} = \frac{\mu(\mu-\alpha)}{\Delta^2} > 0, \quad \frac{\partial \eta_{QI}}{\partial \mu} = -\frac{\alpha\beta}{\Delta^2} < 0.$$

A third channel of positive impact of central examinations on schooling quality runs through the monitoring of teachers and schools. Given central examinations, it becomes evident whether the bad performance of an individual student in a subject is an exception within a class or whether the whole class taught by a teacher is doing badly relative to the country mean. Therefore, parents (and students) have the information they need to initiate action because they can observe whether the teacher (and/or the student) is accountable for the bad performance. If, by contrast, students get marks relative to the class mean only, the performance of the class relative to the country mean will be unobservable and parents will have no information to intervene. As a consequence of the institutional setting, the agents' incentives are fundamentally altered. Given central examinations, the leeway of the teachers to act opportunistically is reduced and the incentives to use resources more effectively are increased. That is, the share d of total resources which teachers can divert from effective teaching is reduced. The same argument can be made for the monitoring of schools as a whole. Through central examinations, agents are made accountable to their principals: parents can assess the performance of their children, of the teachers, and of the schools; the head of a school can assess the performance of her teachers; and the government and administration can assess the performance of different schools.

In the model, the increase in the share $(1-d)$ of resources which are not diverted from teaching caused by a centralization of examinations,

$$(4.21) \quad \frac{\partial (1-d)}{\partial CenExa} > 0,$$

is shown to positively impact on student effort, E, government spending, X, and schooling quality, Q (Table 4.1). Since the elasticities of the endogenous variables with respect to $(1-d)$ are the same as those with respect to I, the effect of the three parameters α, β, and μ on these elasticities can again be derived from equation (4.20).[75]

4.4.2   Distribution of Responsibilities between Schools and Administration

A second institutional feature of the schooling system is the division of decision-making authority between administration and schools. The structure of the institutional system of schooling determines who has the power to decide on which task, which should impact on the effectiveness of resource use in schools. There are two conflicting potential effects of increased decision-making power at the school level. On the one hand, school autonomy establishes freedom to decide within schools, which is a pre-requisite for competition and for the possibility to respond to demands from parents. The actors within the schools should have the decentralized knowledge to choose the best way of teaching for their students (if they have incentives to do so), a kind of knowledge probably not given at the administrative level. Thus, school autonomy, Aut, should increase the informational content of the decisions and thus school effectiveness, I, relative to external decision-making by the administration

$$(4.22) \quad \frac{\partial I}{\partial Aut} > 0,$$

with the ensuing improvements in teaching effectiveness due to the use of local knowledge. As shown by the model of educational production, this is conducive to the levels of student effort, E, government spending, X, and schooling quality, Q (Table 4.1).

---

[75] While it might be argued that central examinations may have a negative effect on schooling quality in some subject areas because they do not allow the potentially fruitful diversification of covered topics which is possible under decentralized examinations, this should not be a major effect in subject areas such as mathematics and science where the topics to be covered are rather standard and where it is thus hard to think of beneficial diversification.

On the other hand, increased school autonomy increases the schools' leeway to act opportunistically, unless decisions can be fully monitored and the extent to which educational objectives are met can be fully evaluated, and unless there is a credible threat of penalties for opportunistic behavior. In addition to leading to more effective teaching, decentralized decision-making might thus also lead to a diversion of schooling resources from teaching students to other objectives of the self-interested producers of education. Hence, schools autonomy may also increase the share of original educational spending which is diverted from teaching activities:

$$(4.23) \quad \frac{\partial d}{\partial Aut} > 0, \quad \text{i.e.,} \quad \frac{\partial (1-d)}{\partial Aut} < 0.$$

This has detrimental consequences for student effort, E, government spending, X, and schooling quality, Q (Table 4.1).

To assess the combined effect of decision-making autonomy of schools on schooling quality, the two tendencies invoked by increased school autonomy—better use of decentralized knowledge and increased scope for resource diversion—have to be compared. Since the elasticity η_{QI} of schooling quality, Q, with respect to school effectiveness, I, and the elasticity $\eta_{Q(1-d)}$ of schooling quality, Q, with respect to the share of non-diverted spending $(1-d)$ are equal (Table 4.1), the net effect of school autonomy on the quality of schooling depends on the relative size of the effects on school effectiveness and on resource diversion in equations (4.22) and (4.23). Which direction of impact is the superior one should depend on the area of decision-making. There are decisions where centralization (decreased school autonomy) may plausibly have positive net effects on student performance, and there are decisions where it is likely to have negative net effects.

If decisions on standard setting and performance control are centralized, a lowering in a school's tuition standards will become easily transparent to parents and administration. This helps in the monitoring of schools' actions, thereby changing the schools' incentives against a misuse of resources. Through a centralized basic curriculum, the amount of what schools should teach is fixed and cannot easily be watered down by the interests of the agents at the school level as long as an external performance control is in place. Thus, the increase in resource diversion, d, caused by school autonomy can be thought to be substantial in these areas of decision-making. Furthermore, the informational advantage, reflected in the teaching effectiveness index, I, of local school personnel on the best curriculum and on the best way to measure performance may be limited. Therefore, the detrimental effect of school autonomy, Aut, of diverted resources should be larger in percentage terms than the conducive effect of local knowledge in the decision-making areas of standard setting and performance control, *Sta*:

$$(4.24) \quad \left| \frac{\partial \ln I}{\partial AutSta} \right| < \left| \frac{\partial \ln(1-d)}{\partial AutSta} \right|.$$

The net effect on schooling quality of school autonomy in standard and control decisions should thus be negative.[76] It may even be argued that knowledge on what students should be taught and on how their achievement should be measured may be equivalent or even superior at the central level relative to the school level. In this setting, $\partial \ln I / \partial AutSta \leq 0$, and the detrimental effect on schooling quality is even larger. Likewise, centralized decisions on the size of the school budget should benefit the overall effectiveness of resource use and thus schooling quality, since actors at the school level have large adverse incentives when it comes to the amount of resources available. It is clearly in the self-interest of decision-makers at the school level to collect additional funds for themselves or for resources which lighten their work load.

In contrast, knowledge on which process and personnel-management decisions are favorable to students' learning should be superior at the school level. Heads of school will have better knowledge than the administration on which tuition structures are best for their schools, which teacher deserves a pay rise or a promotion, and which teacher is the right one to hire for the school. Likewise, individual teachers should be best in choosing the right textbooks and other kinds of supplies and in the organization of instruction. School autonomy should increase the effectiveness, I, of teaching in these decision areas. Furthermore, school autonomy in process and personnel decisions does not generate much leeway to act opportunistically because hiring bad teachers or choosing bad textbooks is not in the interest of school personnel. That is, there is not much room or incentive for local decision-makers to divert resources d in these decision-making areas. Since the local advantage of information and thus effectiveness, I, is large and the scope for resource diversion, d, is small, school autonomy in process and personnel decisions, *AutPro*, should plausibly have a positive net effect on schooling quality:

$$(4.25) \quad \left| \frac{\partial \ln I}{\partial AutPro} \right| > \left| \frac{\partial \ln(1-d)}{\partial AutPro} \right|.$$

---

[76] Additionally, as shown by Costrell (1994), a centralized system of standard-setting will result in higher educational standards than a decentralized system because decentralization reduces a district's marginal benefit of a higher standard and raises its marginal cost.

In the case of process and personnel decisions, one might even think of situations where resource diversion does not occur at all, i.e., $\partial \ln d / \partial AutPro = 0$.

4.4.3 Distribution of Responsibilities between Administrative Levels

The argumentation so far considers "the administration" as one single body. In reality, there are different administrative authorities at the local, regional, state, and national levels in many countries. The division of responsibilities for educational decision-making and for fund allocation between local, intermediate, and central authorities establishes another feature of the institutional system of schooling which may influence the educational outcome. Once responsibility lies with the administration, the question is which level should take over the tasks to ensure the best possible outcome. Again, different effects should run counter to one another.

The lower the level of administrative decision-making, the smaller should be the loss of school effectiveness, I, relative to school autonomy as depicted in equation (4.22). At the local level, more decentralized knowledge is available and the administration is more directly accountable to parents, which might lead to more informed choices (higher I) than central authorities can make. However, the local administration will also have much closer ties with the school personnel, increasing the possibilities for successful lobbying of school-based interest groups and for collusion. Local administrators and school personnel might collude on the determination of the level and use of funds, so that an opportunistic resource allocation and a larger share of diverted spending, d, ensues, just like in the case of school autonomy in equation (4.23).

The central administrative level is more remote from the actors within the school. On the one hand, this should make collusion and thus local resource diversion, d, harder to achieve. On the other hand, monitoring of actions and resource use from the central level is elusive because of information problems (Hoxby 1999).[77] The higher is the level of administrative decision-making, the larger may be the loss of informed teaching, I. Additionally, a self-interested central administration will find it easier to develop an excessive bureaucracy, leading to resource diversion, d, at the central level. Thus, the impact of an allocation of decision-making power to the central administrative level should decrease I, while the effect on d is ambiguous.

---

[77] Hoxby (1999) emphasizes the benefits of decentralized Tiebout residential choices as a solution to the information problem. However, her model does not consider political-economy effects of lobbyism and collusion, and she concedes that there may be serious flaws in the Tiebout process.

Since both the local and the central level of administrative decision-making face serious deficiencies, an intermediate level might be better positioned to run the administration of schools. An intermediate level of administration is too far away from schools for serious local lobbying and collusion (local diversion), but it is possibly superior to the central level in terms of accountability (central diversion) and in monitoring schools. Ultimately, it is an empirical question whether there are differences in the quality of schooling produced under different administrative set-ups and which administrative level performs best.

4.4.4   Teachers' Influence

Teachers are probably the most important external determinants of students' learning. Therefore, an important institutional feature of the schooling system are the incentives which teachers face within schools and their ability to influence the education process. Teachers have a lot of leeway in how to pursue their teaching, since neither their actions in the classroom nor their effort in evaluating student performance and preparation of tuition after class can be easily monitored. Pritchett and Filmer (1999) have shown that if teachers have large influence on expenditure allocation in the schooling sector, they will use it to promote their own interests. The interests which teachers face will often be conflicting. While they will usually derive satisfaction from seeing their students progressing, they also have a genuine interest in increasing their income or decreasing their work load. Furthermore, given their sheer numbers and their ensuing ability to influence the electoral process when acting collectively, they are a potentially powerful political interest group.[78] The institutional setting will determine the incentives which teachers face with respect to actions which are conducive or detrimental to student performance and tip them to behave either in one way or the other.

The general effect of an increase in the decision-making power of teachers should be equivalent to the effect of school autonomy depicted in equations (4.22) and (4.23): The informational content and thus the effectiveness of teaching decisions, I, should rise, but the potential for diversion, d, of resources from teaching to the furthering of other interests should also rise. Thus, the benefits of an increased use of teachers' decentralized knowledge at the classroom level stand against their interest to increase their own financial well-being and to decrease their work load. The relative size of the two effects and hence, the

---

[78]   Given that there is a large number of teachers in many parliaments in the world, the potential of teachers to lobby for their objectives might be substantial.

net effect of teachers' influence should again depend on the specific area of decision-making at hand.

Similar to the argumentation for the distribution of responsibility between schools and administration, a high degree of teacher influence on process decisions, such as what supplies to be bought or which textbooks to be used, should be conducive to student performance, because teachers are the actors who know best how to teach their students (large advantage in *I*) and because there is not much leeway to exploit this kind of decision-making power opportunistically (small disadvantage in *d*). Therefore, an increased influence of teachers on teaching methods, *TeaMet*, should plausibly have a positive net effect:

$$(4.26) \quad \left| \frac{\partial \ln I}{\partial TeaMet} \right| > \left| \frac{\partial \ln(1-d)}{\partial TeaMet} \right|,$$

just like school autonomy on process decisions in equation (4.25).

An additional beneficial effect may spring from the scrutiny with which teachers observe and mark their students' achievement and their monitoring of assigned homework. This scrutiny determines the extent to which studying is rewarded and laziness penalized. That is, teachers' scrutiny of performance examination, *TeaScr*, should have a positive effect on students' rewards for learning, *w*:

$$(4.27) \quad \frac{\partial w}{\partial TeaScr} > 0,$$

with the ensuing positive impact on schooling quality, *Q* (Table 4.1). Equation (4.16) depicts the impact of the parameters α, β, and μ on the size of this effect.

In contrast to the decision-making areas relating to teaching methods, the net effect of a high degree of teacher influence should be different in the decision-making areas relating to teachers' salaries and work loads. Teacher influence in determining teacher salary levels or work load will be detrimental to the quality of schooling, because this creates large incentives for teachers to behave selfishly (large *d*). Thus, as in equation (4.24) for school autonomy on standards, teacher influence on the size of their work load and the size of the rewards for it, *TeaWor*, should have a negative net effect on schooling quality:

$$(4.28) \quad \left| \frac{\partial \ln I}{\partial TeaWor} \right| < \left| \frac{\partial \ln(1-d)}{\partial TeaWor} \right|.$$

Such decision-making areas which enable teachers to increase their salary levels or to decrease their work load may include budgetary decisions and decisions on the amount of subject matters to be covered.

An additional effect of teachers' influence comes into play when teachers act collectively through teacher unions. Teacher unions impact the process of political decision-making both through the voting power of the large number of teachers and through their high degree of ability to organize themselves as an interest group. The very aim of teacher unions is to promote the interests of teachers, and to defend them against the interests of other interest groups.[79] Therefore, they will tend to focus on the interests which are not advanced by the other interest groups. The main interests of teachers which are not advanced by others are to increase their pay and to decrease their work load. Furthermore, teacher unions can exert collective bargaining power—as opposed to individual teachers and to other groups of agents which can less easily be organized—and they will advance the interest of the median teacher, which favors a leveling out of salary scales instead of merit differentiation. Thus, a large influence of teacher unions, *TeaUni*, should not only increase the scope to divert resources, *d*, (as in equation (4.28)), but it should also alter the political priorities, *P*, in the society. A high degree of decision-making power of teacher unions will presumably decrease the political priority, *P*, which the government gives to schooling quality:

$$(4.29) \quad \frac{\partial P}{\partial TeaUni} < 0.$$

A decrease in *P* has a negative impact on the equilibrium levels of student effort, *E*, government spending, *X*, and schooling quality, *Q* (Table 4.1). Hence, by decreasing political priority, *P*, for schooling quality, a large influence of teacher unions tends to lower the educational performance of students. Since the elasticity of the quality of schooling with respect to political priority, η_{QP}, is the same as the one with respect to the school effectiveness index, η_{QI}, the impact of the size of α, β, and μ on the size of this elasticity can be derived from equation (4.20).

4.4.5   Parents' Influence

Just the opposite effect should ensue if parents have a large say in schooling policy. Parents are the only actors within schooling who have a relatively undisturbed interest in the educational performance of their children. They have a clear interest in the schooling system functioning efficiently. Therefore, in-

---

[79]   Hoxby (1996) stresses that teacher unions have both the interest to obtain more generous inputs and the potential to lower the effectiveness of input use.

creased parental influence, *ParInf*, in the political process should increase the political priority, *P*, given to the quality of schooling. A large political power of parents will increase the government's incentives to focus on schooling quality, *Q*, and make it more worthwhile to increase educational spending. Furthermore, increased parental influence at the classroom level should be beneficial to the informational content of teaching and should thus increase the effectiveness of schooling, *I*:

$$(4.30) \quad \frac{\partial P}{\partial ParInf} > 0, \quad \text{and} \quad \frac{\partial I}{\partial ParInf} > 0.$$

Both effects are conducive to the quality, *Q*, of the education produced in the schooling system.

Parents' participation in the educational process is limited by the opportunity cost of their time. Institutions which give parents a greater say both in the political process and in teaching enhance the benefits of participation and make parental involvement more likely. As a result, an institutional setting which ensures increased participation of parents in the political and educational process and gives parents greater influence on decisions on teaching contents and greater monitoring powers should tilt the prevailing incentives in favor of an increased quality of schooling.

It should be noted that this simple depiction of the potential effects of parents' influence rests on the rather strong assumptions that there are no differences between the parents' benefit function and the children's benefit function and that parents do not face costs of tuition. The former assumption is in effect the dynasty assumption that parents care for their children's well-being as much as they care for their own well-being. Considering parents' tuition costs should have an effect on educational production once it is acknowledged that like the other agents, parents are also self-interested. Given parental tuition costs, a greater influence of parents in the schooling system would make them try to shift some of their own costs into the schools, with their decreased own effort impacting negatively on overall schooling quality.

4.4.6 Private Schools

In general, production of basic education is run publicly everywhere in the world. However, in most countries there is also some degree of private provision of schooling. When private schools are available, parents with the aim of increasing their children's educational performance can choose whether to send them to a particular private school. The increased parental choice introduced through the competition of privately managed schools means an increase in the influence of parents in the schooling system. As depicted in equation (4.30), it seems plausible that greater parental influence tilts both the political priority, P, and the informational content and thus effectiveness of schooling decisions, I, in favor of increased schooling quality.

Through the institution of private ownership, the head of a private school also has a clear monetary incentive to make an efficient use of resources so as to maximize the quality of schooling, because this would make parents choose her school. Therefore, she will try to improve the monitoring of her teachers, which should help in reducing resource diversion, d. Furthermore, private provision circumvents many monitoring problems within governmental and administrative entities. While private as opposed to public provision of schooling cannot eliminate all the monitoring problems inherent in the education process, private schools may thus nevertheless decrease the number of difficult-to-monitor principal-agent relationships and face greater incentives to tackle the remaining ones. In effect, private school management, $PrivSc$, should reduce the share of educational spending which is diverted from teaching:

$$(4.31) \quad \frac{\partial d}{\partial PrivSc} < 0.$$

This means that more spending should be available for teaching, and the quality of schooling, Q, should rise (Table 4.1).[80]

By giving parents additional choice, private educational institutions introduce competition into the public schooling system. Because the loss of students to private institutions may have adverse consequences for the heads of public schools which are located close to the private schools, increased competition from private schools should also have a positive effect on quality of schooling in nearby public schools. Thus, private ownership of property rights and competition should generally establish incentives in the schooling system which work in the direction of superior outcomes.

---

[80] In a similar way, Shleifer (1998) shows that from a contracting perspective, private ownership of schools, combined with choice and competition, establishes strong incentives for cost reduction and qualitative innovation which are missing in publicly run schools. Chubb and Moe (1990) argue that public schools tend to be overbureaucratized and ineffective because they are governed by institutions of democratic control, while private schools tend to possess autonomy and the characteristics of an effective organization because they are governed by markets.

4.5 Towards a Model of the Schooling System

The impact of the different institutional features of the schooling system on the quality of schooling which is produced in the system as depicted in the schooling model are summarized in Table 4.2. In general, positive effects should be expected from central examinations, centralization of (as opposed to school autonomy in) standard setting and performance control, school autonomy in process decisions and in personnel management, administrative decision-making at an intermediate (as opposed to local or central) level of administration, influence of teachers on the methods of teaching, regular scrutiny of the performance level achieved by the students, parental influence in the classroom and in the political process, and competition from privately managed schools. In contrast, school autonomy in budgetary matters, teachers' influence on decisions which determine their salaries and work load, and large decision-making powers of teacher unions on the size of teachers' work load and in the political process in general may be expected to influence schooling quality negatively.

Table 4.2: Institutional Effects on Schooling Quality

	Schooling quality	Through:				
		Cost of effort	Rewards	Priority	Effectiveness	Limit to diversion
	Q	c	w	P	I	$(1-d)$
Central examinations	+	−	+		+	+
Centralization of standard and control decisions	+				(−)	+
School autonomy on budget	−				(+)	−
School autonomy in process and personnel decisions	+				+	(−)
Intermediate administration (relative to local/central)	(+)				(−/+)	(+)
Teachers' influence on teaching methods	+				+	(−)
Teachers' scrutiny of student assessment	+		+			
Teachers' influence on work load	−				(+)	−
Teacher unions' influence	−			−		−
Parents' influence	+			+	+	
Private schools	+			+	+	+

Note: + = positive impact, − = negative impact, ( ) = small effect.

The model developed in this chapter is very parsimonious. A more thorough modeling of the process of educational production which goes beyond the restriction on the government and students as the two sole actors seems a promising direction for future research. More actors with additional principal-agent relationships might be introduced into the model. For example, teachers might be introduced as independent actors, who are agents to the government in a contract to teach the students. As rational actors, teachers might choose their level of teaching effort, as well as their level of effort in trying to divert resources from teaching. They would choose these variables in order to maximize their own net benefits. In such a model, the government might not only choose educational spending, but also how much to monitor the behavior of teachers. The chosen level of monitoring would affect teachers' cost of resource diversion. Likewise, parents, the administration, or heads of school might be introduced as further agents who maximize their own respective net benefits. An even further step might be to endogenize the choice of the institutions which prevail in the schooling system. While these institutions are exogenous to the present model, in reality they should develop through the political process.

While abstracting from these issues, the model presented in this chapter is still capable of depicting the main effects of several institutional features on educational production. Furthermore, it throws some light on the empirical literature of resource effects in schooling as described in Chapter 3. The choice of spending levels is endogenous in the model. In a schooling system where institutions are not such that spending would bring much pay-off for the quality of schooling, the optimal resource policy would be not to increase the level of spending (Table 4.1). Furthermore, as long as differences in the institutionally driven parameters are not perfectly controlled for, resource effects found empirically in cross-section or time-series work may be biased. Since an optimizing government would increase resources if institutions are conducive to student performance, beneficial institutions would go hand in hand with higher resources in an optimizing world and the bias would be upwards. However, this need not be the case in reality since actual decision-making of governments may not necessarily be optimal.

Finally, several features depicted in the model can prevent an increase in educational spending, X, from increasing student performance, Q. First, the impact of increased spending on the educational performance of students depends on the institutions prevailing in the schooling system. If X is increased in a way which is easily diverted from being used for teaching, the share of diverted resources, d, may be 100 percent for these additional resources and the marginal effects of increasing X would be 0. Second, increases in X may not lead to large results if students do not face incentives to learn, because student effort, E, would be low in such a setting and the effect of X on Q would thus be small. Third, the expenditure level, X, reached in a schooling system may already be so large that increases in X do not cause a significant increase in schooling quality, Q, given the decreasing returns to educational spending in the education production function.

The central message of this chapter is that institutional policies may be much more promising to increase the quality of schooling than resource policies. Differences in schooling quality as reflected in the performance levels of students may be driven more by differences in the institutional setting of the schooling system than by differences in the level of educational spending. Many institutional features of the schooling system vary substantially around the world but tend to be rather stable within individual countries, both across the schools within a country and over time. Therefore, the importance of institutions as a driving force for schooling quality may especially show up in cross-country differences of students' educational performance.

5 The Link between Institutions and Schooling Quality

5.1 International Evidence on Institutions and Student Performance

Chapter 2 has shown that international differences in schooling quality can account for a large part of the cross-country differences in economic development. However, Chapter 3 has revealed that the international differences in schooling quality cannot be traced back to international differences in expenditure on educational resources. The empirical quest for the sources of schooling quality still remains open. Since Chapter 4 suggested that institutions of the schooling system may be a major determinant of students' educational performance, the current chapter puts these theoretical hypotheses to the empirical test, using cross-country evidence.[81] Thus, the question to be examined is whether and, if so, how differences in institutional incentive mechanisms can add to an explanation of the large international differences in students' cognitive skills.

The Third International Mathematics and Science Study (TIMSS) is the latest international student achievement test for which data is currently available, and it is the most extensive one ever conducted both in its coverage of countries and in the scope of its contents. In addition to testing students' cognitive skills in both mathematics and science, TIMSS gathered a wealth of contextual information about instruction and learning through student, teacher, and school-principal questionnaires. This TIMSS database offers an unprecedented opportunity to examine the determinants of student performance, including the impact of institutions.

Drawing on this pool of data, I have constructed a student-level data set for more than 260,000 individual students in the middle school years, where the broadest sample of countries participated. This new data set forms a representative sample of the students of each of the 39 countries which took part in the test, representing a population of more than 30 million students (Section 5.2). In addition to the TIMSS mathematics and science achievement scores, this micro database gathers data from the different TIMSS background questionnaires

---

[81] Parts of Chapter 5 build on evidence first circulated as a working paper in Wößmann (2000a). Some of the evidence has been referred to in Wößmann (2001).

which enables one to control for individual family background and combines it with student-specific information about the educational circumstances. These include the resource provision at the respective school, the characteristics of the specific teachers who taught mathematics and science classes, and institutional features as discussed in Section 4.4, such as exam regulations, distribution of decision-making responsibilities between schools and different levels of administration, and the influence and incentives of teachers and parents. Furthermore, the data from TIMSS is combined with additional system-level data on the institutional structure of the schooling systems from the educational indicators collected by the OECD, concerning the level of decision-making and the extent of private school management. This database allows an extensive student-level analysis of the determinants of schooling quality through the estimation of microeconometric education production functions.

The institutional structure of educational decision-making processes in the schooling systems differs substantially across the 39 countries covered by the database, creating differences in institutions and incentives which should affect resource allocation decisions and thereby the educational performance of the students. The model of educational production in Chapter 4 has yielded several hypotheses on how different kinds of educational institutions should impact on student performance (Table 4.2). Many of the relationships between institutions and educational performance are very complex in reality, and the interests of the different actors are far from being unidimensional. Therefore, an empirical investigation seems the best step forward to determine the direction and strength of the impact of different institutions and to enhance our understanding of the determinants of student performance. Since there is no significant variation in many institutional features within a single country on which an analysis of institutional effects could be based, within-country evidence can hardly be used to perform a test for institutional determinants of schooling quality. Only international data like the micro database constructed in the present study, which encompass many schooling systems with widely differing institutional structures, have the potential to show whether institutions have important consequences for student performance.

The link between institutions and student performance can be tested by estimating an education production function which includes data on institutions as explanatory variables. Section 5.3 discusses some econometric issues which arise in the estimation of microeconometric education production functions. Since the estimations make use of hierarchically structured survey data, attention has to be given to the use of sampling weights in least-squares regressions and to the estimation of consistent variance-covariance matrices from clustered and stratified data.

The results of the microeconometric student-level investigation in Section 5.4 confirm that many institutional features show strong and significant effects on students' performance in mathematics and science, while different categories of resource inputs reveal no clear positive impact, as the evidence in Chapter 3 already suggested. Controlling for resource and family background effects, the impact on the educational performance of individual students exerted by institutions such as central examinations, school autonomy, teachers' and parents' influence, decision-making authority of different levels of administration, and the size of the private schooling sector is estimated empirically. All in all, the empirical findings support the institutional argumentation of the economic model of educational production in Chapter 4.

To assess the extent to which institutional differences can account for the cross-country differences in student performance levels, country-level education production functions are estimated in Section 5.5. They show that institutions strongly matter for cross-country differences in students' educational performance, while increased resource inputs do not contribute to increased performance. Controlling for indicators of parents' education levels and resource inputs, three indicators of institutional features of the schooling system are shown to exert strong and statistically significant effects on country-level student performance. Together, the variables explain three-quarters of the cross-country variation in mathematics test scores and 60 percent of the variation in science test scores, whereas previous studies which restrained themselves to family and resource effects explained only up to one-quarter of the cross-country variation in student performance tests.

5.2   The International Micro Database Based on TIMSS

As the latest, largest, and most extensive international student achievement test ever conducted, the Third International Mathematics and Science Study (TIMSS) collected both student performance data and student, teacher, and school background data for representative samples of students in about 40 countries. Section 5.2.1 describes TIMSS and motivates the use of international evidence. Section 5.2.2 discusses the use of TIMSS test scores as the dependent variable, while Section 5.2.3 deals with the explanatory variables as they are provided in the micro database constructed for the present study, comprising data on students' family background, school resources, and institutional structures gathered both from TIMSS and from other sources. Section 5.2.4 briefly discusses the issue of missing values in the TIMSS data and the ensuing question of data imputation.

5.2.1 The TIMSS International Student Achievement Test

In order to show that institutions have important consequences for student performance, one has to show that institutional variation leads to a variation in student performance. But there is usually no significant variation in many institutional features within a single country on which an enlightening analysis could be based (Chubb and Moe 1990).[82] However, there are big differences across countries in such institutional features as the centralization of examinations and of other decision-making powers, the responsibilities and influence of different educational actors, and the size of the private schooling sector. Therefore, to test the institutional hypotheses of Chapter 4, I use international evidence.

Until now, the only evidence available on the effects of institutionalized incentive regimes like decentralized management on educational performance is based on case studies of experiments and specific programs (Hanushek et al. 1994). Econometric investigation has not used the huge international evidence that exists, presumably shying away from analyzing educational processes across different countries and cultures. The perspective taken in the present study is that economic principles influence the actions of human beings in any country or culture. People respond to incentives everywhere. Therefore, accounting for the economic and institutional differences, which exist between countries, the international data can be used to analyze determinants within the education process.

In TIMSS, extensive efforts have been made to deal with the challenges associated with comparing achievement across countries, cultures, and languages through careful planning, cooperation among the participating countries, standardized procedures, and rigorous attention to quality control. TIMSS was conducted under the auspices of the International Association for the Evaluation of Educational Achievement (IEA), which has gathered 40 years of experience with international comparative studies on educational achievement and learning contexts. In 1994–95, TIMSS tested representative samples of students in more than 40 countries.[83] In addition to mathematics and science achievement scores,

---

[82] This led Chubb and Moe (1990) to base their empirical analysis on a comparison of the public and the private schooling sector in the United States. This empirical approach and their choice of key concepts and analytical models has been heavily criticized in the literature; see, e.g., Bryk and Lee (1992).

[83] Of the 45 countries participating in TIMSS, three (Argentina, Indonesia, and Italy) were unable to complete the steps necessary to appear in the database. Mexico chose not to release its results. For three countries (Bulgaria, Philippines, and South Africa), no background data are included in the international database because of insufficient quality. Since in Belgium the Flemish and French schooling systems participated separately, data files for 39 schooling systems are available: Australia, Austria, Canada, Colombia, Cyprus, Czech Republic, Denmark, England, Flemish Belgium, France, French Belgium, Germany, Greece, Hong Kong, Hungary, Iceland,

the TIMSS international database contains a myriad of educational variables representing background information about teaching and learning collected from students, teachers, and heads of school. Altogether, TIMSS tested and gathered contextual data for more than half a million students and administered question-naires to teachers and heads of school in 15,000 schools, thereby providing the largest wealth of information on student performance across countries ever available.[84]

Countries participating in the study were required to administer tests to the students in the middle school years, but could choose whether or not to partici-pate at the primary and final school years. Therefore, this chapter focuses on the middle school years, where students enrolled in the two adjacent grades contain-ing the largest proportion of 13-year-old students were tested, which are seventh- and eighth-grade students in most countries. More than a quarter of a million students were tested in the middle school years, which form a representative sample of a population of more than 30 million students.

The TIMSS achievement tests used the experience gained by their earlier studies. They were developed through an international consensus-building pro-cess involving input from international experts in mathematics, science, and measurement, and were endorsed by all participating countries. Based on a cur-riculum framework developed by educators from around the world, test speci-fications were developed which included items representing a wide range of mathematics and science topics and eliciting a range of skills from students. The TIMSS tests include items requiring students both to select the appropriate response, to provide a short answer to a question or problem, and to provide a more elaborate response or explanation.

In addition to testing students, TIMSS collected contextual information about instruction and learning through student, teacher, and school questionnaires. The database includes information on approximately 1,500 instructional, school, and home background variables. The students who participated in TIMSS completed questionnaires about their demographics, home background, and classroom and out-of-school activities. The mathematics and science teachers of sampled students responded to questions about their professional training and education, their instructional practices, their responsibilities for decision-making in several areas, and about class sizes and the availability of materials. The heads of schools provided information on school characteristics and resources, the degree of centralization of decision-making, the allocation of responsibility for different

---

Iran, Ireland, Israel, Japan, Korea, Kuwait, Latvia, Lithuania, Netherlands, New Zealand, Norway, Portugal, Romania, Russian Federation, Scotland, Singapore, Slovak Republic, Slovenia, Spain, Sweden, Switzerland, Thailand, and United States.

[84]   For more information about the design, development, implementation, and analyses of TIMSS, see the internet homepage at http://timss.bc.edu/.

tasks, and topics like the extent of parents' participation. Additionally, some system-level information was provided by the national research coordinators of each participating country.

Basic results of TIMSS have been published in international achievement reports (see, e.g., Beaton et al. 1996a, 1996b). They have usually shown that while home factors are strongly related to mathematics and science achievement, the relationship is less clear between achievement and various instructional variables. However, these reports contain mainly univariate, within-country analyses.

5.2.2   Test Scores in Mathematics and Science as Performance Measures

While test scores of cognitive achievement in mathematics and science may be reasonable measures of the output in central areas of schooling and may thus capture important aspects of the human capital of students, they certainly do not reflect the whole array of socially and economically valuable human capital. First, there are many problems with constructing meaningful and internationally comparable standardized tests of cognitive skills. Second, there are many other subjects in school apart from mathematics and science—many of which do not easily lend themselves to standardized achievement tests. And third, there are many valuable, partly noncognitive skills formed outside schools, mainly in families and later in advanced educational institutions and in firms.

However, many arguments warrant an analysis based on the test scores of cognitive achievement in mathematics and science. First of all, much care was taken with the TIMSS test design, so that it used probably the best technique available up to now to measure cognitive skills in mathematics and science. TIMSS tried to remedy shortcomings of earlier approaches. The study implemented rigorous procedures to prevent bias, to ensure comparability in school and student sampling, and to assure quality in test design and development, data collection, scoring procedures, and analysis. TIMSS covered a wide range of topics and capabilities in the two subjects and elicited a range of skills from the students. In mathematics, the content areas included fractions and number sense, geometry, algebra, measurement, proportionality, and data representation, analysis, and probability. In science, they included earth science, life science, physics, chemistry, and environmental issues and the nature of science. Many different kinds of performances were expected from students, encompassing categories such as understanding simple information, performing routine procedures, using complex procedures, solving problems, proving, communicating, and investigating the natural world.

In their assessment of the relative merits of standardized multiple-choice tests and authentic open-ended-response tests, Hanushek et al. (1994: 137) point out that both have (often offsetting) advantages and disadvantages and thus recommend the utilization of a combination of both. This is exactly the strategy used by TIMSS. Approximately one-fourth of the questions (designed to represent approximately one-third of students' response time) were in the free-response format, requiring students to generate and write their own answers. Some free-response questions asked for short answers while others required extended responses where students needed to show their work. The remaining questions used a multiple-choice format.

Combining the performance in the different questions of a subject, proficiency was mapped onto an international scale with a mean of 500 and a standard deviation of 100, yielding the international achievement scores. TIMSS was designed to ensure international comparability. The curriculum framework on which the TIMSS achievement test is based takes care that the achievement items are appropriate for the students of all participating countries and reflect their current curriculum.[85] All in all, the TIMSS test results are most probably the best one can currently get in measuring student achievement in mathematics and science.

In a modern economy where economic success is increasingly attributed to advances in research and development, high levels of cognitive skills in mathematics and science are important to provide for able engineers and scientists. At the aggregate, cross-country level, Hanushek and Kimko (2000) show that schooling quality as measured by comparative tests in mathematics and science has a consistent, stable, and strong influence on economic growth. Furthermore, many studies have shown that there are large returns to higher achievement test scores in mathematics and science in the labor market (Boissiere et al. 1985; Bishop 1989, 1992). These earnings advantages to higher achievement on standardized mathematics tests have grown recently (Murnane et al. 1995). For students dropping out of school, basic cognitive skills are also an important determinant of later earnings (Tyler et al. 2000). Earnings in the labor market are the most reasonable measure of the economically valuable human capital of a person, encompassing the returns to several dimensions of human capabilities. Therefore, the fact that measures of cognitive skills in mathematics and science are a good predictor of future earnings suggests that this measure can actually serve as a—possibly weak—proxy for other skills.

Finally, it is widely accepted that it is much harder to quantify and measure performance in other subjects and noncognitive skills than it is to measure performance in mathematics and science. Consequently, it is sensible to confine

---

[85]   A test-curriculum matching analysis conducted by TIMSS showed that omitting those items for each country which measure topics not addressed in the curriculum had little effect on the overall pattern of achievement results across countries.

the application of econometric methods to the production of those skills which are readily quantifiable, keeping in mind the limitations which may be implied.

Therefore, the test scores should be taken for what they are good: They give a reasonable measure of the cognitive achievement of students in mathematics and in science. An analysis of the production of these cognitive skills is of interest in itself as they constitute an important part of socially and economically valuable human capital. Furthermore, there is evidence suggesting that implications derived from the analysis of these cognitive skills expand well into other parts of human capital.

5.2.3   Data on Student Background, Resources, and Institutions

The sources of the explanatory variables are TIMSS student, teacher, and school background questionnaires and country-level data on the schooling systems. Section 5.7 describes the construction of the micro database used in this study. It gives a complete exposition of the variables used and includes their descriptive statistics in Table A5.1.

Student-level information obtained from the TIMSS student background questionnaires is used to control for students' background and family characteristics. Teacher questionnaire data give class-level information on class size and the class teacher's characteristics, behavior, and influence. To assess the impact of institutional features like the decision-making influence of teachers and schools, dummy variables are created from the qualitative survey data (Section 5.7). Data obtained from school questionnaires, answered by the principals of the schools tested, are used to show further effects of school resources and institutional features.

Country-level institutional and resource data was taken from statistics of different international organizations. TIMSS reported some country-level data on decision-making centralization, while some resource data at the country level came from UNESCO and World Bank statistics. Finally, the OECD educational indicators presented several institutional features of the schooling system at large, dealing with the organization of the schooling system with respect to levels of decision-making and private school management.

5.2.4   Data Imputation

For the explanatory variables from the TIMSS questionnaires, missing data was a problem. While some students, teachers, and school principals failed to answer individual questions, some other questions were not at all administered in some countries. Since dropping students with missing data on some explanatory variables altogether from the regression analysis would severely reduce the sample size, delete the information available on the other explanatory variables, and introduce sample selection bias, imputation of missing values was chosen.[86] I imputed values using the data of those students with nonmissing values on the variable of interest and data on a set of "fundamental" explanatory variables available for all students.

For each student, i, with missing data on a specific variable A, a set of "fundamental" explanatory variables, F, with data available for all students was used to impute the missing data in the following way. Let S denote the set of students with available data for A. Using the students in S, the variable A was regressed on F. For A being a discrete variable, ordinary least squares estimation was used for the regression. For A being a dichotomous (binary) variable, the probit model was used. If A was originally (before deriving dummies) a polychotomous qualitative variable with multiple categories, an ordered probit model was estimated. The coefficients from these regressions and the data $F(i)$ were then used to impute the value of $A(i)$ for the students with missing data. For the probit models, the estimated coefficients were used to forecast the probability of occurrence associated with each category for the students with missing data, and the category with the highest probability was imputed.

The set of "fundamental" explanatory variables, F, included: the student's sex, the student's age, two dummies on the grade level which the student attended, four dummies on the parents' education level, four dummies on the number of books in the student's home, three dummies on the type of community in which the school was located, gross domestic product (GDP) per capita of the country, and educational expenditure per student in secondary education in the country. The small amount of missing data within F was imputed by taking the average value at the lowest level available, that is, class average, school average, or country average. For the three countries which did not administer one of the variables in F, these missing data were imputed by the method outlined above, using the remaining variables in F for the regression.

The data imputation procedures were implemented in *SPSS* (Release 9.0). The coefficients of the probit and ordered probit regressions were estimates in *EViews* (Version 3.1) and then used in *SPSS* to compute probabilities of categorical occurrence. The percentage of imputed values for each variable is given in Table A5.1, as well as the names of the countries which did not provide internationally comparable data for each variable. Results of robustness tests

---

[86] Data on individual students for whom nonimputed data were available for less than 25 variables of the standard regression specification of Table 5.1 were dropped from the sample. This excluded 614 students from the original sample of 267,159.

against dropping from the sample observations with imputed data for each individual variable are reported in Section 5.4.4.

5.3 Econometric Issues in Estimating Micro Education Production Functions

5.3.1 Micro Education Production Functions

To determine the influence of student background, resources, and institutions on students' educational performance, the education production function of equation (3.1) can be extended to

$$(5.1) \quad Q_{ic} = B'_{ic}\beta_1 + R'_{ic}\beta_2 + I'_{ic}\beta_3 + \varepsilon_{ic},$$

where Q is schooling quality as measured by the TIMSS test score of student i in school c, B is a vector of measures of the student's background, R is a vector of measures of resource use, I is a vector of measures of institutional features surrounding the student's learning (the variables in R and I are measured at the classroom, school, or country level), ε is an error term, and β_1, β_2, and β_3 are vectors of parameters to be estimated.[87] The parameters β_3 reflect the impact of schooling institutions on student performance.

Studies such as Hanushek and Kimko (2000) and Lee and Barro (2001) have used country-level data to analyze the determinants of students' performance. By definition, macro education production functions cannot control for individual influences on a student's performance. Apart from the impossibility of properly controlling for other influences, investigations at the country or provincial level are restrained to the analysis of system-level institutional determinants like central examinations (as performed by Bishop 1997, 1999), but they cannot deal with institutional features working at lower levels. Bishop (1999: 395) concedes that, "important as [curriculum-based external exit examination systems] may be, they are not the only or even the most important determinant of achievement

---

[87] Note that the TIMSS data does not allow for a value-added specification which controls for students' performance at the beginning of a grade (Section 3.1.2) because it was conducted only once for each student. While there are reasons to believe that a value-added specification might yield superior estimates of the effects of resource endowment which is measured for a given point in time, the level specification applied here seems most suitable to estimate the effects of institutional features which are relatively constant over time and have influenced a student's learning for longer than just the current grade.

levels." To assess other institutional determinants of students' achievement, one has to look below the country level.

Hence, the relevant level at which to perform the analysis is the individual student (not the class, school, district, or country), because this directly links a student's performance to her teaching environment. The estimation of such a microeconometric education production function provides the opportunity to control for individual background influences on student performance when looking at the influence of resources and institutions, to assess the influence of the relevant resource and teacher characteristics with which a student is faced, and to look at the institutional features relevant to the individual student.

5.3.2   Consequences of Hierarchically Structured Survey Data

In using student-level data, attention has to be given to the complex data structure given by the survey design and the multi-level nature of the explanatory variables. As is common in educational survey data, the TIMSS sampling design includes varying sampling probabilities for different students as well as clustered and stratified data (Martin and Kelly 1998). Varying sampling probabilities may bias the parameter estimates of an ordinary least squares (OLS) regression. Weighted least squares (WLS) regression utilizing sampling weights can be used to solve this econometric problem (Section 5.3.2.1). Data clustering and stratification may bias the estimated standard errors, since the error structure in clustered data may differ from the assumptions of the classical OLS model. Clustering-robust linear regression (CRLR) accommodates the error structure of hierarchically structured data and provides robust standard errors in the presence of clustered and stratified data (Section 5.3.2.2).

5.3.2.1 Sampling Weights and Weighted Least Squares Estimation

The TIMSS sampling procedure was designed to achieve nationally representative student samples by stratified sampling within each country. As a result, students from different within-country strata may have differing probabilities of being selected. TIMSS reports sampling weights for each student which are equal to the inverse of the probability of being sampled. These stratum weights ensure that each within-country stratum of students is weighted in accordance with its relative size in the real population.

To avoid bias in the estimated equation and to obtain nationally representative coefficient estimates in regressions with stratified survey data, WLS estimation using the stratum weights has to be employed so that the proportional contribution of each stratum in the sample to the parameter estimates is the same as would have been obtained in a complete census enumeration (Klein 1974: 409–412). Putting the vectors of explanatory variables B, R, and I from equation (5.1) together into one matrix of explanatory variables, X, and combining the parameter vectors β_1, β_2, and β_3 into one parameter vector β, the corresponding weighted coefficient estimator is

$$(5.2) \quad \hat{\beta} = (X'WX)^{-1}X'WQ,$$

where $W = diag(w_i)$ is a diagonal matrix which contains the sampling weight w_i for each student i on its diagonal.

DuMouchel and Duncan (1983) show that the use of a WLS estimator is especially relevant in an omitted-predictor model. This condition is certainly given in the estimation of an education production function, where the innate ability of each student remains unmeasured. The WLS regressions in Section 5.4 use weights which assure that each student is weighted according to her probability of selection so as to yield representative samples within each country and to give each country the same weight in the international estimation. To allow a comparison of OLS and WLS estimates, both estimates are presented in the results tables of Section 5.4.

5.3.2.2 *Clustered Data and Robust Variance Estimation*

The TIMSS sampling procedure had a two-stage clustered sample design within each country, with the first stage yielding a sample of schools and the second stage yielding a sample of classrooms (Gonzalez and Smith 1997). Thus, the primary sampling units (PSUs) or clusters in TIMSS were the schools. Individual students who go to the same school may share some characteristics which are not perfectly captured by the included observable variables. Furthermore, the data set is characterized by a hierarchical structure with data collected at different levels. Since the resource and institutional variables are not measured at the student level but at the classroom level or the school level (see above), these variables are identical for students who share the same class or school. As a result, observations in the same PSU are not independent, so that the structure of the error term in equation (5.1) may be more complicated than conventional econometric methods assume. The problem with the conventional formulas for the computation of standard errors, which ignore the cluster design of the data, is that they overstate precision by ignoring the dependence of observations within the same PSU. As shown by Moulton (1986, 1990), ignoring the consequences of the hierarchical data structure in the estimation of standard errors can lead to serious danger of spurious regression.

To solve this problem, a different modeling of the error term than in the conventional least squares estimation of equation (5.1) is required.[88] Kloek (1981) analyzes the simplest case, where two special features of the data structure are given. First, the number of observations within each PSU, m, is equal for all PSUs, so that the cluster design is balanced. Second, all explanatory variables are constant within each PSU and vary only between PSUs. Given these two features, and ignoring sampling weights for the moment, equation (5.1) for the schooling quality measure, Q, of student i in school (PSU, cluster) c can be rewritten as

$$(5.3) \quad Q_{ic} = X_c'\beta + \varepsilon_{ic} = X_c'\beta + \mu_c + v_{ic},$$

where the Xs are common to all students in a school. Here, the error term, ε_{ic}, consists of two error components, where μ_c is constant within each PSU, and v_{ic} is an individual error component. The following assumptions apply:

$$(5.4) \quad \begin{aligned} E(\varepsilon_{ic}) &= E(\mu_c) = E(v_{ic}) = 0 \\ E(\varepsilon_{ic}^2) &= \sigma^2 = \sigma_\mu^2 + \sigma_v^2 \\ E(\varepsilon_{ic}\varepsilon_{jc}) &= \sigma_\mu^2 = \left(\frac{\sigma_\mu^2}{\sigma_\mu^2 + \sigma_v^2} \right)\sigma^2 = \rho\sigma^2, i \neq j \\ E(\varepsilon_{ic_a}\varepsilon_{jc_b}) &= 0, c_a \neq c_b. \end{aligned}$$

That is, both error components have an expected mean of 0. The variance-covariance structure of the error terms is given by the assumptions that the μs are uncorrelated across PSUs and that the vs are uncorrelated both within and across PSUs. ρ is the intra-cluster correlation coefficient.

Kloek (1981) shows that in this setting, the OLS estimator is efficient, and the variance-covariance matrix of the OLS estimator has to be scaled up by the design effect, d:[89]

$$(5.5) \quad V(\hat{\beta}) = \sigma^2(X'X)^{-1}d,$$

where $d = 1 + (m-1)\rho$.

Scott and Holt (1982) and Pfefferman and Smith (1985) show that equation (5.5) provides an upper bound for the true variance-covariance matrix which is usually not tight both when the explanatory variables differ within clusters and

---

[88]   The following exposition builds on Deaton (1997: 74–78).

[89]   A second, less serious effect is that the estimate of the regression standard error σ^2 also requires a design-effect adjustment to be unbiased.

when there are unequal numbers of observations within each PSU (with the size of the largest PSU replacing m). They also show that the efficiency losses of the least squares estimator due to explanatory variables varying within PSUs are typically small. This justifies the use of the least squares model to yield point estimates of the parameters, while the estimation of the variance-covariance matrix of the parameters needs correction.

Deaton (1997: 76–77) suggests a method—here referred to as clustering-robust linear regression (CRLR)—which yields this correction in the more general case where the size of the clusters may vary and where not all explanatory variables are constant within the clusters. His derivation of a consistent estimate of the variance-covariance matrix $V(\hat{\beta})$ in the general case can be presented by starting with the general definition of the variance-covariance matrix:

$$
\begin{aligned}
V(\hat{\beta}) &= E\left[(\hat{\beta}-\beta)(\hat{\beta}-\beta)'\right] \\
&= E\left[\left((X'X)^{-1}X'\varepsilon\right)\left((X'X)^{-1}X'\varepsilon\right)'\right] \\
&= E\left[(X'X)^{-1}X'\varepsilon\varepsilon'X(X'X)^{-1}\right] \\
&= (X'X)^{-1}X'E(\varepsilon\varepsilon')X(X'X)^{-1}.
\end{aligned}
$$

(5.6)

The conventional OLS regression model uses the assumption that the variance-covariance matrix of the error terms can be expressed as a constant error variance σ^2 times an identity matrix I:

(5.7) $E(\varepsilon\varepsilon') = \sigma^2 I.$

This disturbance variance-covariance matrix assumes independence between the error terms of all observations. Given the intra-cluster dependence of the error term in our case, this assumption no longer holds.

Therefore, CRLR uses the following procedure to correct the estimated standard errors of the least squares regression in the presence of hierarchically structured data. As an estimate of the disturbance variance-covariance matrix $E(\varepsilon\varepsilon')$, a block-diagonal matrix $\tilde{\Lambda}$ is constructed with one block for each PSU. For each PSU c ($c = 1, ..., n$), the block on the diagonal of $\tilde{\Lambda}$ is given by the matrix $e_c e_c'$ based on the vector of residuals e_c from an OLS estimation within each PSU:

(5.8) $E(\varepsilon\varepsilon') = \tilde{\Lambda} = \begin{bmatrix} e_1 e_1' & 0 & 0 & 0 \\ 0 & e_2 e_2' & 0 & 0 \\ 0 & 0 & \ddots & 0 \\ 0 & 0 & 0 & e_n e_n' \end{bmatrix}$

$$
= \begin{bmatrix}
\begin{matrix} e_{11}^2 & e_{11}e_{12} & \cdots & e_{11}e_{1m_1} \\ e_{12}e_{11} & e_{12}^2 & \cdots & e_{12}e_{1m_1} \\ \vdots & \vdots & \ddots & \vdots \\ e_{1m_1}e_{11} & e_{1m_1}e_{12} & \cdots & e_{1m_1}^2 \end{matrix} & & 0 & & 0 & & 0 \\[2em]
& \begin{matrix} e_{21}^2 & e_{21}e_{22} & \cdots & e_{21}e_{2m_2} \\ e_{22}e_{21} & e_{22}^2 & \cdots & e_{22}e_{2m_2} \\ \vdots & \vdots & \ddots & \vdots \\ e_{2m_2}e_{21} & e_{2m_2}e_{22} & \cdots & e_{2m_2}^2 \end{matrix} & & 0 & & 0 \\[2em]
0 & & 0 & \ddots & & 0 \\[2em]
& & & & \begin{matrix} e_{n1}^2 & e_{n1}e_{n2} & \cdots & e_{n1}e_{nm_n} \\ e_{n2}e_{n1} & e_{n2}^2 & \cdots & e_{n2}e_{nm_n} \\ \vdots & \vdots & \ddots & \vdots \\ e_{nm_n}e_{n1} & e_{nm_n}e_{n2} & \cdots & e_{nm_n}^2 \end{matrix} \\
0 & & 0 & & 0 &
\end{bmatrix}
$$

where e_{ci} is the error term of the ith observation in cluster c and m_c is the size of cluster c.

Based on this estimate of the variance-covariance matrix of the error terms, the robust variance-covariance matrix of the coefficient estimates $\hat{\beta}$ can be written as

$$(5.9) \quad \tilde{V}(\hat{\beta}) = (X'X)^{-1}\left(\sum_c X_c' e_c e_c' X_c \right)(X'X)^{-1}.$$

This CRLR method relaxes the independence assumption and requires only that the observations be independent across the PSUs, allowing any given amount of correlation within the PSUs. Thus, CRLR allows one to estimate appropriate standard errors when many cases share the same value on some but not all independent variables.[90]

---

[90]   A related method often used in educational research to account for the hierarchical data structure are hierarchical linear models (HLM), also known as multi-level models (Bryk and Raudenbush 1992; Goldstein 1999). HLM accommodates the intra-cluster dependence by explicitly modeling the different levels of the hier-archical data structure. Cohen and Baldi (1998) show that CRLR is superior to HLM because it does not require HLM's assumptions of random and normally distributed effects. When these assumptions are violated by outliers or by a skewed error distribution, HLM significantly underestimates the standard errors of higher-level parameters and gives biased parameter estimates, respectively, while CRLR provides estimates of parameters and standard errors which are both consistent and robust. Only when the assumptions are met that errors at all levels are truly normally distributed, estimates of lower-level coefficients are slightly more efficient under HLM than CRLR. This greater efficiency is purchased with HLM's stronger assump-tions. Thus, while CRLR may sacrifice some efficiency at the lower level relative to

As is shown by White's (1984: 134–142) exposition on estimating asymptotic covariance matrices, equation (5.9) provides a consistent estimate of the variance-covariance matrix of the least squares estimator.[91] For this estimate to be consistent, it is neither supposed nor required that the matrices $e_c e_c'$ are consistent estimates of the cluster variance-covariance matrices.[92] The property of consistency of the variance-covariance matrix of the parameters holds even if the error variances differ across PSUs and even in the face of arbitrary correlation patterns within PSUs.

When WLS estimators based on sampling weights are used to yield unbiased coefficient estimates, as outlined in the previous subsection, the consistent CRLR estimate of the variance-covariance matrix can be derived as

$$(5.10) \quad \tilde{V}(\hat{\beta}) = (X'WX)^{-1} \left(\sum_c X_c' W_c e_c e_c' W_c X_c \right) (X'WX)^{-1},$$

with weight matrix W from equation (5.2).

The robust variance estimation for clustered data, combined with weighted coefficient estimates, is implemented in the econometric program *Stata* (StataCorp 1999) by the *svyreg* procedure for the estimation of regressions from complex survey data. Since each country was sampled separately in TIMSS, sampling was done independently across countries, fixing the division into countries in advance. In consequence, the TIMSS data is stratified by country. The *svyreg* procedure also contains an adjustment of equation (5.10) for this data stratification.

In the results tables of Section 5.4, robust standard errors based on CRLR are presented in addition to conventional (raw) standard errors. The robust standard errors are based on countries as strata and schools as PSUs. As the highest level of clustering, schools were chosen as PSUs, thereby allowing any degree of dependence within schools. Therefore, the reported robust standard errors are actually upper bounds for the coefficients of those explanatory variables which are measured at the student or classroom level. The marks signaling significance levels in the results tables are based on these robust variance estimates.

HLM and thus lead to overly conservative estimates, HLM can lead to invalid inference under moderate violations of its assumptions.

[91] This statement holds provided that the cluster size remains fixed as the sample size becomes larger, which is usually the case in practice.

[92] It is obviously impossible to estimate the cluster variance-covariance matrices consistently from a single realization of the cluster residuals.

5.4   Microeconometric Results

Table 5.1 shows OLS and WLS regression results for the mathematics achieve-ment score. The results apply to a sample of 266,545 students in the middle school years from 39 schooling systems. While the results do not differ consider-ably between the OLS and the WLS estimation, the following discussion refers to the WLS estimates. Furthermore, significance statements are based on the robust variance estimation which accounts for the clustered data structure.

5.4.1   Family Background and Resource Effects

5.4.1.1 Student and Family Characteristics

Before being able to test the hypotheses of the institutional economics in the schooling sector, effects of differences in student characteristics and school resources have to be controlled for. Students in higher grades perform consider-ably better than students in lower grades. In mathematics, students in 8th grade scored 40.3 points above students in 7th grade (holding all other influences constant), and 9th-grade students scored 100.3 points above 7th-grade students. After controlling for these differences in grade levels, the age of students is negatively related to performance, probably reflecting a grade repetition effect. After controlling for the other influences, girls performed 7.6 points lower than boys. Students being born in the country in which they attend school, students living with both parents, and students who had at least one parent born in the country where they attend school performed better than otherwise.

The educational level achieved by the students' parents was strongly positive-ly related to the students' educational performance. Relative to students whose parents had only primary education, students with parents finishing secondary or higher education performed considerably better. Parents' attending of some sec-ondary schooling without finishing it did not make a sizable difference relative to having only primary education. The effect captured by the variable "books at home," which proxies for the educational and social background of the family, was even stronger than that of the highest educational level achieved by the parents. The performance level increased steadily from students having up to 10 books at home over up to 25, 100, and 200 books to more than 200 books. For example, students with more than 200 books at home scored 54.3 test score points higher in mathematics than students with up to 10 books at home. Students in schools located in geographically isolated communities performed worse than students from more urban areas. Finally, as a control for the overall level of development of the country in which the student lives, GDP per capita is positively related to mathematics achievement. All these effects of student and family characteristics are statistically highly significant.

Student and family background effects on science achievement, reported in Table 5.2, are very similar to the case of mathematics achievement. While being qualitatively identical, the quantitative effect differs to some extent for some variables. For example, the lead of boys' performance over girls' performance was 8.5 points larger in science than in mathematics.

5.4.1.2 *Resources and Teacher Characteristics*

The estimated effects of the amount of resources used on student performance are consistent with most of the literature in that no strong positive relationship exists between resources and student performance (Chapter 3). In fact, instead of resulting in higher student performance, higher educational expenditure per student (measured at the country level) and smaller class sizes (measured at the classroom level) are statistically significantly related to inferior TIMSS mathematics and science results. The same holds for the effect of smaller ratios of students to total professional staff at the school, which is statistically insignificantly different from zero.[93] For all three of these resource variables, the observed effects show an adverse direction.[94]

There are two ambiguities with the estimate for educational expenditure per student. First, the calculation of the error variance should take account of the fact that expenditure per student is measured at the country level. When calculating robust standard errors on the basis of countries as PSUs, the expenditure effect turns statistically insignificant in mathematics. Second, the presented estimations are based on expenditure measured in international dollars, i.e., converted on the basis of purchasing power parities (Section 3.2.2). Following the argumentation of Baumol's cost-disease model (Section 3.3.2.2), the international comparison of educational expenditure should also take into account differences in economy-wide labor productivity, which affects the wage level of the education sector. To take account of this effect, I divided educational expenditure per student in nominal terms through nominal GDP per worker for each country. Using this

---

[93] Note that the results here are presented in terms of the student-teacher ratio to show the resemblance to the class size variable, while the discussion of resource effects in Chapter 3 was carried out in terms of the teacher-student ratio, which is the inverse of the student-teacher ratio.

[94] These estimates do not directly address the potential problem of resource endogeneity (Section 3.1.3). However, the country-level results of Section 5.5.2, which should aggregate out the endogenous variation, yield results equivalent to these microeconometric estimates.

Table 5.1: Microeconometric Results for Mathematics Performance

(Dependent variable: TIMSS international mathematics test score)

	OLS		WLS			
	Coeffi-cient	Raw SE[a]	Coeffi-cient	Raw SE[a]	Robust SE[a]	Stand. co.[b]
Constant	426.985	(4.360)	482.793*	(4.211)	(13.916)	
Student and family characteristics						
Upper grade	38.773	(0.425)	40.342*	(0.424)	(1.086)	0.202
Above upper grade	99.486	(1.464)	100.313*	(1.513)	(3.906)	0.127
Age	−9.884	(0.244)	−14.183*	(0.231)	(0.779)	−0.135
Sex	−7.229	(0.343)	−7.634*	(0.346)	(0.878)	−0.038
Born in country	8.372	(0.813)	9.199*	(0.816)	(1.338)	0.021
Living with both parents	15.276	(0.514)	12.099*	(0.519)	(0.814)	0.040
Parent born in country	5.132	(0.715)	3.983†	(0.722)	(1.602)	0.011
Parents' education						
Some secondary	0.069	(0.707)	−3.989*	(0.702)	(1.553)	−0.014
Finished secondary	25.755	(0.654)	26.475*	(0.660)	(1.454)	0.123
Some after secondary	12.046	(0.695)	15.130*	(0.700)	(1.515)	0.066
Finished university	36.600	(0.734)	39.724*	(0.746)	(1.619)	0.152
Books at home						
11–25	10.999	(0.755)	10.326*	(0.749)	(1.360)	0.037
26–100	37.317	(0.705)	35.846*	(0.701)	(1.444)	0.168
101–200	47.570	(0.761)	46.713*	(0.756)	(1.543)	0.186
More than 200	55.145	(0.753)	54.269*	(0.750)	(1.562)	0.235
Community location						
Geographically isolated area	−14.707	(1.040)	−18.502*	(1.085)	(3.385)	−0.030
Close to the center of a town	2.451	(0.361)	1.598	(0.363)	(1.479)	0.008
GDP per capita	0.004	(5.9e-5)	0.004*	(5.8e-5)	(2.1e-4)	0.240
Resources and teacher characteristics						
Expenditure per student	−0.009	(2.1e-4)	−0.006*	(2.1e-4)	(6.9e-4)	−0.106
Class size	0.912	(0.018)	1.176*	(0.019)	(0.090)	0.122
Student-teacher ratio	0.011	(0.003)	0.006	(0.003)	(0.007)	0.004
No shortage of materials	8.525	(0.387)	7.230*	(0.394)	(1.585)	0.036
Great shortage of materials	−1.480	(0.563)	−5.925†	(0.554)	(2.393)	−0.020
Instruction time	3.7e-4	(2.3e-5)	3.1e-4*	(2.3e-5)	(8.4e-5)	0.025
Teacher characteristics						
Teacher's sex	5.634	(0.372)	5.727*	(0.374)	(1.345)	0.029
Teacher's age	−0.712	(0.033)	−0.667*	(0.033)	(0.124)	−0.062
Teacher's experience	1.075	(0.032)	1.038*	(0.033)	(0.121)	0.097
Teacher's education						
Secondary	11.151	(1.674)	15.682*	(1.569)	(5.206)	0.062
BA or equivalent	10.919	(1.648)	10.571†	(1.542)	(5.105)	0.050
MA/PhD	20.860	(1.694)	25.576*	(1.596)	(5.411)	0.090

[a]SE = standard error. — [b]Stand. co. = standardized coefficient. — Significance level based on robust standard errors: *1 percent. — †5 percent. — ‡10 percent.

Table 5.1 continued

	OLS		WLS			
	Coefficient	Raw SE[a]	Coefficient	Raw SE[a]	Robust SE[a]	Stand. co.[b]
Institutional settings						
Central examinations						
Central examinations	17.842	(0.434)	16.062*	(0.402)	(0.402)	0.045
External exams influence curriculum	10.740	(0.539)	4.271‡	(0.524)	(0.524)	0.016
Distribution of responsibilities between schools and administration						
Central curriculum	15.585	(0.539)	10.776*	(0.519)	(0.519)	0.048
Central textbook approval	10.053	(0.474)	9.559*	(0.460)	(0.460)	0.078
School responsibility						
School budget	−5.362	(0.663)	−5.852†	(0.683)	(0.683)	−0.017
Purchasing supplies	−2.288	(0.976)	0.538	(0.997)	(0.997)	0.001
Hiring teachers	13.959	(0.454)	12.723*	(0.471)	(0.471)	0.055
Determining teacher salaries	6.539	(0.455)	10.588*	(0.464)	(0.464)	0.046
Teachers' influence						
Teachers' responsibility						
School budget	−15.478	(1.032)	−13.318*	(1.100)	(1.100)	−0.022
Purchasing supplies	11.361	(0.602)	14.148*	(0.642)	(0.642)	0.040
Hiring teachers	−4.317	(5.413)	−10.294	(6.197)	(6.197)	−0.003
Determining teacher salaries	−16.874	(5.153)	−11.069	(5.492)	(5.492)	−0.003
Strong influence on curriculum						
Teacher individually	9.709	(0.442)	11.952*	(0.446)	(0.446)	0.051
Subject teachers	−2.980	(0.473)	−6.855*	(0.476)	(0.476)	−0.034
School teachers collectively	−9.333	(0.459)	−12.659*	(0.459)	(0.459)	−0.063
Teacher unions	−27.532	(1.367)	−32.329*	(1.370)	(1.370)	−0.042
Class teacher has strong influence on						
Money for supplies	2.800	(0.905)	−0.815	(0.909)	(0.909)	−0.002
Kind of supplies	−2.701	(0.593)	−0.627	(0.606)	(0.606)	−0.002
Subject matter	−0.613	(0.414)	−0.830	(0.420)	(0.420)	−0.004
Textbook	−0.322	(0.480)	2.687	(0.478)	(0.478)	0.011
Scrutiny of exams	4.410	(0.109)	4.749*	(0.110)	(0.110)	0.078
Homework	−0.006	(0.002)	0.001	(0.002)	(0.002)	0.001
Parents' influence						
Parents influence curriculum	−0.949	(1.314)	3.714	(1.390)	(1.390)	0.005
Uninterested parents limit teaching	−12.546	(0.672)	−10.107*	(0.656)	(0.656)	−0.029
Interested parents limit teaching	−8.879	(0.871)	−10.860*	(0.825)	(0.825)	−0.025
Parent-teacher meetings	−5.966	(0.277)	−6.152*	(0.283)	(0.283)	−0.039
Observations	266,545		266,545			
Schools (PSUs)	6,107		6,107			
Countries	39		39			
R^2 (adj.)	0.22		0.22			

[a]SE = standard error. — [b]Stand. co. = standardized coefficient. — Significance level based on robust standard errors: *1 percent. — †5 percent. — ‡10 percent.

Table 5.2: Microeconometric Results for Science Performance

(Dependent variable: TIMSS international science test score)

	OLS		WLS			
	Coeffi-cient	Raw SE[a]	Coeffi-cient	Raw SE[a]	Robust SE[a]	Stand. co.[b]
Constant	409.230	(4.525)	455.626*	(4.315)	(11.881)	
Student and family characteristics						
Upper grade	43.897	(0.434)	46.568*	(0.433)	(0.990)	0.235
Above upper grade	99.908	(1.491)	105.354*	(1.544)	(3.536)	0.134
Age	−6.128	(0.249)	−10.116*	(0.236)	(0.708)	−0.097
Sex	−15.546	(0.349)	−16.130*	(0.352)	(0.753)	−0.081
Born in country	10.428	(0.828)	11.195*	(0.831)	(1.305)	0.026
Living with both parents	9.320	(0.524)	7.437*	(0.529)	(0.800)	0.025
Parent born in country	13.686	(0.728)	12.536*	(0.736)	(1.400)	0.034
Parents' education						
Some secondary	−2.142	(0.720)	−5.226*	(0.715)	(1.469)	−0.019
Finished secondary	17.830	(0.667)	20.067*	(0.674)	(1.284)	0.094
Some after secondary	8.421	(0.708)	10.423*	(0.714)	(1.330)	0.046
Finished university	30.827	(0.747)	34.304*	(0.760)	(1.424)	0.132
Books at home						
11–25	12.381	(0.769)	12.251*	(0.763)	(1.153)	0.044
26–100	35.629	(0.718)	34.174*	(0.715)	(1.248)	0.161
101–200	50.483	(0.775)	48.862*	(0.770)	(1.348)	0.196
More than 200	59.954	(0.767)	57.494*	(0.764)	(1.370)	0.250
Community location						
Geographically isolated area	−4.163	(1.058)	−7.371†	(1.106)	(3.397)	−0.012
Close to the center of a town	−0.958	(0.369)	−2.215‡	(0.371)	(1.306)	−0.011
GDP per capita	0.004	(6.0e-5)	0.004*	(5.9e-5)	(2.0e-4)	0.264
Resources and teacher characteristics						
Expenditure per student	−0.011	(2.2e-4)	−0.010*	(2.2e-4)	(6.4e-4)	−0.186
Class size	0.362	(0.019)	0.477*	(0.020)	(0.060)	0.047
Student-teacher ratio	0.010	(0.003)	0.009	(0.003)	(0.007)	0.006
No shortage of materials	6.998	(0.394)	6.543*	(0.402)	(1.374)	0.032
Great shortage of materials	−7.375	(0.573)	−11.595*	(0.565)	(2.138)	−0.039
Instruction time	3.4e-4	(2.3e-5)	3.0e-4*	(2.4e-5)	(6.8e-5)	0.024
Teacher characteristics						
Teacher's sex	5.947	(0.377)	7.801*	(0.378)	(1.166)	0.039
Teacher's age	−0.272	(0.033)	−0.216‡	(0.033)	(0.113)	−0.020
Teacher's experience	0.457	(0.033)	0.445*	(0.033)	(0.115)	0.041
Teacher's education						
Secondary	19.882	(2.032)	24.243*	(1.801)	(4.940)	0.091
BA or equivalent	11.241	(1.993)	12.378†	(1.758)	(4.859)	0.059
MA/PhD	25.575	(2.034)	32.106*	(1.806)	(5.042)	0.119

[a]SE = standard error. — [b]Stand. co. = standardized coefficient. — Significance level based on robust standard errors: * 1 percent. — † 5 percent. — ‡ 10 percent.

Table 5.2 continued

	OLS		WLS			
	Coeffi-cient	Raw SE[a]	Coeffi-cient	Raw SE[a]	Robust SE[a]	Stand. co.[b]
Institutional settings						
Central examinations						
Central examinations	8.598	(0.437)	10.650*	(0.405)	(1.302)	0.024
External exams influence curriculum	2.329	(0.550)	−4.364†	(0.536)	(1.881)	−0.016
Distribution of responsibilities between schools and administration						
Central curriculum	5.319	(0.552)	5.573*	(0.530)	(1.649)	0.031
Central textbook approval	5.563	(0.474)	6.157*	(0.460)	(1.346)	0.052
School responsibility						
School budget	−2.065	(0.674)	−3.451	(0.695)	(2.356)	−0.010
Purchasing supplies	1.939	(0.996)	2.867	(1.016)	(3.308)	0.006
Hiring teachers	6.235	(0.461)	5.247*	(0.478)	(1.473)	0.023
Determining teacher salaries	11.381	(0.462)	15.162*	(0.473)	(1.817)	0.067
Teachers' influence						
Teachers' responsibility						
School budget	−9.172	(1.048)	−4.583	(1.116)	(3.025)	−0.008
Purchasing supplies	7.052	(0.613)	6.837*	(0.653)	(2.062)	0.019
Hiring teachers	6.817	(5.518)	7.595	(6.315)	(6.002)	0.002
Determining teacher salaries	−9.640	(5.249)	−6.048	(5.600)	(16.342)	−0.002
Strong influence on curriculum						
Teacher individually	8.711	(0.450)	10.768*	(0.455)	(1.536)	0.046
Subject teachers	−2.129	(0.481)	−4.573*	(0.485)	(1.625)	−0.023
School teachers collectively	−3.084	(0.468)	−5.034*	(0.468)	(1.575)	−0.025
Teacher unions	−18.901	(1.393)	−18.395*	(1.395)	(5.533)	−0.024
Class teacher has strong influence on						
Money for supplies	3.764	(0.764)	6.876*	(0.791)	(2.255)	0.018
Kind of supplies	3.871	(0.516)	4.566*	(0.530)	(1.520)	0.018
Subject matter	−0.429	(0.382)	−1.213	(0.380)	(1.186)	−0.006
Textbook	−0.978	(0.453)	−1.016	(0.459)	(1.379)	−0.004
Scrutiny of exams	0.513	(0.116)	0.444	(0.117)	(0.406)	0.007
Homework	−0.031	(0.004)	−0.043*	(0.005)	(0.014)	−0.017
Parents' influence						
Parents influence curriculum	0.264	(1.339)	5.041	(1.416)	(4.411)	0.006
Uninterested parents limit teaching	−12.980	(0.776)	−11.003*	(0.758)	(2.649)	−0.028
Interested parents limit teaching	−0.295	(0.952)	−1.333	(0.922)	(3.394)	−0.003
Parent-teacher meetings	−2.293	(0.289)	−2.662*	(0.290)	(0.859)	−0.017
Observations	266,545		266,545			
Schools (PSUs)	6,107		6,107			
Countries	39		39			
R^2 (adj.)	0.18		0.19			

[a]SE = standard error. — [b]Stand. co. = standardized coefficient. — Significance level based on robust standard errors: * 1 percent. — † 5 percent. — ‡ 10 percent.

measure of real expenditure per student in the estimations, the coefficient is statistically insignificant (based on robust variance estimation with countries as PSUs) both in mathematics and in science, with the one having a positive sign and the other having a negative sign. Thus, a positive effect of expenditure per student seems to be absent in the international TIMSS results.

In contrast to the measured effects of the size of the teaching staff, the equipment with facilities has the expected effect when measured by the subjective assessment of the principals of the schools. Students in schools whose principals reported that the capacity to provide instruction is not affected by the shortage or inadequacy of instructional materials scored 7.2 points higher in mathematics relative to students in schools with a little or some limitation (6.5 in science), while students in schools with great shortage of materials scored 5.9 (11.6) points worse. However, these findings should be interpreted with care since inadequate supplies may have led to poor achievement, or principals of low-achieving schools may tend to blame their poor achievement on inadequate supplies.

Instruction time (in minutes per year) at the relevant grade level of the school is statistically significantly positively related to student performance in mathematics and science. While the relative importance of the explanatory dummy variables can be directly evaluated on the basis of their regression coefficients (the coefficient of dummies reports the conditional test score difference between students with and without the characteristic of interest), standardized coefficients (reported in the last column of Tables 5.1 and 5.2 for the WLS estimation) can be used to compare the relative importance of the discrete explanatory variables. For example, a change of 1 standard deviation in instruction time is related to a change of only 0.025 standard deviations in the mathematics test score, while a 1 standard-deviation change in the mathematics class size is related to a change of 0.122 standard deviations in mathematics performance.

As for teacher characteristics, students of female teachers score statistically significantly higher than students of male teachers in both mathematics and science. Controlling for the teacher's age, more years of experience are positively related to students' performance. Conversely, controlling for the teacher's experience, the teacher's age is negatively related to students' performance. This may reflect positive effects of teaching experience in combination with negative effects of age differences between teachers and students, presumably due to increasing difficulties of intergenerational understanding and declining motivation of aging teachers. Teachers' level of education is positively related to students' performance. Relative to students of teachers who did not complete secondary education, students of teachers who finished secondary education scored considerably better. While the effect was largest for teachers with a masters or doctorate degree (25.6 points in mathematics and 32.1 points in science), teachers with a bachelor degree or equivalent (10.6 and 12.4) did not achieve the same results for their students as teachers who just completed secondary education plus perhaps some teacher training (15.7 and 24.2). Overall, the effects of teachers' education levels were larger in science than in mathematics.

In sum, the relationship between school resources and student performance remains ambiguous, as was also the conclusion of the evidence presented in Chapter 3. Class size and most measures of expenditure per student show adverse effects, while equipment with instructional materials and teachers' experience and education show positive effects. What is clear is that there certainly is no strong and systematic relationship between resource use and student performance. In light of the theory presented in Chapter 4, this is actually not surprising: Within the institutional setting of public schooling systems, the incentives of the actors involved do not clearly point in the direction of increased student performance. So the next sections investigate whether differences in the incentive structures determined by the institutional features of the schooling systems have significant effects on student performance.

5.4.2   Institutional Effects: TIMSS Evidence

The effects of different institutions of the schooling system on student performance relate to the same institutional features which were considered in Section 4.4. The educational institutions which can be analyzed on the basis of the TIMSS questionnaire data alone (Section 5.4.2) are centralized examinations, the distribution of decision-making power between schools and administration, the influence of teachers in the schooling system, and the influence of parents. The OECD educational indicators give additional evidence on the distribution of decision-making power between schools and administration (Section 5.4.3). Furthermore, they allow an analysis of the distribution of decision-making power between different levels of administration and of the extent of competition from privately managed schools in the schooling system.

5.4.2.1 *Central Examinations*

Of the 39 schooling systems analyzed in this study, 15 have some kind of centralized examination in the sense that a central decision-making authority has exclusive responsibility for or gives final approval of the content of examinations. Students in countries with centralized examination systems scored 16.1 points higher in mathematics and 10.7 points higher in science than students in countries without centralized examinations.[95] The evidence suggests that central examinations matter in explaining international differences in the productivity of schooling systems. Hence, the international micro evidence corroborates the findings of Bishop (1997, 1999) at the country and provincial level.

Furthermore, students in schools where external examinations or standardized tests had a lot of influence in determining the curriculum had test scores 4.3 points higher in mathematics than students in schools where this was not the case. In science, the effect is negative when imputed observations are included, while it is positive but insignificant when the observations with imputed data on this variable are dropped from the sample (Section 5.4.4). The weaker effect of standardized tests in science than in mathematics may reflect that science tests lend themselves less readily to standardization.

5.4.2.2 *Distribution of Responsibilities between Schools and Administration*

The responsibility for decision-making in several areas of the schooling system is distributed differently between administration and schools across countries. For example, schools have a very high degree of decision-making autonomy in the Netherlands, while they do not have much autonomy in Greece, Norway, or Portugal.[96] The question is whether schools are free to decide or whether decision-making is centralized. With respect to centralized decisions on standard setting, two country-level dummies report whether decision-making responsibilities for the syllabi for courses of study ("central curriculum") and for the list of approved textbooks ("central textbook approval") are centralized. Students in countries both with centralized curriculum setting and centralized textbook approval score higher in mathematics and science than students in countries without these decisions being centralized.[97] However, the absolute size of both these effects is smaller than the effect of centralized examinations.

---

95 With only 39 independent observations, the effect of this country-level variable entails some degree of uncertainty. Calculating robust standard errors with countries as PSUs leaves the effect of central examinations in mathematics statistically significant only at the 15 percent level, while it turns statistically insignificant in science. When increasing the threshold of nonimputed data to a sample size of 255,018 (Section 5.4.4), the mathematics effect is significant at the 10 percent level based on robust standard errors with countries as PSUs.

96 As measured by the OECD indicator on the distribution of decision-making responsibilities in the schooling systems, less than 25 percent of educational decisions are taken at the school level in Greece, Norway, and Portugal, while the Netherlands have the highest degree of school autonomy with 73 percent of decisions taken at the school level (see Section 5.7 for more information on this indicator).

97 With robust standard errors calculated on the basis of countries as PSUs—taking account of the fact that there are only 39 independent observations on these two

The division of decision-making authority between administration and schools is also relevant in financial and process decisions. These have been measured at the school level, and the category of school responsibility encompasses the decision-making powers of teachers, department heads, principals, and schools' governing boards. Students in schools which had primary responsibility in determining the size of their school budget had lower scores in mathematics (5.9 points) and science (3.5 points) than students in schools which did not primarily determine the size of their own budget.[98] That is, taking away responsibility for the amount of resources available from the school level is conducive to student performance. By contrast, school autonomy in process decisions on purchasing supplies goes hand in hand with superior achievement of students.[99] This also holds for decisions on hiring teachers, where students in schools which had freedom to decide on the hiring of teachers performed statistically significantly better in mathematics (12.7 points) and science (5.2 points) than students in schools without primary responsibility in the hiring of teachers. Likewise, students in schools which could determine teacher salaries themselves scored 10.6 points higher in mathematics (15.2 points higher in science) than students in schools without decision autonomy in this regard. Thus, school autonomy in personnel management seems highly conducive to student performance, and centralization of these decision-making powers robs schools of the opportunity to make decisions which favor their students.

In sum, the evidence supports the hypothesis that the distribution of responsibilities between schools and administration matters for the efficiency of resource use in the schooling system and for the educational performance of students. On the one hand, centralized decisions on standard setting, performance control, and the size of the school budget help to assure that the producers of education look for the performance of students. On the other hand, school autonomy (decentralized decisions at the school level) seems to be the best way to guarantee high student performance in process and personnel-management decisions. While centralized decision-making can add coherence in curriculum coverage and control output from the center, an easing of process and personnel-management regulations may help schools' flexibility in tailoring instruction to the different needs of students. Thus, the most conducive combination seems to

---

variables—these effects cannot be statistically significantly distinguished from zero, however.

[98] While the mathematics effect is statistically significant, the science effect is not.

[99] The low level of significance of the "purchasing supplies" coefficient in the WLS estimation for science is due to multicollinearity. Running the same regression without the other "responsibility" variables, the coefficient on "purchasing supplies" is 5.813 and statistically significant at the 10 percent level (with a robust standard error of 3.180).

be a mechanism of external target-setting and control to limit school-level opportunistic behavior combined with a high degree of freedom to decide at the
school level on subjects where school-level knowledge is important.[100]

5.4.2.3 Teachers' Influence

When looking at the decision-making power of specific groups of actors, the
degree of freedom of teachers to decide independently on several educational
topics should impact on student performance by affecting the decision-making
outcome in the schooling system. Correspondingly, students in schools whose
principals reported that teachers had primary responsibility for the size of the
school budget scored 13.3 points worse in mathematics (4.6 points in science)
than students in schools where primary responsibility for the school budget was
not with teachers.[101] Conversely, students scored 14.1 points better in mathematics (6.8 in science) if teachers had primary responsibility for purchasing
supplies. These two findings reflect effects similar to those reported in the
previous section for school autonomy in these two decision-making areas. There,
the school category included department heads, the principal, and the school's
governing board in addition to teachers. Decisions on the total amount of money
to be spent should be centralized, i.e., taken away from schools and teachers,
while decisions on the purchase of specific supplies should be decentralized to
schools and teachers.[102]

With regard to teachers' influence on the curriculum which is taught in the
school, a significant difference arises between teachers acting individually and
teachers acting collectively. On the one hand, students in schools where each
teacher individually had a lot of influence on the curriculum performed considerably better than otherwise (12.0 points in mathematics and 10.8 points in
science). On the other hand, students in schools where school teachers collec-

---

[100] Section 5.4.3 presents further evidence on the distribution of responsibilities between
schools and administration obtained on the basis of the OECD educational indicators.

[101] The low degree of significance of the effect in science is due to a mixture of
multicollinearity and data imputation. Both if the other "responsibility" variables are
dropped and if observations with nonoriginal data on the variable of teachers' responsibility for the school budget are dropped, the effect gets statistically significant and
larger in absolute terms.

[102] The effects of teachers being responsible for the hiring of teachers and for the determination of teacher salaries are statistically insignificant in both mathematics and
science, with negative coefficients in mathematics and opposing signs of coefficients
in science. This insignificance is due to the fact that only in 4 schools with a total of
less than 300 tested students (out of the total of 266,545 students), heads of school
reported that teachers had primary responsibility for hiring teachers (6 schools in the
case of teacher salaries).

tively or teacher unions exercised a lot of influence on the curriculum performed statistically significantly worse than in the case where these groups of teachers did not exercise a lot of influence on the curriculum. This detrimental effect of teachers influencing the curriculum collectively is strongest in the case of teacher unions (−32.3 points in mathematics and −18.4 points in science).[103]

Concerning specific influence areas of individual teachers, statistically significant results are confined to science. Students of teachers with a lot of influence on money for supplies and on the kind of supplies which are purchased showed statistically significantly better science performance. By contrast, students of teachers with a lot of influence on the subject matter to be taught, determining the teachers' work load, performed worse in science.[104] Whether the class teacher is allowed to decide on the specific textbook to be used does not seem to have a significant effect on students' performance. These findings suggest that a high degree of individual teacher influence is conducive to student performance in the case of process decisions related to the choice of supplies, while it is detrimental in the case of decisions on the choice of subject matters to be taught which determine the work load of the teacher.

An additional effect on schooling quality should stem from teachers' scrutiny of their students' educational progress. The scrutiny with which teachers observe and mark student achievement determines the extent to which studying is rewarded and laziness penalized. Achievement scrutiny is measured by the amount of time outside the formal school day which the class teacher spends on preparing or grading student tests or exams each week. This scrutiny of exams has a statistically significantly positive effect on student performance in mathematics, while the positive effect in science is not statistically significant.

The amount of homework assigned by the class teacher is another measure influencing the amount of time which students spend studying. However, minutes of homework per week assigned by the class teacher is statistically insignificantly related to students' performance in mathematics and negatively to students' performance in science. This may reflect that minutes of homework assigned by the teacher may be very different from minutes of homework spent by each student. Alternatively, it may reflect a nonlinear, more complex relation-

---

[103] This finding of a negative effect of teacher unions' influence in the schooling system corresponds to Hoxby's (1996) result that teacher unionization can explain how schools can simultaneously have worse student performance and bigger school budgets including more generous inputs. Hoxby has shown on the basis of panel data for US school districts that teacher unions increase school inputs but reduce the productivity with which these inputs are used sufficiently to have a negative overall effect on student performance, so that their primary effect is rent seeking.

[104] When observations with imputed data on this variable are dropped from the regression, the effect turns larger and statistically significant (Section 5.4.4).

ship between minutes of homework assigned and student performance. The variable reflecting minutes of homework per week is combined from two original variables reflecting how often homework is assigned per week and how many minutes it takes for an average student to complete one homework assignment. Both in mathematics and in science, homework frequency is negatively related to student performance, while homework length is positively related to student performance. It seems that assigning homework less often but on a more ambitious scale each is particularly conducive to students' learning. This should be more of a question for educationists, however. In any event, there is clearly no direct positive relationship between minutes of assigned homework per week and test score performance.

Overall, the findings on teachers' influence give a clear picture. If individual teachers can make use of their decentralized knowledge on which teaching method may be best for their students and if they regularly scrutinize their students' educational progress, this will help students to perform better. This conclusion is corroborated by the positive effects of individual teachers influencing the curriculum which is taught in the school, of teachers having responsibility for the purchase of supplies, and of teachers scrutinizing student achievement. However, if teachers can use their decision-making powers primarily to reduce their work load and advance their own interests, this will hurt students' learning opportunities. This conclusion is corroborated by the negative effects of teachers' responsibility for the school budget and for the teaching load and of teachers exerting collective power over the curriculum. Especially the power wielded by teacher unions, which have the explicit purpose of furthering teachers' own interests against the interests of other actors involved in the education process, is a clear example of agents acting opportunistically to further goals different from students' performance.[105]

5.4.2.4 Parents' Influence

Evidence was previously reported that parents' education and the number of books in a student's home were strongly positively related to the student's educational performance. Apart from the learning environment at home, the influence which parents have on curricular matters and on teaching in the formal education system should also impact on students' learning opportunities. Accordingly, students in schools where parents had a lot of influence in determining

---

[105] The empirical results on teachers' influence support the evidence presented by Pritchett and Filmer (1999) that inputs which provide teachers with direct benefits are generally over-used in educational production relative to inputs which contribute only to student performance.

the curriculum scored higher both in mathematics and in science than students in schools where parents did not strongly influence the curriculum; however, these effects are not statistically significantly different from zero.

With regard to parents' influence on teaching, the class teacher reported whether parents uninterested in their children's learning and progress strongly limited how she was teaching her class, e.g., because she then could not rely on parents in scrutinizing homework. The class teacher also reported whether interested parents limited class teaching, presumably by preventing her from teaching in the way she judged most suitable. Students in classes with uninterested parents strongly limiting class teaching performed 10.1 points worse in mathematics and 11.0 points worse in science relative to students in classes where teaching was not a great deal limited by uninterested parents. When interested parents were deemed a cause of limitation, students scored 10.9 points worse in mathematics. However, this effect is very small and statistically insignificantly different from zero in science. That is, even though science teachers maintained that their teaching was greatly limited by parents being excessively interested in their children's learning, this interference did not cause inferior performance of the students.

These positive effects of parents' involvement were not replicated in a positive effect of the time parents spent on meeting with teachers. In fact, the number of hours outside the formal school day reported by the class teacher to be spent on meetings with parents each week ("parent-teacher meetings") was actually negatively related to student performance. However, this may reflect the fact that teachers have more to discuss with parents of poor students than with parents of good students, so that the time spent on parent-teacher meetings is not exogenous to the students' performance. Furthermore, the hours for parent-teacher meetings are preventing teachers from doing other useful work like the preparation and evaluation of classes and exams.

5.4.3   Institutional Effects: OECD Evidence

Additional evidence on the effects of the institutional setting of the schooling system, encompassing features related to administration and schools, can be obtained from the institutional measures of the OECD educational indicators. Table 5.3 reports the WLS mathematics results for these indicators, which are all measured in percentages within a country. Since the OECD indicators are country-level variables, the number of countries equals the number of independent observations for these effects. Consequently, the standard errors reported are robust standard errors based on countries as PSUs. To save degrees of freedom, given that the OECD variables are available only for a limited number

Table 5.3: Microeconometric Results in Mathematics: OECD Data

(Dependent variable: TIMSS international mathematics test score)

	Coeffi-cient	Robust SE[a]	Stand. co.[b]	Obser-vations	Countries	R^2 (adj.)
Distribution of responsibilities between schools and administration						
School autonomy	0.120	(0.469)	0.015	136,478	21	0.19
School level decisions:						
Overall	0.227	(0.463)	0.042	134,004	21	0.20
Organization of instruction	0.891[†]	(0.368)	0.131	134,004	21	0.20
Personnel management	−0.043	(0.295)	−0.014	134,004	21	0.20
Planning and structures	0.136	(0.502)	0.027	134,004	21	0.20
Resources	−0.002	(0.320)	−4.4e-4	134,004	21	0.20
Distribution of responsibilities between administrative levels						
Central government decisions:						
Overall	−0.447	(0.271)	−0.097	134,004	21	0.20
Organization of instruction	−1.734[*]	(0.436)	−0.203	134,004	21	0.21
Personnel management	−0.234	(0.197)	−0.078	134,004	21	0.20
Planning and structures	−0.114	(0.189)	−0.037	134,004	21	0.20
Resources	−0.371	(0.210)	−0.108	134,004	21	0.20
Government level of funds:						
Funds provided at local level	−0.410[*]	(0.120)	−0.150	160,615	22	0.20
Funds provided at central level	−0.346[†]	(0.161)	−0.126	160,615	22	0.19
Private schools						
Private enrollment	0.594[†]	(0.243)	0.105	170,846	23	0.19
Independent private enrollment	2.909[*]	(0.824)	0.195	170,846	23	0.20
Public expenditure on private institutions	0.621[*]	(0.159)	0.132	185,786	26	0.20
Public expenditure on independent private institutions	12.124[‡]	(6.658)	0.101	185,786	26	0.20

Note: WLS regression. Each row contains the result of a separate regression. Controlling for all variables of Table 5.1. Robust standard errors based on countries as primary sampling units in parentheses.

[a]SE = standard error. — [b]Stand. co. = standardized coefficient. — Significance level based on robust standard errors: [*] 1 percent. — [†] 5 percent. — [‡] 10 percent.

of countries participating in TIMSS and because most of the indicators are available for a different sample of countries, each row in Table 5.3 reports the results for a different regression, with the number of included student observations and countries and the adjusted R^2 of the regression given at the end of each row. All results reported in Table 5.3 again control for all the student background, resource, and other institutional variables reported in Table 5.1. Table 5.4 reports equivalent results for science performance.

Table 5.4: Microeconometric Results in Science: OECD Data

(Dependent variable: TIMSS international science test score)

	Coefficient	Robust SE[a]	Stand. co.[b]	Observations	Countries	R^2 (adj.)
Distribution of responsibilities between schools and administration						
School autonomy	0.523‡	(0.300)	0.062	136,478	21	0.19
School level decisions:						
Overall	0.779*	(0.272)	0.142	134,004	21	0.19
Organization of instruction	0.808†	(0.358)	0.116	134,004	21	0.19
Personnel management	0.429‡	(0.215)	0.133	134,004	21	0.19
Planning and structures	0.578†	(0.272)	0.113	134,004	21	0.19
Resources	0.393	(0.253)	0.076	134,004	21	0.18
Distribution of responsibilities between administrative levels						
Central government decisions:						
Overall	−0.554†	(0.239)	−0.117	134,004	21	0.19
Organization of instruction	−1.178†	(0.462)	−0.134	134,004	21	0.19
Personnel management	−0.411†	(0.148)	−0.133	134,004	21	0.19
Planning and structures	−0.153	(0.172)	−0.049	134,004	21	0.18
Resources	−0.417*	(0.112)	−0.118	134,004	21	0.19
Government level of funds:						
Funds provided at local level	0.023	(0.116)	0.008	160,615	22	0.17
Funds provided at central level	−0.196	(0.159)	−0.070	160,615	22	0.17
Private schools						
Private enrollment	0.539*	(0.138)	0.093	170,846	23	0.17
Independent private enrollment	1.257†	(0.522)	0.082	170,846	23	0.17
Public expenditure on private institutions	0.138	(0.284)	0.029	185,786	26	0.18
Public expenditure on independent private institutions	4.569	(4.149)	0.037	185,786	26	0.18

Note: WLS regressions. Each row contains the result of a separate regression. Controlling for all variables of Table 5.2. Robust standard errors based on countries as primary sampling units in parentheses.

[a]SE = standard error. — [b]Stand. co. = standardized coefficient. — Significance level based on robust standard errors: * 1 percent. — † 5 percent. — ‡ 10 percent.

5.4.3.1 Distribution of Responsibilities between Schools and Administration

Evidence based on TIMSS questionnaire measures showed that the distribution of responsibilities between schools and administration in different educational decision-making areas has a statistically significant impact on student performance (Section 5.4.2.2). An OECD indicator of school autonomy reports the percentage of educational decisions in a country taken at the school level in full autonomy without consultations or preset frameworks. Decisions which are not taken at the school level are taken by the administration at the central, state, provincial, subregional, or local level of government. The general indicator of full school autonomy ("school autonomy" in Tables 5.3 and 5.4)—which comprises the decision-making domains of organization of instruction, personnel management, planning, and resources—is statistically significantly positively related to student performance in science, and statistically insignificantly positively in mathematics. The standardized coefficients show that if the percentage of decisions taken at the school level in full autonomy increased by 1 standard deviation (equivalent to 11.3 percentage points), students scored 0.062 standard deviations (equivalent to 6.1 test score points) higher in science.

Likewise, including decisions at the school level which have been taken within frameworks from or after consultation with other levels of administration ("school level decisions"), increased decision-making authority at the school level—as opposed to different administrative levels—is also conducive to student performance, with the positive coefficient being statistically significant only in science.

The variables on school responsibility are also given for the four subgroups of decisions separately. For science performance, the coefficients on school level decisions are statistically significantly positive in the decision-making domains of organization of instruction, personnel management, and planning and structures. For example, an increase of 1 standard deviation (equivalent to 13.1 percentage points) in the percentage of decisions on organization of instruction taken at the school level is related to an increase of 0.113 standard deviations (equivalent to 11.2 test score points) in students' science performance. For mathematics performance, the coefficients on school level decisions in the subdomains are not statistically different from zero except for the decision-making domain of organization of instruction. These results on the four subgroups of decision-making authority at the school level are the only ones with considerable differences between mathematics and science.

The fact that the effects of school responsibility are positive for science but statistically insignificant for mathematics may indicate that mathematics lends itself much easier to standardization, so that taking away responsibilities for mathematics teaching from the school level does not cause much harm in terms of decreased use of decentralized knowledge. Since the benefits of school-level knowledge may therefore be small in mathematics, the deficiencies of school-level opportunism could bring the net effects close to zero. However, even in mathematics these effects are subject to the controlling for the school-responsibility variables measured at the school level as reported in Table 5.1. While the coefficient on the OECD indicator of personnel management is small and statistically insignificant, the strong positive effects of schools' primary responsibility for hiring teachers and for determining teacher salaries render the combined effect of decentralized personnel decisions positive even in the case of mathematics.

5.4.3.2 Distribution of Responsibilities between Administrative Levels

When decision-making authority lies with the administration (as opposed to the school level), the remoteness of this authority from the school level establishes another feature of the institutional system of schooling. Both the level of administrative decision-making and the control over educational funding may mainly be at the local, intermediate, or central level of government. The dominant level of administrative decision-making in schooling differs widely across countries. For example, Portugal (69 percent) and Greece (56 percent) have large percentages of educational decisions taken at the central level of government,[106] while in Belgium and the United States, the central level of government has basically no decision-making power in schooling matters. In Belgium, most of the decisions (61 percent) are taken at the lower regional level, and in the United States, the majority of decisions (69 percent) are taken at the local level. The distribution of educational funding (final purchasing of educational resources) between administrative levels follows a similar pattern. In Greece and New Zealand, virtually all educational funding is done by the central level of government, while in Belgium, Japan, Korea, Switzerland, and the United States, less than 1 percent of funding is undertaken by the central government. In Belgium and Korea, virtually all funding is done by the regional level of government. Local governments allocate virtually all final funds in the United States, and the overwhelming part of funds in Canada, Hungary, Norway, and the United Kingdom.

Tables 5.3 and 5.4 report the effect of the extent of decision-making at the central level of government ("central government decisions"), where the residual category (the percentage of decisions not taken at the central level) encompasses the decisions taken at the school level and at the local and intermediate (subregional, provincial, and state) levels of government. Students in countries with a higher percentage of decisions taken at the central level of government scored lower in both the mathematics and the science tests, with only the science effect being statistically significant.

The effects in each of the four subgroups of decision-making in both mathematics and science are also negative, with the effects of instructional and resource decisions in both mathematics and science and the personnel management effect in science being statistically significant. For example, all other things equal, increasing the amount of decisions on organization of instructions taken at the central level by 1 standard deviation resulted in 0.203 standard deviations lower performance in mathematics (0.134 in science). By contrast, the per-

---

[106] In Greece, all decisions on personnel management are taken at the central level. In Portugal, all decisions on planning and structures are taken at the central level.

centage of decisions taken at an intermediate level of government (part of the residual category in the regressions presented in the tables) were positively related to student performance.

In a similar way to the distribution of decision-making authority, the distribution of responsibility for and control over funding between the different government levels is related to student performance. The larger the share of funds provided at the local or the central level of government in a country (as final purchasers of educational resources),[107] the lower was students' performance in mathematics.[108] Consequently, students performed considerably better the more funding was decided on at an intermediate level of government (the residual category). Once responsibility for decision-making in and funding of education lies with the administration, an administrative level distant enough from individual schools to limit opportunistic and collusive behavior but not as remote as the center, where decision-makers are no longer familiar with local needs, seems to be most conducive to focusing attention on student performance.

5.4.3.3 Private Schools

The extent of competition from private institutions in the schooling system differs considerably across countries, leading to differences in the market structure prevailing in the schooling systems. The Netherlands have by far the highest share of privately managed schools (76 percent of all schools), followed by the United Kingdom (36 percent) and Korea (35 percent). However, less than one percent of Dutch schools are financially independent in the sense that they receive less than half of their core funding from government agencies. The countries with the largest shares of financially independent private schools are Japan (24 percent), Korea (18 percent), and the United States (16 percent). At the other extreme, Australia, Austria, the Czech Republic, Denmark, France, Germany, Hungary, Iceland, Norway, Spain, and Sweden have virtually no financially independent private schools. As the results in Tables 5.3 and 5.4 show, students in countries with larger shares of enrollment in privately managed educational institutions ("private enrollment") scored statistically significantly higher in both mathematics and science. That is, countries with a larger share of private management control over schools performed better. This effect was even larger when only those privately managed institutions were considered which were also

---

[107] Qualitatively similar results arise when focusing at the level of government which is the initial source of funds, i.e., before transfers between the different government levels.

[108] The effects in science are statistically insignificantly negative for centrally provided funds and virtually zero for locally provided funds.

financially independent of funding from government sources for their basic educational services ("independent private enrollment").

The Netherlands (75 percent) and Belgium (63 percent) are the countries with by far the largest share of public educational expenditure going to private institutions, while in Austria, Greece, Ireland, New Zealand, the Russian Federation, and the United States, less than half a percent of public expenditure goes to private schools. Similar to the results for private enrollment, countries with a larger share of (public) educational expenditure going to private institutions ("public expenditure on private institutions") performed better both in mathematics and in science (with only the mathematics effect being statistically significant). Again, this effect was even stronger when only those expenditures were counted which went to independent private institutions which received less than half of their core funding from the government ("public expenditure on independent private institutions"). Thus, student performance is higher in schooling systems where private schools take over resource allocation from public decision-makers.

These effects of private school management are measured at the country level. This does not allow for an assessment of the relative performance of public and private schools, for which the relevant data is not available in the TIMSS case. However, measuring the system-level effect of private school management is the appropriate way to estimate the general effects of the competitive environment and the market structure prevailing in the different schooling systems, because increased competition from private schools is expected to have a positive effect also on the effectiveness of resource use in nearby public schools which may otherwise lose students to the private schools. As Hoxby (1994) has shown empirically, increased competition from private schools raises the performance of students in public school in U.S. metropolitan areas, so that positive effects of private school competition on nearby public schools seem to be given. Furthermore, Hoxby (1996) has shown that in the United States, the negative effect of teacher unionization is smaller when a school faces competition from private schools. Hoxby (1996) interprets her findings as suggesting that teacher unions may actually be a primary means whereby a lack of competition among schools translates into more generous school inputs and worse student performance in the U.S. schooling system.[109] In any case, a structure of the schooling system

---

[109] As direct evidence on the relative performance of private schools in the United States, Rouse (1998) has shown that gains in mathematics scores of students who participated in the Milwaukee Parental Choice Program to attend nonsectarian private schools were statistically significantly higher than those of unsuccessful applicants to the program and of other public school students, controlling for student fixed effects. A collection of contributions to the discussion whether private schools are superior to public schools is contained in Cohn (1997: Part II). Concerning competition among public schools, Hoxby (2000a) has shown that easier choice among public schools in

characterized by competition through private institutions appears to be highly conducive to students' learning, as the performance of students is found to be statistically significantly positively related to the share of private management control over educational institutions.

5.4.4   Summary and Robustness of Microeconometric Results

Overall, the microeconometric results suggest that both family and institutional factors have strong and unambiguous effects on the quality of schooling, while the impact of resource factors appears to be dubious and weak at best. The students' family background has the strongest impact on students' educational performance. Especially the educational background of parents was strongly conducive to students' learning in mathematics and in science. By contrast, resource effects are very weak, and many even imply that a superior provision with resources can go hand in hand with inferior student performance. There is certainly no general positive effect of educational spending on the quality of schooling. Smaller student-teacher ratios in the classroom or at the school level do not in general lead to increased student performance. However, a sufficient equipment with instructional material and a sufficient level of teachers' formal education seem to render positive effects.

Taken together, the features of the institutional system governing the schooling process strongly influence the quality of schooling. The effects of the dummies characterizing institutional settings in Tables 5.1 and 5.2 sum up to more than 210 test score points in mathematics and to about 150 test score points in science. That is, a student who faced institutions that were all conducive to student performance would have scored more than 200 points higher in mathematics than a student who faced institutions that were all detrimental to student performance. This test score advantage in mathematics equals about 2 standard deviations in test scores and compares to an average test score difference between seventh and eighth grade of 40 points. In addition to that, there are the effects of the discrete variables and the system-level results reported in Tables 5.3 and 5.4.

Table 5.5 summarizes the individual institutional effects and relates them to the reasoning of the theoretical model of educational production of Chapter 4. Central examinations as well as centralized control mechanisms with respect to standards and budgets favor educational performance. School autonomy favors educational performance in the domains of personnel management like choice

---

U.S. metropolitan areas leads to greater productivity of these schools, both in the form of improved student performance and of lower expenditure per student.

Table 5.5: Theoretical Reasoning and Microeconometric Results on Institutional Effects

	Influence on student performance	
	theoretical reasoning (Section 4.4)	microeconometric evidence (Section 5.4)
Central examinations	+	+
Central control of standards	+	+
School autonomy on budget	−	−
School autonomy in personnel management	+	+
School autonomy in process decisions	+	+
Intermediate level of administration and funding	(+)	+
Individual teachers' influence on teaching methods	+	+
Teachers' scrutiny of student assessment	+	+
Teachers' influence on work load	−	−
Teacher unions' influence on curriculum	−	−
Parents' influence	+	+ / −
Private schools	+	+

Note: + = positive impact. − = negative impact. + / − = ambiguous impact.

and rewarding of teachers and of process decisions like purchase of supplies and organization of instruction. Once responsibility for decision-making in and funding of education lies with the administration, intermediate levels seem to fare better than both central and local authorities in focusing attention on student performance. An individual teacher having decision-making power over her teaching methods and devoting extra time to student assessment is conducive to students' learning. By contrast, teachers' influence on the subject matter to be taught (as a measure of the size of their work load) and a strong influence of teacher unions in the schooling system—or more generally teachers acting collectively—seems to have negative impacts on student performance. The influence of parents on classroom teaching is ambiguous, but uninterested parents clearly have a negative effect on their children's learning. A competitive environment in the schooling sector characterized by large shares of privately managed schools helps to assure that the producers of education focus on the performance of students. All in all, the reasonings of the theoretical model of the schooling system presented in Chapter 4 are supported by the microeconometric evidence presented in this chapter.

A comparison between performance in mathematics and in science shows that all of these results are very robust across the two subjects. Family and resource effects as well as institutional effects are qualitatively the same for mathematics and science learning. The only difference is that standardization effects seem to be more positive in mathematics than in science. This shows up in the facts that the effects of centralized examinations, curricula, and textbook approval are larger for mathematics than for science, that a strong influence of external examinations on the school curriculum has a positive effect on mathematics scores but an ambiguous one on science scores, and that school authority in the four decision-making domains reported by the OECD impacts positively on science performance but is unrelated to mathematics performance (with the exception of the organization of instructions). This difference may indicate a higher propensity for standardization in the case of mathematics than in the case of science.

Since some of the variables of the TIMSS data set included a substantial amount of missing values and therefore had to be imputed, it remains to be tested whether the reported results are sensitive to the imputation. The robustness can be tested by dropping observations with imputed data individually for each variable and rerunning the regressions. The only changes either in significance or direction of the relationships occur in the regressions for the following institutional variables.[110] The effect of external exams' influence on the curriculum turns positive (albeit statistically insignificant) in science, replicating the mathematics result. The negative effect of teachers' responsibility for the school budget turns strongly statistically significant in science, while it is statistically significant only at the 15 percent level in mathematics. The coefficient on subject teachers' influence on the curriculum turns statistically insignificant and positive in both mathematics and science, as does the coefficient on school teachers' influence on the curriculum in science. The coefficient on the class teacher having strong influence on the subject matter taught turns statistically significant in science, while the insignificant coefficient on the choice of textbooks turns positive in science (as it is in mathematics). The effect of homework in mathematics and the effect of parents' influence on the curriculum in both mathematics and science turn statistically insignificantly negative.

Since the negative impact of teachers exercising collective influence over the curriculum is anyway best represented by the strong negative effect of teacher unions, and since a statistically significant impact of parents' involvement in teaching is shown by the strong negative impact of uninterested parents, it can in sum be stated that none of the findings relevant for the argumentation in this study depend on the data imputation. Furthermore, increasing the threshold of nonimputed variables for a student to be included in the sample (Section 5.2.4)

---

[110] The only changes for background and resource effects are that the negative coefficient on parents having some secondary education turns statistically insignificant both in mathematics and in science (and positive in mathematics), that the coefficient on the community location close to the center of a town turns statistically insignificantly positive in science and statistically significantly positive in mathematics, and that the positive effect of the teacher's highest education level being the BA turns statistically insignificant in the mathematics regression.

by another 10 variables—reducing the total sample size to 255,018 students in mathematics and to 251,292 students in science—does not lead to any change in significance or sign of the coefficients.

5.5   Understanding Cross-Country Differences in Student Performance

5.5.1   Macro Education Production Functions

In their country-level regressions of test scores on various measures of family and school inputs, Hanushek and Kimko (2000) and Lee and Barro (2001) achieve very low explanatory power as measured by the adjusted R^2 (the proportion of the variation in test scores explained by the explanatory variables). Hanushek and Kimko report R^2s between 0.19 and 0.26 for different estimations, while the average R^2 of Lee and Barro's panel estimation is 0.23. In microeconometric (student-level) estimations like the ones reported in Section 5.4, the omission of measures of innate ability leads to relatively low R^2s since unobserved heterogeneity in the innate ability of students enters the error term. However, assuming that the average level of innate ability does not vary across countries (as Hanushek and Kimko explicitly do), the proportion of the variation in test scores explained by measurable variables should be considerably higher in country-level regressions than in microeconometric regressions. Put differently, the low R^2s of the available country-level studies reveal that their measures of family and school inputs cannot explain much of the cross-country differences in the performance levels of students.

If the hypotheses presented in Chapter 4 are correct and institutional features are important in determining student performance, incorporating aggregated institutional variables into a macro education production function should increase the explained proportion of the variation in test scores considerably. By aggregating institutional variables to reflect the percentage of students in a country for whom an institutional feature is given[111] and by combining this institutional data with country-level data on average test scores, family background, and resource endowment for each country, one can devise a rough-and-ready method for estimating institutional effects at the country level. In a country-level

---

[111] The aggregation of the variables takes care of the stratification of the TIMSS data by weighting each student to yield nationally representative aggregated data for each country.

estimation, a lot of the valuable information of the student-level estimation, which links the teaching environment of each individual student directly to her performance, is lost. This forgoes much of the valuable insights attainable in the microeconometric analysis. But performing a country-level estimation yields a test whether institutions matter for the observed cross-country differences in schooling quality and provides some indication of the explanatory power of institutional features.

5.5.2   Country-Level Results

Table 5.6 reports the results of such a country-level regression for student performance in mathematics and in science. The regressions include the share of parents who finished secondary education and the share of parents who had education beyond secondary education[112] as indicators of the family background of the students of each country, average class size as a resource indicator, and three indicators of institutional features of the schooling systems. The first institutional indicator is the extent of school autonomy in supply choice in the country as measured by the percentage of students in schools which had primary responsibility for purchasing supplies. The second one is an indicator of teacher unions' influence as measured by the percentage of students in schools where teacher unions had a strong influence on the curriculum. The third institutional indicator is a proxy for the scrutiny of assessment as measured by the average time class teachers spent outside the formal school day on preparing or grading student tests or exams. The aggregated (country-level) variables give the average manifestation of a characteristic in a country or the percentage of students in the country for which a characteristic is given, while micro (student-level) variables directly link the characteristic to each student. To emphasize this difference between micro and aggregated variables, the aggregated variables of Table 5.6 have names adapted to, but different from, the micro variables.

The indicators of family background have a strong positive impact on the average educational performance of the students in a country. The share of parents who finished secondary education has the largest standardized coefficient both in the mathematics and in the science regression. It actually appears that a completed basic education of the parents at the secondary level is far more important for students' learning than parents having education beyond the secondary level.

---

[112] To save degrees of freedom, the latter share combines the information contained in the two dummies in the student-level estimation on parents who had some education beyond the secondary level and on parents who finished university.

Table 5.6: Country-Level Results for Student Performance

(Dependent variable: TIMSS international mathematics/science test score)

I. Mathematics	Coefficient	Standard error	Standardized coefficient
Constant	144.424[†]	(63.234)	
Parents' education: finished secondary	176.271[*]	(23.308)	0.725
Parents' education: beyond secondary	91.367	(22.557)	0.429
Class size	3.873[*]	(0.720)	0.524
School autonomy in supply choice	98.464[‡]	(49.381)	0.170
Teacher unions' influence	−467.790[*]	(90.000)	−0.455
Scrutiny of assessment	26.911[*]	(6.610)	0.355
Observations	39		
F	19.31		
R^2 (adj.)	0.74		
II. Science	**Coefficient**	**Standard error**	**Standardized coefficient**
Constant	234.843[*]	(62.028)	
Parents' education: finished secondary	136.873[*]	(23.448)	0.705
Parents' education: beyond secondary	60.989[†]	(23.174)	0.359
Class size	2.557[*]	(0.856)	0.370
School autonomy in supply choice	106.307[†]	(48.440)	0.230
Teacher unions' influence	−369.327[*]	(92.859)	−0.450
Scrutiny of assessment	12.428[‡]	(6.963)	0.197
Observations	39		
F	10.49		
R^2 (adj.)	0.60		

Significance level: [*] 1 percent. — [†] 5 percent. — [‡] 10 percent.

As an indicator of the amount of resources used in the schooling system, average class size is again statistically significantly positively related to student performance. The test score levels in mathematics and science were higher in schooling systems with larger classes, unambiguously implying that resources are more effectively used in countries with larger classes. As an alternative measure of resource effects, expenditure per student entered statistically insignificantly and with a negative sign into the equation both in mathematics and in science.[113] Thus, higher resource use in schooling clearly does not contribute to an explanation of international differences in educational performance levels.

---

[113] This holds both for the PPP-adjusted expenditure measure and for the one deflated by GDP per worker (Section 5.4.1.2).

This finding on resource effects in the TIMSS data set corroborates the evidence presented by Hanushek and Kimko (2000), where the estimated resource effects are also either statistically insignificant or statistically significant but with the wrong sign (Section 3.2.1). However, this finding contrasts with the finding of Lee and Barro (2001) that smaller class sizes are related to superior student performance.[114]

The three institutional indicators included in the country-level regressions are all statistically significantly related to student performance in both mathematics and science. School autonomy in supply choice is positively related to student performance, indicating that decentralized decision-making on process decisions is beneficial to teaching outcomes. The indicator of teacher unions' influence in the schooling system shows a strong negative effect on student performance in both mathematics and science. An increase of 1 standard deviation in the teacher union indicator is related to a decrease of 0.46 standard deviations in the mathematics test score (0.45 in science). The proxy for scrutiny of assessment has a positive impact on the student performance, which is larger in mathematics than in science.

The six variables together explain the international variation in student test scores far better than previous studies. They yield an adjusted R^2 of 0.74 in mathematics and of 0.60 in science. This indicates that even with the rather crude country-level method, where the indicators can only proxy for actual features of the schooling systems across the 39 countries but cannot link them microeconometrically to individual student performance, three-quarters of the cross-country variation in mathematics test scores and 60 percent of the variation in science test scores can be explained when including the three indicators of institutional features of the schooling systems.

Cross-country differences in student performance are not a mystery. They are related to policy measures. However, the policy measures which matter for schooling output are not simple resource inputs. Instead, differences in the institutions of the schooling systems help in understanding cross-country differences in students' educational performance. Institutions set incentives and thereby determine the effectiveness with which schooling resources are put to use. Success in educational production does not primarily depend on the amount of resources spent, but on the institutional features governing the education process.

---

[114] As their measure of class size, Lee and Barro (2001) use the average student-teacher ratio in primary schools of a country, while their test scores mainly reflect performance in secondary education. This measurement seems inferior to using the actual class sizes of the students tested, as was done in the present study. Lee and Barro also report a statistically insignificant negative coefficient on expenditure per student.

5.6   Institutions Matter

Microeconometric student-level estimates reveal that differences in the incentive structures determined by the institutional features of the schooling systems matter for the quality of schooling. The combined effect of performance-conducive educational institutions amounts to a test score difference in student performance of more than 200 points in mathematics (150 points in science), which is five times as large as the conditional test score difference between seventh and eighth grade. Aggregated country-level estimates show that institutional differences can explain a major part of the international differences in average student performance levels. They help to explain 74 percent of the cross-country variation in mathematics test scores and 60 percent in science test scores in the present study, whereas previous studies which constrained themselves to family and resource effects reached only a maximum of 25 percent of explained variation.

For schooling policy, this means that the crucial question is not one of more resources but one of improving the institutional environment of schooling to ensure an efficient use of resources. Student performance is influenced by the productivity of resource use in schools. This productivity is determined by the behavior of the people who act in the educational process. These people respond to incentives. And their incentives are set by the institutional structure of the system. In short, by setting proper institutions, schooling policy can favorably affect student performance. By contrast, spending more money within an institutional system that sets adverse incentives will not improve student performance. The only policy that promises positive effects is to create an institutional system where all the people involved have an incentive to improve student performance and to save costs.

The empirical results identify the specific institutional features of the schooling system which are favorable to student performance. Among these features are:

- central examinations,
- centralized control mechanisms in curricular and budgetary affairs,
- school autonomy in process and personnel decisions,
- an intermediate level of administration performing administrative tasks and educational funding,
- individual teachers having both incentives and powers to select appropriate teaching methods and to scrutinize their students' educational performance,
- no freedom of teachers to determine their own work load,
- limited influence of teacher unions,
- encouragement of parents to take interest in teaching matters, and
- competition from private educational institutions.

Once these favorable institutional features are implemented in a country, this should allow considerable improvements in the educational performance of students, conceivably at the given size of the educational budget. One of the most pleasant features of institutional reforms—as opposed to resource expansions—is in fact that institutional effects are "for given resources." That is, they mostly come at no or low recurrent operation costs.

These results open several questions which may be dealt with in future empirical research. A more complex empirical model could analyze a system of equations where both educational performance and the amount, composition, and effectiveness of the resources used are a function of particular institutional features of the schooling system. The interaction between different institutional features of the schooling system and between institutional and resource effects could also be scrutinized by including interaction terms in the estimation.

Additionally, the wealth of information given in the TIMSS database allows for an empirical analysis in other fields than economics. Educationists might be interested in the effect of different instructional modes on students' performance, possibly differentiated by the institutional setting in which they are applied. Sociologists might analyze peer effects on individual students' educational achievement. While the present study has focused on test scores as outcomes of schooling, it should also be of interest whether the institutional features conducive to student performance in mathematics and science have (positive or negative) effects on the social behavior of students such as use of violence or attitudes towards societal values.

Other important empirical topics include the impact of performance-related pay for teachers and of voucher systems on student performance. The negative effect of increased influence of teacher unions found in this chapter might actually proxy for the effect of a standard salary scale as opposed to merit differentials in teacher pay. Since neither performance-related pay nor voucher systems have yet been implemented on a wide-ranging scale, their effects cannot be estimated with the TIMSS data. However, case-study evidence may increasingly become available and complement the analysis of the present study.

5.7   Appendix: The International Micro Student Performance Database

A list of the variables used in this chapter and their descriptive statistics is given in Table A5.1. The sources of the variables—as reported in the column labeled "Origin"—are TIMSS student, teacher, and school background questionnaires, as well as country-level data on the schooling systems obtained also from OECD educational indicators. For dummy variables, the column labeled "True" reports the percent of students for which the state expressed by the dummy is true. For discrete variables, the international means and standard deviations are reported.

All programs for completing the several steps of the construction of the database were implemented in *SPSS* (Releases 9.0 and 10.0).

Data from TIMSS Student, Teacher, and School Questionnaires

Student-level information (marked "St" in the column "Origin" of Table A5.1) is used to control for students' background and family characteristics. To capture the fact that performance should differ between the two adjacent grades in which students were tested, the dummy "upper grade" is set equal to one for each student in the upper one of the two grades tested. In addition, two countries (Sweden and Switzerland) have tested students in a third grade above the other two, which is captured by the dummy "above upper grade". Data on the students' age and sex are included, as well as dummies showing whether the student was born in the country where she goes to school, whether she lives with both parents, and whether at least one parent was born in the country. Furthermore, four dummies are included representing the highest educational level achieved by the students' parents, as well as four dummies for the number of books in the students' home, which acts as a proxy for the educational and social background of the family. In the estimated production functions, the coefficients on the dummies for parents' education show the performance of students with parents who achieved some secondary education, finished secondary education, had some education beyond the secondary level, and finished university relative to students with parents who only had primary education. Likewise, the dummies for books at home show the performance of students with four ranges of numbers of books (11–25 or enough to fill one shelf, 26–100 or enough to fill one bookcase, 101–200 or enough to fill two bookcases, and more than 200 or enough to fill three or more bookcases) relative to students with none or very few (up to 10) books at home.

Data obtained from TIMSS teacher and school questionnaires are used to show effects of school resources and institutional features. To do so, the student-specific data on achievement test scores and student characteristics was merged with the class-level teacher data and with the school-level data. Teacher data are available separately for mathematics and science teachers. If a student had more than one teacher in either mathematics or science, the teacher who taught the most minutes per week to that student was chosen when merging student and teacher data.

The teacher data, T, give class-level information on class size and the class teacher's characteristics, behavior, and influence. Teacher characteristics considered are the teacher's sex, age, years of teaching experience, and education. The teacher's education is again given in dummy form, showing the effect of the completion of secondary education, bachelor degree, and masters or doctorate degree relative to teachers without completing secondary education. The relevant data on institutional features which are used to deal with the hypotheses of Section 4.4 is derived from qualitative survey data. Teachers were asked how much influence they had on the amount of money to be spent on supplies, on what supplies to be purchased, on the subject matter to be taught, and on specific textbooks to be used. The four-item response possibilities of the questionnaire ranged from "none" to "a lot". To be able to assess the impact of teachers' influence in the different decision-making areas on students' performance, dummy variables were created from these qualitative data which are set equal to one for each teacher who answered that she had "a lot" of influence in the respective field. In the same way, a dummy variable was created signifying that parents uninterested in their children's learning and progress limited "a great deal" how the teacher teaches his class, as well as one for limitations by parents interested in their children's learning. Further data gives information on the scrutiny of exams as measured by the time (in hours per week) which the teacher spent outside the formal school day on preparing or grading exams, on minutes of homework per week assigned by the teacher, and on the time which the teacher spent outside the formal school day on parent-teacher meetings.

The school-level information, Sc, was given by the principals of the schools tested. It includes dummies for schools located in geographically isolated communities and for schools located close to the center of a town (the residual category being schools located in villages or on the outskirts of a town), as well as dummies for schools whose principal thought that the capacity to provide instruction is "not" or "a lot" affected by the shortage or inadequacy of instructional materials like textbooks. Data is given on the ratio of total student enrollment to professional staff at the school, where the latter includes principals, assistant principals, department heads, classroom teachers, teacher aides, laboratory technicians, and learning specialists. An instruction-time variable combines information on the duration of a typical instructional period in minutes, on the number of instructional periods of an average school day, and on the number of instructional days in the school year, each reported separately for the lower and the upper grade. Apart from these resource-related data, qualitative assessment of the institutional setting is given. Principals were asked who, with regard to their school, had primary responsibility for different activities, including formulating the school budget, purchasing supplies, hiring teachers, and determining teacher salaries. Possible answers were "teachers," "department heads," "the principal," "the school's governing board," and "not a school responsibility." Dummies were created for each activity showing whether primary responsibility was with the school and whether it was with teachers. Finally, six dummies show whether external examinations/standardized tests, each teacher individually, teachers of the same subject as a group, teachers collectively for the school, teacher unions, and parents had "a lot" of influence in determining the curriculum which is taught in the school.[115]

Country-Level Data

At the country level, C, TIMSS reported the degree of centralization regarding decision-making about examinations, curriculum syllabi, and textbooks (Beaton et al. 1996a: 17–19). Dummies report whether the central level of decision-making authority within the (national or regional) schooling system had exclusive responsibility for or gave final approval of the content of examinations, the syllabi for courses of study, and the list of approved textbooks. As a measure of the country's level of development which sets the general background for the educational opportunities of the students, data on GDP per capita (in current international dollars, 1994) is included, obtained from World Bank (1999b) statistics. Unfortunately, the TIMSS database does not contain expenditure data. In lack of expenditure data at the local level, current public expenditure per student in secondary education at the national level in 1994 was calculated on the basis of data from UNESCO, *Statistical Yearbooks*, converted into international dollars with purchasing-power-parity exchange rates from the World Bank (1999b).

Further country-level data on institutional features of the schooling system—concerning the level of decision-making and private involvement—were obtained from the 1997 and 1998 volumes of the OECD educational indicators, CO, which are devised to provide a quantitative description of the comparative functioning of schooling systems. Most of these indicators were gathered in the UNESCO/OECD World Education Indicators (WEI) program, which includes a number of non-OECD member countries. The number of countries for which each OECD indicator is available is reported in Table A5.1.

With regard to the organization of the schooling system, the OECD gathered information on the distribution of decision-making responsibilities among key shareholders of education. These shareholders are central, state, provincial, sub-regional, and local authorities as well as schools.[116] The indicator relates to public lower secondary education and is available for the school year 1997/98

---

[115] The method of data imputation for missing values in the TIMSS questionnaires is described in Section 5.2.4.

[116] Information on names and numbers of decision-making units per decision-making level for each country can be found in Annex 3 of the 1998 issue of the OECD *Education at a Glance: OECD Indicators*.

only.[117] It is based on 35 decision items included in a survey completed by panels of national experts and refers to actual decision-making practice (not to nonbinding formal regulations). The variables used in the present study represent the percentages of educational decisions taken at the school level and at the central government level (OECD 1998: Tables E5.1 and E5.2). The general indicator (termed "overall" in Table A5.1) is calculated to give equal importance to each of the following four decision-making domains: organization of instruction, personnel management, planning and structures, and resource allocation and use. Data is also available for each of the four domains separately. Decisions on the organization of instruction include the determination of school attendance, promotion, repetition, and teaching and assessment methods. Decisions on personnel management comprise the hiring, dismissal, career influence, and duties of staff as well as the fixing of salary scales. As for planning and structures, decisions such as the creation and closure of schools and grades, the design of programs of study, and the setting of qualifying examinations for a certificate are combined. Resource decisions include the allocation and use of resources for different kinds of expenditure. Finally, the variable "school autonomy" captures what percentage of decisions are taken at the school level in full autonomy, as opposed to after consultations with or within frameworks from other educational authorities (OECD 1998: Table E5.3).

Another OECD educational indicator reports which share of final public funds is spent by the different levels of government (after transfers between the different government levels), showing whether local, intermediate, or central authorities are the final purchasers of educational resources (OECD 1998: Table B6.1a). The variables on the "government level of final funds" report the respective shares of total public funds provided at the local level and at the central level, giving information on the division of responsibility for and control over the funding of education between local, intermediate, and national authorities.

Data on the share of private enrollment in total enrollment refer to the school year 1994/95 (derived from OECD 1997: Table C1.1a). Educational institutions are classified as either public or private according to whether a public agency or a private entity has the ultimate power to make decisions concerning the institution's affairs (ultimate management control). That is, public institutions are institutions controlled and managed directly by a public education authority or agency or controlled by a body whose members are appointed by a public authority, while private institutions are controlled and managed by a nongovernmental organization (e.g., a church or a business enterprise). As a subgroup of the private institutions, government-independent private institutions are those

---

[117] This should not be a problem, however, since organizational structures in the schooling system are relatively stable.

Table A5.1: Descriptive Statistics on the International Micro Database

Variable	Origin[a]	True (percent)	Mean	Std. dev.	Imputed (percent)	Countries missing[b]
Test scores						
Mathematics score	St		507.6	99.3	0.0	—
Science score	St		506.8	98.4	0.0	—
Student and family characteristics						
Upper grade	St	51.3			0.0	—
Above upper grade	St	1.8			0.0	—
Age (years)	St		13.8	0.9	1.4	—
Sex (female)	St	50.2			0.4	—
Born in country	St	94.1			7.6	FRA JPN
Living with both parents	St	87.3			7.3	JPN
Parent born in country	St	91.9			7.7	JPN
Parents' education	St				13.2	GBR JPN
Some secondary		14.2				
Finished secondary		31.8				
Some after secondary		24.4				
Finished university		18.1				
Books at home	St				6.0	JPN
11–25		14.8				
26–100		33.0				
101–200		19.4				
More than 200		24.9				
Community location	Sc				10.2	KWT
Geographically isolated area		3.0				
Close to the center of a town		39.7				
GDP per capita (international $)	C		15404.0	6993.1	0.0	—
Resources and teacher characteristics						
Expenditure per student (inernat. $)	C		3242.8	1941.7	0.0	—
Mathematics class size (no. of stud.)	T		28.4	10.7	26.8	—
Science class size (no. of students)	T		28.8	10.2	35.8	—
Student-teacher ratio	Sc		25.7	61.2	21.0	GBR
No shortage of materials	Sc	41.0			12.3	SCO
Great shortage of materials	Sc	12.5			12.3	SCO
Instruction time (minutes per year)	Sc		47226.5	8248.6	30.0	GRC JPN KWT
Mathematics teacher characteristics	T					
Teacher's sex (female)		54.1			12.0	—
Teacher's age (years)			40.8	9.3	12.0	—
Teacher's experience (years)			16.2	9.4	13.2	—
Teacher's education					22.2	AUS BFL/R DNK JPN
Secondary		18.8				
BA or equivalent		64.8				
MA/PhD		15.3				
Science teacher characteristics	T					
Teacher's sex (female)		52.4			15.0	—
Teacher's age (years)			40.7	9.2	15.0	—
Teacher's experience (years)			15.7	9.3	16.3	—
Teacher's education					24.9	AUS BFL/R DNK JPN
Secondary		15.9				
BA or equivalent		66.6				
MA/PhD		16.7				

Table A5.1 continued

Variable	Origin[a]	True (percent)	Mean	Std. dev.	Imputed (percent)	Countries missing[b]
Institutional settings						
Central examinations						
Central examinations	C	34.2				—
External exams influence curriculum	Sc	15.2			20.0	BFL/R GBR KWT NOR
Distribution of responsibilities between schools and administration						SCO
Central curriculum	C	77.2				—
Central textbook approval	C	51.3				—
School responsibility	Sc					
School budget		90.5			20.4	GBR NOR SCO
Purchasing supplies		96.2			21.3	GBR NOR SCO
Hiring teachers		73.1			17.4	GBR NOR SCO
Determining teacher salaries		27.9			20.3	GBR NOR SCO BFL/R
Teachers' influence						
Teachers' responsibility	Sc					
School budget		3.2			20.4	GBR NOR SCO
Purchasing supplies		10.0			21.3	GBR NOR SCO
Hiring teachers		0.1			17.4	GBR NOR SCO
Determining teacher salaries		0.1			20.3	GBR NOR SCO BFL/R
Strong influence on curriculum	Sc					BFR GBR KWT NOR SCO
Teacher individually		24.3			17.5	
Subject teachers		48.9			18.0	
School teachers collectively		45.0			17.4	
Teacher unions		1.7			17.9	
Math. teacher has strong influence on	T					GBR
Money for supplies		4.9			13.7	
Kind of supplies		13.2			13.7	
Subject matter		28.5			13.3	
Textbook		19.9			13.6	
Science teacher has strong influence on	T					GBR ISR
Money for supplies		7.4			17.0	
Kind of supplies		20.1			16.8	
Subject matter		40.6			16.5	
Textbook		24.8			16.9	
Mathematics	T					
Scrutiny of exams (hours p. w.)			2.5	1.6	14.1	DNK
Homework (minutes per week)			99.3	80.0	22.4	—
Science	T					
Scrutiny of exams (hours p. w.)			2.4	1.6	16.9	DNK
Homework (minutes per week)			38.8	40.9	32.9	AUT
Parents' influence						
Parents' influence on curriculum	Sc	1.8			17.1	BFR GBR KWT NOR SCO
Mathematics	T					
Uninterested parents limit teaching		8.3			25.9	JPN
Interested parents limit teaching		4.8			24.2	FRA
Parent-teacher meetings (hours p. w.)			0.6	0.6	15.6	DNK
Science	T					
Uninterested parents limit teaching		6.4			34.3	JPN
Interested parents limit teaching		4.2			32.5	FRA
Parent-teacher meetings (hours p. w.)			0.6	0.6	18.8	DNK

Table A5.1 continued

Variable (in percent)	Origin[a]	True (percent)	Mean	Std. dev.	Imputed (percent)	Number of countries available
Distribution of responsibilities between schools and administration						
School autonomy	CO		16.5	11.3		21
School level decisions	CO					21
Overall			40.1	16.9		
Organization of instruction			80.1	13.1		
Personnel management			29.9	29.0		
Planning and structures			24.2	18.3		
Resources			26.2	19.4		
Distribution of responsibilities between administrative levels						
Central government decisions	CO					21
Overall			25.2	21.5		
Organization of instruction			9.9	11.1		
Personnel management			31.8	32.7		
Planning and structures			41.0	30.6		
Resources			18.2	28.9		
Government level of final funds	CO					22
Funds provided at local level			38.0	36.4		
Funds provided at central level			28.1	34.4		
Private schools	CO					
Private enrollment			13.8	14.0		23
Independent private enrollment			4.3	6.9		23
Public exp. on private institutions			10.6	17.2		26
Public exp. on indep. private inst.			0.4	0.9		26

[a]St = student, T = class teacher, Sc = school, C = country, CO = OECD country data. — [b]BFL = Flemish Belgium, BFR = French Belgium, BFL/R = Belgium (both parts), for further country abbreviations see Figure 3.5. — Statistics are unweighted.

private institutions which receive less than 50 percent of its core funding from government agencies, while government-dependent private institutions primarily depend on funding from government sources for their basic educational services. The variable "public expenditure on (independent) private institutions" contains the share of public educational expenditure going to (independent) private educational institutions in the financial year 1995 (OECD 1998: Table B6.2).

6   Implications for Schooling Policy

This study has dealt with the production of education in schools. School education takes central stage in the process of economic growth and development through the formation of high-quality human capital. "With human capital being a major determinant of economic growth, the organizational conditions for human capital formation are an important element of a strategy for growth" (Siebert 2000a: 3). As outlined in the introductory chapter, political advisors and policymakers have stressed the importance of a sound basic education everywhere in the world, but there are controversial debates about the appropriate means to achieve this end. The findings of this study contribute to the educational policy debate from an economic point of view.

6.1   Ensuring High-Quality Schooling as Growth Policy

The main policy implications of the findings obtained in this study concern the conduct of schooling policy, but as will be argued, schooling policy is actually a central ingredient of any promising long-run strategy for economic policy focusing on growth and development. An efficient schooling policy which ensures a high-quality education will necessarily have wider implications for the economic prospects of countries in an integrating world economy. The main policy implications of the findings of this study are summarized in the following eight statements.

1. Schooling policy is growth policy.

The quality of a country's stock of human capital is decisive for the country's long-run economic development (Chapter 2). Hence, politicians aiming at a sustainable growth strategy should focus on the schooling system, where a major part of the national human capital stock is produced. As the rates of return to education decrease with the amount of education already accumulated by a person, and as there are synergies and complementarities in the learning process which cause learning to beget learning, basic education produced in schools can be expected to have the largest growth impact. Policy initiatives which aim to ensure a sound basic education, especially in the early years, are—intended or not—inherently part of a country's growth policy. Schooling policy and economic policy are therefore inextricably linked. Success in schooling is the foundation for economic success, and failure in schooling depletes a country of its economic potential.

Even more, the beneficial effects of education go beyond the economic payoffs to expanded human capabilities more generally. These additional payoffs are stressed by Sen (1999), who understands development as a broader concept of freedom expansion, where economic growth is not an end in itself but a means to expanding the freedoms which people enjoy. In this perspective, education is not only important for human capital in the narrow sense that it augments future production possibilities, but it is also important for human capabilities in the broader sense that it expands the ability and freedom of people to lead the kind of lives they value. These additional benefits of education as valued by the broader human-capability perspective include the abilities to read, communicate, and argue, to choose in a more informed way, and to be taken more seriously by others. In a development strategy thus understood, the focus on schooling policy should be underscored even further, not only in developing countries.

2. Schooling policy should focus on quality rather than on quantity.

In much of the literature on the empirics of growth, education is defined in quantitative terms: How many years of education does somebody have? The findings in this study imply that how long a person attends a school is far less important than how much the person really learns during that time. Put differently, it is schooling quality rather than schooling quantity which matters for economic performance. Qualitative differences in a year of schooling may be so large that they can dwarf the consequences of any potential quantitative differences. A promising schooling policy should focus on improving the quality of each year of schooling a student receives, rather than on increasing the number of years the student spends in school.

6.2 Making Good Use of the Money

3. Money cannot buy schooling quality in present schooling systems.

First of all a warning on what schooling policies should *not* do: they should not throw money at failing schools (Hanushek 1981). A large literature suggests that increasing educational spending without implementing incentives which ensure that resources are allocated efficiently will not lead to an increase in the quality of students' education (Chapter 3). More money is not the answer to the quest for high-quality schooling. While there are some schools which will be able and willing to make beneficial use of additional resources, and while additional resources may be useful under specific circumstances, there is no evidence that gives reason to expect that general across-the-board increases in educational spending will result in increases in schooling quality.

This does not mean that additional resources will never help in bringing about increased educational performance of students. Especially in developing countries, where many schools have to work with class sizes of 50 students and more, where many teachers have not received a sufficient level of education themselves, and where educational budgets do not suffice to provide a decent basic education to every child, additional spending may have positive payoffs and may actually be indispensable for ensuring education for all. But as long as the schooling system is not constituted in a way which secures an efficient use of additional resources, increased educational spending is not a sufficient condition to ensure increases in students' educational performance, even in developing countries. In the schooling systems as presently constituted in most countries, and at the resource levels currently reached in the developed world, a general increase in educational spending will not lead to improved schooling quality, if past experience is any guide.

Furthermore, it must be stressed that resource policies are costly. Any potential benefit of increased educational spending has to be valued against its costs. The critical question is whether increased spending will increase students' future productivity with its ensuing benefits enough to warrant the cost of a resource policy. For policy decisions, it is essential to see whether the benefits of any initiative measure up to its costs. The evidence currently available suggests that this is not the case for increased educational spending per student because the costs by far outweigh even the most favorable estimates of returns (Heckman 2000: 22). In addition, alternative resource policies have to be valued against each other. For example, class-size reductions are among the most expensive policies considered in schooling, and there is an economic trade-off between the use of money to decrease class sizes and other potential uses of the money. The evidence suggests that while increased overall per-student spending and lower class sizes do not render positive effects on student performance, providing schools with the proper instructional materials and supplies and with experienced, well-educated teachers does impact positively on the quality of schooling (Chapter 5). This raises the question of *how* the money is spent, which is again a question of the institutions governing the schooling system.

4. Incentives are the key to success in the schooling sector.

Schooling policies have to consider the incentives which result from the institutions of the schooling sector. A central reason for the lack of positive resource effects in the current schooling systems is that the agents who act in the education process and who decide on the allocation of resources do not have sufficient incentives to increase the quality of schooling (Chapter 4). Spending more money in an institutional system that sets adverse incentives will mainly lead to the advancement of other objectives than increasing schooling quality. Additional funds will be used opportunistically to further the agents' own interests, as opposed to furthering the educational performance of students. The crucial question for schooling policy is not one of more resources, but one of creating an institutional system in which all the people involved have incentives to improve on performance and to save on costs (see also Hanushek et al. 1994). People respond to incentives; they alter their individual behavior in accordance with the incentives which they have. Thus, institutions which increase the benefits of behavior conducive to student performance and which increase the costs of behavior detrimental to student performance will ultimately result in the production of higher-quality schooling.

Even those researchers who doubt that there is no genuine positive input-output relationship in schooling, like Krueger (1999b: 32), do "not dispute that a change in incentives and enhanced competition among schools could possibly improve the efficiency of public schools." But Krueger adds that "such a conclusion should rest on direct evidence that private schools are more efficacious than public schools, or on evidence that competition improves performance, not on a presumption that public schools as currently constituted fail to transform inputs into outputs." Chapter 5 provides such direct evidence on which institutional settings are most conducive to schooling quality.

6.3 Incentive-Based Institutional Reforms

5. Schools should be allowed to decide autonomously on operational tasks.

School autonomy in operational areas contributes to a high level of schooling quality. The bureaucratic obstacles introduced by centralized process regulations inhibit schools from tailoring their instruction in ways that fit their students. Schools need a high degree of autonomy in making decisions on teaching techniques and purchase of supplies in order to respond to the demands of parents—a prerequisite for competition. Also, the educators in a school should have more knowledge of effective teaching strategies for their specific students than central administrators (World Bank 1999a: 49–50).

Likewise, heads of schools should have more knowledge than central administrators of which teachers to hire and which teachers to promote or give a raise in salary. Hence, personnel-management decisions should lie with schools, not with central administrations. For instance, the allocation of teachers to schools by central bureaucratic authorities, as in some German states, comes close to the allocation of workers to firms in centrally planned economies and is probably not very different in its productivity effects.

Schooling policy has to recognize that any kind of knowledge is possessed by individuals at a decentralized level. The "knowledge of the particular circumstances of time and place" (Hayek 1945: 522) is not available to a central planning agency. To make use of this specific local knowledge, an easing of process and personnel-management regulations is necessary. A high degree of freedom to decide at the school level is necessary for tasks where school-level knowledge is important. School personnel must be able to search out what will work in their specific situation.

6. Schools must be made accountable.

However, increased autonomy at the school level also increases the potential for local opportunistic behavior. Local decision-makers may use their autonomy to reduce their work load or to further objectives divergent from increasing the quality of schooling—unless the right incentives are in place. Therefore, schools must be subject to external monitoring and evaluation which focus their incentives on furthering schooling quality. The more flexibility a school has, the more important it is to have external standards and assessments.

External supervision should take the form of central examinations, central standard setting, and external monitoring of budgetary decisions. Performance control mechanisms such as external examinations supervise the achievements reached in terms of schooling quality, thereby making students, teachers, and schools accountable and focusing their incentives on educational performance. Centralized decision-making on curriculum issues sets the educational standards which schools have to meet and prevents schools from seeking to reduce their work load. External decision-making on the size of the school budget and external control of budgetary affairs prevents actors at the school level from using additional funds to further their own interests or to employ them on resources which lighten their work load. Centralization of decisions on standard setting, performance control, and budgetary matters helps to make schools accountable for their actions, thereby furthering the quality of schooling.

Simply decentralizing decision-making regarding every educational task is not sufficient to ensure efficient resource allocation in the schooling system. There has to be clarity about the objectives, i.e., which level of performance is aimed for. The incentives of the actors at the school level need to be focused on students' educational performance. And they must be directly accountable for their actions. The evidence suggests that in order to govern the schools, the supervisory authority should be at a level far enough from schools to make lobbying difficult, yet close enough to understand the local needs and to be able to effectively monitor the schools.

7. Teachers' incentives have to focus on improving student performance.

Teachers have a central role in the schooling system. On a day-to-day basis, they instruct their students in the classroom and monitor the students' educational progress. However, the behavior of teachers can hardly be directly monitored, so that they have a great deal of freedom to pursue their teaching to their own liking. The degree of freedom of teachers to make teaching decisions independently affects the decision-making outcome in the schooling system. Thus, their ability to influence the process and the focus of their incentives are decisive for the outcome of the education process. The schooling system has to ensure that teachers have incentives which are conducive to student performance. Otherwise teachers may tend to decrease their work load or increase their payoffs without looking at educational results. Generating the former and avoiding the latter is an intriguing task given the importance and the interests of teachers.

It means that the influence of teachers has to be restricted where and when it pertains mainly to act on objectives which diverge from schooling quality. When teachers have the power to determine how much they have to teach and how much they receive for it, there is a great danger that this influence is used to the detriment of students' learning opportunities. Therefore, external standards on these issues have to focus teachers' incentives on the goal of advancing students' learning. It seems especially vital to curb the power of teacher unions in determining their own work load, e.g., by setting the curriculum. Given their numbers and their ensuing ability to influence the electoral process when acting collectively, teacher unions are a potentially powerful political interest group. In promoting the special interests of teachers, they tend to aim at increasing their pay and decreasing their work load, which also means decreasing the amount of subject matter to be covered. Teacher unions can also exert collective bargaining power. In doing so, they tend to advance the interest of the median teacher, which favors a leveling of salary scales instead of differentiation by merit. Such decisions are to the disadvantage of students' educational performance.

Bringing teachers' incentives in line with student performance also means that individual teachers have to be allowed to search for the best teaching methods for their classes, as long as their incentives are focused on students' learning through external standards and monitoring. For example, a high degree of teacher leeway in making decisions about which textbooks to buy should be conducive to student learning, since teachers know best how to teach their students. Areas where increased influence of individual teachers will have positive payoffs also include the regular scrutiny of students' advances in educational achievement.

If schools and teachers can use their intimate knowledge of their students to choose the best teaching method, then they can teach more effectively. But if they can use their influence, whether acting collectively or individually, to reduce their work load, then students' learning opportunities will suffer. The challenge for schooling policy is to create a set of incentives which encourages school personnel to behave in ways that do not necessarily further their own interests. The incentive structure must aim to secure that teachers put aside their other interests and focus mainly on raising student achievement.

8. Competition between schools creates performance-conducive incentives.

Introducing competition into the schooling system gives parents the possibility to choose the school which they deem the best, and creates incentives favorable to high educational achievement. As in other sectors of the economy, competition imposes penalties on suppliers who fail to use their resources effectively. Inefficiency leads to higher costs and lower quality, which is practically an invitation to competitors to lure away customers. But the relative lack of competition in the schooling sectors of most countries tends to dull the incentives to improve quality while holding down costs. Competition could help to wipe out inefficiencies in the current schooling systems.

Moreover, in the public schooling system, the ability of parents and students to ensure that they receive high-quality schooling is constrained by the enormous obstacles to leaving a bad school. Parents and students have to rely almost exclusively on the government, school administrators, and school personnel to monitor one another's behavior and to create appropriate quality-control measures. Giving parents choice and encouraging parents to take interest in their children's educational advancement will increase the pressure on schools to produce a high quality of schooling and to use available resources efficiently to reach this objective.

Parents can be allowed to choose between public schools, increasing competition between them. Furthermore, the existence of more private schools gives parents who want to raise their children's achievement the ability to choose whether to send them to a particular private school or to a public school. Private schools have monetary incentives to use resources efficiently, and they change the incentives for public schools by introducing competition into the public schooling system. When private schools take over resource allocation and school management from public decision-makers, incentives are altered in favor of furthering students' educational performance.

This policy implication for the system of basic education mirrors the success story of the institutions of higher education in the United States, whose attractiveness to foreign students results from the competitive market structure in U.S. higher education which ensures its high educational standards compared to other countries (Heckman 2000: 23–26). Given that countries stand in locational competition with each other, replacing the bureaucratic organization of the university systems in European countries with an organization based on the concept of competition has been deemed the greatest challenge for European countries (Siebert 2000c: 22). Thus, the policy implication of allowing greater competition in the system of basic education is in line with the reform proposal of the German Council of Economic Experts (Sachverständigenrat 1998: 247–256) for the German system of higher education (Section 1.1).

To sum up, the formation of high-quality human capital is essential for the economic success both of individuals and of society at large in a modern economy. If the schooling system manages to produce sound basic education for all, the country builds the potential for sustainable long-run economic development. To ensure high-quality education, schooling policy has to pay attention to the incentives which affect the quality of the schooling system. The crucial question for schooling policy is not one of adding resources to the system but one of creating an institutional system where all actors involved have incentives to improve student performance and to save on costs.

References

Acemoglu, D., and J. Angrist (2000). How Large Are Human Capital Externalities? Evidence from Compulsory Schooling Laws. *NBER Macroeconomics Annual 2000*. Cambridge, Mass.: MIT Press.

African Development Bank (1998). *African Development Report 1998: Human Capital Development*. Oxford: Oxford University Press.

Aghion, P., and P. Howitt (1998). *Endogenous Growth Theory*. Cambridge, Mass.: MIT Press.

Akerhielm, K. (1995). Does Class Size Matter? *Economics of Education Review* 14(3): 229–241.

Angrist, J.D., and V. Lavy (1999). Using Maimonides' Rule to Estimate the Effect of Class Size on Scholastic Achievement. *Quarterly Journal of Economics* 114(2): 533–575.

Ashenfelter, O., C. Harmon, and H. Oosterbeek (1999). A Review of Estimates of the Schooling/Earnings Relationship, with Tests for Publication Bias. *Labour Economics* 6(4): 453–470.

Asian Development Bank (1998). *Asian Development Outlook 1998: Population and Human Resources*. Oxford: Oxford University Press.

Azariadis, C., and A. Drazen (1990). Threshold Externalities in Economic Development. *Quarterly Journal of Economics* 105(2): 501–526.

Barro, R.J. (1991). Economic Growth in a Cross Section of Countries. *Quarterly Journal of Economics* 106(2): 407–443.

Barro, R.J. (1997). *Determinants of Economic Growth: A Cross-Country Empirical Study*. Cambridge, Mass.: MIT Press.

Barro, R.J. (1999). Human Capital and Growth in Cross-Country Regressions. *Swedish Economic Policy Review* 6(2): 237–277.

Barro, R.J., and J.-W. Lee (1993). International Comparisons of Educational Attainment. *Journal of Monetary Economics* 32(3): 363–394.

Barro, R.J., and J.-W. Lee (1996). International Measures of Schooling Years and Schooling Quality. *American Economic Review (Papers and Proceedings)* 86(2): 218–223.

Barro, R.J., and J.-W. Lee (2001). International Data on Educational Attainment: Updates and Implications. *Oxford Economic Papers* 53(3): 541–563.

Barro, R.J., and X. Sala-i-Martin (1995). *Economic Growth*. New York: McGraw-Hill.

Baumol, W.J. (1967). Macroeconomics of Unbalanced Growth: The Anatomy of Urban Crisis. *American Economic Review* 57(3): 415–426.

Beaton, A.E., M.O. Martin, I.V.S. Mullis, E.J. Gonzalez, T.A. Smith, and D.L. Kelly (1996a). *Science Achievement in the Middle School Years: IEA's Third International Mathematics and Science Study (TIMSS)*. Chestnut Hill, Mass.: Boston College.

Beaton, A.E., I.V.S. Mullis, M.O. Martin, E.J. Gonzalez, D.L. Kelly, and T.A. Smith (1996b). *Mathematics Achievement in the Middle School Years: IEA's Third International Mathematics and Science Study (TIMSS)*. Chestnut Hill, Mass.: Boston College.

Becker, G.S. ([1964]1993). *Human Capital: A Theoretical and Empirical Analysis, with Special Reference to Education*. Chicago: University of Chicago Press.

Behrman, J.R. (1999). Schooling in Asia: Selected Microevidence on Determinants, Effects, and Policy Implications. *Journal of Asian Economics* 10(2): 147–194.

Behrman, J.R., and M.R. Rosenzweig (1994). Caveat Emptor: Cross-Country Data on Education and the Labor Force. *Journal of Development Economics* 44(1): 147–171.

Benhabib, J., and M.M. Spiegel (1994). The Role of Human Capital in Economic Development: Evidence from Aggregate Cross-Country and Regional U.S. Data. *Journal of Monetary Economics* 34(2): 143–173.

Betts, J.R. (1998). The Impact of Educational Standards on the Level and Distribution of Earnings. *American Economic Review* 88(1): 266–275.

Bils, M., and P.J. Klenow (2000). Does Schooling Cause Growth? *American Economic Review* 90(5): 1160–1183.

Bishop, J.H. (1989). Is the Test Score Decline Responsible for the Productivity Growth Decline? *American Economic Review* 79(1): 178–197.

Bishop, J.H. (1992). The Impact of Academic Competencies on Wages, Unemployment, and Job Performance. *Carnegie-Rochester Conference Series on Public Policy* 37 (December): 127–194.

Bishop, J.H. (1997). The Effect of National Standards and Curriculum-Based Exams on Achievement. *American Economic Review (Papers and Proceedings)* 87(2): 260–264.

Bishop, J.H. (1998). Are National Exit Examinations Important for Educational Efficiency? Mimeo. Cornell University, Ithaca, N.Y.

Bishop, J.H. (1999). Are National Exit Examinations Important for Educational Efficiency? *Swedish Economic Policy Review* 6(2): 349–398.

Boissiere, M., J.B. Knight, and R.H. Sabot (1985). Earnings, Schooling, Ability, and Cognitive Skills. *American Economic Review* 73(5): 1016–1030.

Boozer, M., and C. Rouse (2001). Intraschool Variation in Class Size: Patterns and Implications. *Journal of Urban Economics* 50(1): 163–189.

Bryk, A.S., and V.E. Lee (1992). Is Politics the Problem and Markets the Answer? An Essay Review of Politics, Markets, and America's Schools. *Economics of Education Review* 11(4): 439–451.

Bryk, A.S., and S.W. Raudenbush (1992). *Hierarchical Linear Models: Applications and Data Analysis Methods.* Advanced Quantitative Techniques in the Social Sciences 1. Newbury Park: Sage Publications.

Card, D. (1999). The Causal Effect of Education on Earnings. In O. Ashenfelter and D. Card (eds.), *Handbook of Labor Economics.* Volume 3A. Amsterdam: North-Holland.

Card, D., and A.B. Krueger (1992). Does School Quality Matter? Returns to Education and the Characteristics of Public Schools in the United States. *Journal of Political Economy* 100(1): 1–40.

Case, A., and A. Deaton (1999). School Inputs and Educational Outcomes in South Africa. *Quarterly Journal of Economics* 114(3): 1047–1084.

Case, A., and M. Yogo (1999). Does School Quality Matter? Returns to Education and the Characteristics of Schools in South Africa. NBER Working Paper 7399. National Bureau of Economic Research, Cambridge, Mass.

Chiswick, B.R. (1998). Interpreting the Coefficient of Schooling in the Human Capital Earnings Function. *Journal of Educational Planning and Administration* 12(2): 123–130.

Chubb, J.E., and T.M. Moe (1990). *Politics, Markets, and America's Schools.* Washington, D.C.: The Brookings Institution.

Ciccone, A., and G. Peri (2000). Human Capital and Externalities in Cities. Mimeo. Universitat Pompeu Fabra, Barcelona.

Coase, R.H. (1984). The New Institutional Economics. *Journal of Institutional and Theoretical Economics* 140(1): 229–231.

Cohen, J., and S. Baldi (1998). An Evaluation of the Relative Merits of HLM vs. Robust Linear Regression in Estimating Models with Multi-Level Data. Mimeo. American Institutes for Research, Washington, D.C.

Cohn, E. (ed.) (1997). *Market Approaches to Education. Vouchers and School Choice.* Oxford: Pergamon.

Coleman, J.S., E.Q. Campbell, C.J. Hobson, J. McPartland, A.M. Mood, F.D. Weinfeld, and R.L. York (1966). *Equality of Educational Opportunity: Summary Report.* Washington, D.C.: U.S. Government Printing Office.

Costrell, R.M. (1994). A Simple Model of Educational Standards. *American Economic Review* 84(4): 956–971.

Council of Economic Advisors (1999). *Economic Report of the President 1999.* Washington, D.C.: U.S. Government Printing Office.

Deaton, A. (1997). *The Analysis of Household Surveys: A Microeconometric Approach to Development Policy.* (Published for the World Bank.) Baltimore: The Johns Hopkins University Press.

de la Fuente, A., and R. Doménech (2000). Human Capital in Growth Regressions: How Much Difference Does Data Quality Make? CEPR Discussion Paper 2466. Centre for Economic Policy Research, London.

Denison, E.F. (1967). *Why Growth Rates Differ: Postwar Experience in Nine Western Countries.* Washington, D.C.: The Brookings Institution.

DuMouchel, W.H., and G.J. Duncan (1983). Using Sample Survey Weights in Multiple Regression Analyses of Stratified Samples. *Journal of the American Statistical Association* 78(383): 535–543.

EBRD (European Bank for Reconstruction and Development) (2000). *Transition Report 2000: Employment, Skills and Transition.* London.

The Economist (1997). A Hard Choice for Mr Blair. October 18: 17–18.

The Economist (1999). A Contract on Schools. January 16: 21.

The Economist (2000). America's Education Choice. April 1: 13.

EIB (European Investment Bank) (2000). *Annual Report 1999.* Luxembourg.

Epple, D., and R.E. Romano (1998). Competition Between Private and Public Schools, Vouchers, and Peer-Group Effects. *American Economic Review* 88(1): 33–62.

Federal Reserve Bank of New York (1998). Excellence in Education. Views on Improving American Education. Special Issue of *Economic Policy Review*, Volume 4, Number 1.

Furubotn, E.G., and R. Richter (1997). *Institutions and Economic Theory. The Contribution of the New Institutional Economics.* Ann Arbor: University of Michigan Press.

Gallup, A. (2000). Education: A Vital Issue in Election 2000. Poll Releases, October 2. Gallup News Service. Princeton: Gallup Organization.

Gemmell, N. (1996). Evaluating the Impacts of Human Capital Stocks and Accumulation on Economic Growth: Some New Evidence. *Oxford Bulletin of Economics and Statistics* 58(1): 9–28.

Goldstein, H. (1999). *Multilevel Statistical Models.* Kendall's Library of Statistics 3. (Revised Internet edition of the second print edition as of September 11, 2000. http://www.arnoldpublishers.com/support/goldstein.htm). London: Edward Arnold.

Gollin, D. (1998). Getting Income Shares Right: Self Employment, Unincorporated Enterprise, and the Cobb-Douglas Hypothesis. Mimeo. Williams College, Williamstown, Mass.

Gonzalez, E.J., and T.A. Smith (eds.) (1997). *User Guide for the TIMSS International Database: Primary and Middle School Years.* Chestnut Hill, Mass.: International Association for the Evaluation of Educational Achievement, TIMSS International Study Center, Boston College.

Griliches, Z. (1996). The Discovery of the Residual: A Historical Note. *Journal of Economic Literature* 34(3): 1324–1330.

Grissmer, D.W., S.N. Kirby, M. Berends, and S. Williamson (1994). *Student Achievement and the Changing American Family.* Santa Monica, Calif.: Rand.

Gundlach, E. (1994). Accounting for the Stock of Human Capital: Selected Evidence and Potential Implications. *Weltwirtschaftliches Archiv* 130(2): 350–374.

Gundlach, E. (1995). The Role of Human Capital in Economic Growth: New Results and Alternative Interpretations. *Weltwirtschaftliches Archiv* 131(2): 383–402.

Gundlach, E., and L. Wößmann (2001). The Fading Productivity of Schooling in East Asia. *Journal of Asian Economics* 12(3): 401–417.

Gundlach, E., D. Rudman, and L. Wößmann (2002). Second Thoughts on Developing Accounting. *Applied Economics* 34(11): 1359–1369.

Gundlach, E., L. Wößmann, and J. Gmelin (2001). The Decline of Schooling Productivity in OECD Countries. *Economic Journal* 111(471): C135–C147.

Hall, R.E., and C.I. Jones (1999). Why Do Some Countries Produce So Much More Output per Worker than Others? *Quarterly Journal of Economics* 114(1): 83–116.

Hanushek, E.A. (1981). Throwing Money at Schools. *Journal of Policy Analysis and Management* 1(1): 19–41.

Hanushek, E.A. (1986). The Economics of Schooling: Production and Efficiency in Public Schools. *Journal of Economic Literature* 24(3): 1141–1177.

Hanushek, E.A. (1994). Money Might Matter Somewhere: A Response to Hedges, Laine, and Greenwald. *Educational Researcher* 23(4): 5–8.

Hanushek, E.A. (1995). Interpreting Recent Research on Schooling in Developing Countries. *World Bank Research Observer* 10(2): 227–246.

Hanushek, E.A. (1996a). Measuring Investment in Education. *Journal of Economic Perspectives* 10(4): 9–30.

Hanushek, E.A. (1996b). School Resources and Student Performance. In G. Burtless (ed.), *Does Money Matter? The Effect of School Resources on Student Achievement and Adult Success*. Washington D.C.: Brookings Institution.

Hanushek, E.A. (1997a). The Productivity Collapse in Schools. In W. Fowler, Jr. (ed.), *Developments in School Finance 1996*. Washington, D.C.: U.S. Department of Education, National Center for Education Statistics.

Hanushek, E.A. (1997b). Assessing the Effects of School Resources on Student Performance: An Update. *Educational Evaluation and Policy Analysis* 19(2): 141–164.

Hanushek, E.A. (1998). Conclusions and Controversies about the Effectiveness of School Resources. *Economic Policy Review* (Federal Reserve Bank of New York) 4(1): 11–27.

Hanushek, E.A. (1999a). Some Findings from an Independent Investigation of the Tennessee STAR Experiment and from Other Investigations of Class Size Effects. *Educational Evaluation and Policy Analysis* 21(2): 143–163.

Hanushek, E.A. (1999b). The Evidence on Class Size. In S.E. Mayer and P.E. Peterson (eds.), *Earning and Learning: How Schools Matter*. Washington, D.C.: Brookings Institution Press.

Hanushek, E.A. (2000). Evidence, Politics, and the Class Size Debate. Mimeo. Stanford University, Stanford, Calif.

Hanushek, E.A., and D.D. Kimko (2000). Schooling, Labor-Force Quality, and the Growth of Nations. *American Economic Review* 90(5): 1184–1208.

Hanushek, E.A., S.G. Rivkin, and L.L. Taylor (1996). Aggregation and the Estimated Effects of School Resources. *Review of Economics and Statistics* 78(4): 611–627.

Hanushek, E.A., C.S. Benson, R.B. Freeman, D.T. Jamison, H.M. Levin, R.A. Maynard, R.J. Murnane, S.G. Rivkin, R.H. Sabot, L.C. Solmon, A.A. Summers, F. Welch, and B.L. Wolfe (1994). *Making Schools Work. Improving Performance and Controlling Costs.* Washington, D.C.: Brookings Institution.

Harbison, R.W., and E.A. Hanushek (1992). *Educational Performance of the Poor: Lessons from Rural Northeast Brazil.* (Published for the World Bank.) Oxford: Oxford University Press.

Hayek, F.A. von (1945). The Use of Knowledge in Society. *American Economic Review* 35(4): 519–530.

Heckman, J.J. (2000). Policies to Foster Human Capital. *Research in Economics* 54(1): 3–56.

Heckman, J.J., and P.J. Klenow (1997). Human Capital Policy. Mimeo. University of Chicago.

Heckman, J.J., A. Layne-Farrar, and P. Todd (1996). Human Capital Pricing Equations with an Application to Estimating the Effect of Schooling Quality on Earnings. *Review of Economics and Statistics* 78(4): 562–610.

Hedges, L.V., R.D. Lane, and R. Greenwald (1994). Does Money Matter? A Meta-Analysis of Studies of the Effects of Differential School Inputs on Student Outcomes. *Educational Researcher* 23(3): 5–14.

Hoxby, C.M. (1994). Do Private Schools Provide Competition for Public Schools? NBER Working Paper 4978. National Bureau of Economic Research, Cambridge, Mass.

Hoxby, C.M. (1996). How Teachers' Unions Affect Education Production. *Quarterly Journal of Economics* 111(3): 671–718.

Hoxby, C.M. (1999). The Productivity of Schools and Other Local Public Goods Producers. *Journal of Public Economics* 74(1): 1–30.

Hoxby, C.M. (2000a). Does Competition among Public Schools Benefit Students and Taxpayers? *American Economic Review* 90(5): 1209–1238.

Hoxby, C.M. (2000b). The Effects of Class Size on Student Achievement: New Evidence from Population Variation. *Quarterly Journal of Economics* 115(4): 1239–1285.

IDB (Inter-American Development Bank) (1998). *Facing Up to Inequality in Latin America: Economic and Social Progress in Latin America, 1998/1999 Report.* Washington, D.C.: Johns Hopkins University Press.

IEA (International Association for the Evaluation of Educational Achievement) (1998). *Third International Mathematics and Science Study: International Achievement Reports.* http://timss.bc.edu/timss1995i/TIMSSPublications.html.

IMF (International Monetary Fund) (2000). *International Financial Statistics Yearbook.* Washington, D.C.: IMF.

Islam, N. (1995). Growth Empirics: A Panel Data Approach. *Quarterly Journal of Economics* 110(4): 1127–1170.

Jorgenson, D.W. (1995). *Productivity. Volume 1: Postwar U.S. Economic Growth. Volume 2: International Comparisons of Economic Growth.* Cambridge, Mass.: MIT Press.

Jorgenson, D.W., and Z. Griliches (1967). The Explanation of Productivity Change. *Review of Economic Studies* 34(3): 249–283.

Jorgenson, D.W., F.M. Gollop, and B.M. Fraumeni (1987). *Productivity and U.S. Economic Growth.* Cambridge, Mass.: Harvard University Press.

Journal of Economic Perspectives (1996). Special Issue: Symposium on Primary and Secondary Education. 10(4): 3–72.

Jovanovic, B., and R. Rob (1999). Solow vs. Solow. Mimeo. New York University.

King, R.G., and R.E. Levine (1994). Capital Fundamentalism, Economic Development, and Economic Growth. *Carnegie-Rochester Conference Series on Public Policy* 40 (June): 259–292.

Klein, L.R. (1974). *A Textbook of Econometrics.* Englewood Cliffs, N.J.: Prentice-Hall.

Klenow, P.J., and A. Rodríguez-Clare (1997a). Economic Growth: A Review Essay. *Journal of Monetary Economics* 40(3): 597–617.

Klenow, P.J., and A. Rodríguez-Clare (1997b). The Neoclassical Revival in Growth Economics: Has It Gone Too Far? *NBER Macroeconomics Annual 1997.* Cambridge, Mass.: MIT Press.

Kloek, T. (1981). OLS Estimation in a Model Where a Microvariable Is Explained by Aggregates and Contemporaneous Disturbances Are Equicorrelated. *Econometrica* 49(1): 205–207.

Krueger, A.B. (1999a). Experimental Estimates of Education Production Functions. *Quarterly Journal of Economics* 114(2): 497–532.

Krueger, A.B. (1999b). An Economist's View of Class Size Research. Mimeo. Princeton University.

Krueger, A.B., and M. Lindahl (2001). Education for Growth: Why and For Whom? *Journal of Economic Literature* 39(4): 1101–1136.

Krueger, A.B., and D.M. Whitmore (2001). The Effect of Attending a Small Class in the Early Grades on College-Test Taking and Middle School Test Results: Evidence from Project STAR. *Economic Journal* 111(468): 1–28.

Krueger, A.O. (1968). Factor Endowments and Per Capita Income Differences among Countries. *Economic Journal* 78(311): 641–659.

Kyriacou, G.A. (1991). Level and Growth Effects of Human Capital: A Cross-Country Study of the Convergence Hypothesis. *Economic Research Reports* 19–26, C.V. Starr Center for Applied Economics, New York University.

Landsburg, S.E. (1993). *The Armchair Economist: Economics and Everyday Life.* New York: Free Press.

Lau, L.J., D.T. Jamison, and F.F. Louat (1991). Education and Productivity in Developing Countries: An Aggregate Production Function Approach. PRE Working Paper 612. World Bank, Washington, D.C.

Lazear, E.P. (2001). Educational Production. *Quarterly Journal of Economics* 116(3): 777–803.

Lee, J.-W., and R.J. Barro (2001). Schooling Quality in a Cross Section of Countries. *Economica* 68(272): 465–488.

Levine, R.E., and D. Renelt (1992). A Sensitivity Analysis of Cross-Country Growth Regressions. *American Economic Review* 82(4): 942–963.

Lucas, R.E., Jr. (1988). On the Mechanics of Economic Development. *Journal of Monetary Economics* 22(1): 3–42.

Maddison, A. (1987). Growth and Slowdown in Advanced Capitalist Economies: Techniques of Quantitative Assessment. *Journal of Economic Literature* 25(2): 649–698.

Mankiw, N.G. (1995). The Growth of Nations. *Brookings Papers on Economic Activity* (1): 275–326.

Mankiw, N.G., D. Romer, and D.N. Weil (1992). A Contribution to the Empirics of Economic Growth. *Quarterly Journal of Economics* 107(2): 408–437.

Marshall, A. ([1890]1922). *Principles of Economics: An Introductory Volume*. London: Macmillan.

Martin, M.O., and D.L. Kelly (eds.) (1998). *TIMSS Technical Report Volume II: Implementation and Analysis, Primary and Middle School Years*. Chestnut Hill, Mass.: Boston College.

Mincer, J. (1974). *Schooling, Experience, and Earnings*. New York: National Bureau of Economic Research.

Mingat, A. (1998). The Strategy Used by High-performing Asian Economies in Education: Some Lessons for Developing Countries. *World Development* 26(4): 695–715.

Mosteller, F. (1995). The Tennessee Study of Class Size in the Early School Grades. *The Future of Children* 5(2): 113–127.

Moulton, B.R. (1986). Random Group Effects and the Precision of Regression Estimates. *Journal of Econometrics* 32(3): 385–397.

Moulton, B.R. (1990). An Illustration of a Pitfall in Estimating the Effects of Aggregate Variables on Micro Units. *Review of Economics and Statistics* 72(2): 334–338.

Mulligan, C.B., and X. Sala-i-Martin (1997). A Labor Income-Based Measure of the Value of Human Capital: An Application to the States of the United States. *Japan and the World Economy* 9(2): 159–191.

Mulligan, C.B., and X. Sala-i-Martin (2000). Measuring Aggregate Human Capital. *Journal of Economic Growth* 5(3): 215–252.

Murnane, R.J., J.B. Willett, and F. Levy (1995). The Growing Importance of Cognitive Skills in Wage Determination. *Review of Economics and Statistics* 77(2): 251–266.

Nehru, V., E. Swanson, and A. Dubey (1995). A New Database on Human Capital Stock in Developing and Industrial Countries: Sources, Methodology, and Results. *Journal of Development Economics* 46(2): 379–401.

Nelson, R.R., and E.S. Phelps (1966). Investment in Humans, Technological Diffusion, and Economic Growth. *American Economic Review* 56(2): 69–75.

North, D.C. (1994). Economic Performance Through Time. *American Economic Review* 84(3): 359–368.

OECD (Organisation for Economic Co-Operation and Development) (various issues). *Education at a Glance: OECD Indicators*. Paris: OECD.

Olson, M., Jr. (1996). Big Bills Left on the Sidewalk: Why Some Nations are Rich, and Others Poor. *Journal of Economic Perspectives* 10(2): 3–24.

O'Neill, D. (1995). Education and Income Growth: Implications for Cross-Country Inequality. *Journal of Political Economy* 103(6): 1289–1301.

Pfeffermann, D., and T.M.F. Smith (1985). Regression Models for Grouped Populations in Cross-Section Surveys. *International Statistical Review* 53(1): 37–59.

Pritchett, L. (2001). Where Has All the Education Gone? *World Bank Economic Review* 15(3): 367–391.

Pritchett, L., and D. Filmer (1999). What Education Production Functions Really Show: A Positive Theory of Education Expenditure. *Economics of Education Review* 18(2): 223–239.

Psacharopoulos, G. (1994). Returns to Investment in Education: A Global Update. *World Development* 22(9): 1325–1343.

Psacharopoulos, G. (2000). Economics of Education à la Euro. *European Journal of Education* 35(1): 81–95.

Psacharopoulos, G., and A.M. Arriagada (1986). The Educational Composition of the Labour Force: An International Comparison. *International Labour Review* 125(5): 561–574.

Quibria, M.G. (1999). Challenges to Human Resource Development in Asia. *Journal of Asian Economics* 10(3): 431–444.

Rao, M.G. (1998). Accommodating Public Expenditure Policies: The Case of Fast Growing Asian Economies. *World Development* 26(4): 673–694.

Review of Economics and Statistics (1996). Special Issue: Symposium on School Quality and Educational Outcomes. 78(4): 559–691.

Romer, P.M. (1990a). Endogenous Technological Change. *Journal of Political Economy* 98(5): S71–S102.

Romer, P.M. (1990b). Human Capital and Growth: Theory and Evidence. *Carnegie-Rochester Conference Series on Public Policy* 32 (Spring): 251–286.

Rothstein, R., and K.H. Miles (1995). *Where's the Money Gone? Changes in the Level and Composition of Education Spending*. Washington, D.C.: Economic Policy Institute.

Rothstein, R., and L. Mishel (1997). Alternative Options for Deflating Education Expenditures Over Time. In W. Fowler, Jr. (ed.), *Developments in School Finance 1996*. Washington, D.C.: U.S. Department of Education, National Center for Education Statistics.

Rouse, C.E. (1998). Private School Vouchers and Student Achievement: An Evaluation of the Milwaukee Parental Choice Program. *Quarterly Journal of Economics* 113(2): 553–602.

Sachverständigenrat zur Begutachtung der gesamtwirtschaftlichen Entwicklung (1998). *Vor weitreichenden Entscheidungen*. Jahresgutachten 1998/99. Stuttgart: Metzler-Poeschel.

Sachverständigenrat zur Begutachtung der gesamtwirtschaftlichen Entwicklung (2000). *Chancen auf einen höheren Wachstumspfad*. Jahresgutachten 2000/01. Stuttgart: Metzler-Poeschel.

Sander, W. (1999). Endogenous Expenditures and Student Achievement. *Economics Letters* 64(2): 223–231.

Schettkat, R. (2001). In Bildung investieren? Die Bildungs-Laffer-Kurve. *Beihefte der Konjunkturpolitik (Applied Economics Quarterly)* 51: 307–317.

Schimmelpfennig, A. (2000). *Structural Change of the Production Process and Unemployment in Germany*. Kieler Studien 307. Tübingen: Mohr Siebeck.

Schultz, T.W. (1961). Investment in Human Capital. *American Economic Review* 51(1): 1–17.

Scott, A.J., and D. Holt (1982). The Effect of Two-Stage Sampling on Ordinary Least Squares Methods. *Journal of the American Statistical Association* 77(380): 848–854.

Sen, A. (1999). *Development as Freedom*. Oxford: Oxford University Press.

Shleifer, A. (1998). State versus Private Ownership. *Journal of Economic Perspectives* 12(4): 133–150.

Siebert, H. (1997). Labor Market Rigidities: At the Root of Unemployment in Europe. *Journal of Economic Perspectives* 11(3): 37–54.

Siebert, H. (1999a). *The World Economy*. London: Routledge.

Siebert, H. (1999b). How Can Europe Solve Its Unemployment Problem? Kiel Discussion Paper 342. Kiel Institute for World Economics, Kiel.

Siebert, H. (2000a). Building a Growth Strategy. Paper presented at the World Economic Forum, Davos. Mimeo. Kiel Institute for World Economics, Kiel.

Siebert, H. (2000b). The New Economy—What Is Really New? Kiel Working Paper 1000. Kiel Institute for World Economics, Kiel.

Siebert, H. (2000c). The Paradigm of Locational Competition. Kiel Discussion Paper 367. Kiel Institute for World Economics, Kiel.

Siebert, H. (2000d). What Does Globalization Mean for the World Trading System? In The WTO Secretariat (ed.), *From GATT to the WTO: The Multilateral Trading System in the New Millennium*. The Hague: Kluwer Law International.

Smith, A. ([1776]1976). *An Inquiry into the Nature and Causes of the Wealth of Nations.* Glasgow Edition (R.H. Campbell and A.S. Skinner, eds.). Oxford: Clarendon Press.

Solow, R.M. (1956). A Contribution to the Theory of Economic Growth. *Quarterly Journal of Economics* 70(1): 65–94.

Solow, R.M. (1957). Technical Change and the Aggregate Production Function. *Review of Economics and Statistics* 39(3): 312–320.

StataCorp (1999). *Stata Statistical Software: Release 6.0.* College Station, Tex.: Stata Corporation.

Summers, R., and A.W. Heston (1988). A New Set of International Comparisons of Real Product and Price Levels: Estimates for 130 Countries, 1950–1985. *The Review of Income and Wealth* 34(1): 1–25.

Summers, R., and A.W. Heston (1991). The Penn World Table (Mark 5): An Expanded Set of International Comparisons, 1950–1988. *Quarterly Journal of Economics* 106(2): 327–368.

Temple, J.R.W. (1999a). The New Growth Evidence. *Journal of Economic Literature* 37(1): 112–156.

Temple, J.R.W. (1999b). A Positive Effect of Human Capital on Growth. *Economics Letters* 65(1): 131–134.

Temple, J.R.W. (2001a). Generalizations That Aren't? Evidence on Education and Growth. *European Economic Review* 45(4–6): 905–918.

Temple, J.R.W. (2001b). Growth Effects of Education and Social Capital in the OECD Countries. *OECD Economic Studies* 33(2): 57–101.

Tinbergen, J. (1942). Zur Theorie der langfristigen Wirtschaftsentwicklung. *Weltwirtschaftliches Archiv* 55(1): 511–549.

Topel, R. (1999). Labor Markets and Economic Growth. In O. Ashenfelter and D. Card (eds.), *Handbook of Labor Economics.* Volume 3C. Amsterdam: North-Holland.

Tyler, J.H., R.J. Murnane, and J.B. Willett (2000). Do the Cognitive Skills of School Dropouts Matter in the Labor Market? *Journal of Human Resources* 35(4): 748–754.

UN (United Nations) (various issues). *National Accounts Statistics: Main Aggregates and Detailed Tables.* New York.

UNDP (United Nations Development Programme) (2000). *Human Development Report 2000. Human Rights and Human Development.* Oxford: Oxford University Press.

UNESCO (United Nations Educational, Scientific and Cultural Organization) (2000a). *World Education Indicators.* http://unescostat.unesco.org/en/stats/stats0.htm.

UNESCO (United Nations Educational, Scientific and Cultural Organization) (2000b). *World Education Report 2000. The Right to Education: Towards Education for All Throughout Life.* Paris: UNESCO.

UNESCO (United Nations Educational, Scientific and Cultural Organization) (various issues). *Statistical Yearbook.* Paris: UNESCO.

U.S. Department of Education, National Center for Educational Statistics (1997). *The Condition of Education 1997*. Washington, D.C.: U.S. Government Printing Office.

U.S. Department of Education, National Center for Educational Statistics (1998). *Digest of Education Statistics 1997*. Washington, D.C.: U.S. Department of Education.

Weiss, A. (1995). Human Capital vs. Signalling Explanations of Wages. *Journal of Economic Perspectives* 9(4): 133–154.

White, H. (1984). *Asymptotic Theory for Econometricians*. Orlando: Academic Press.

Wolfensohn, J.D. (1999). A Proposal for a Comprehensive Development Framework—A Discussion Draft. Mimeo. World Bank. http://www.worldbank.org/cdf.

World Bank (1992). *World Development Report 1992: Development and the Environment*. Oxford: Oxford University Press.

World Bank (1993). *The East Asian Miracle: Economic Growth and Public Policy*. Oxford: Oxford University Press.

World Bank (1999a). *World Development Report 1998/99: Knowledge for Development*. Oxford: Oxford University Press.

World Bank (1999b). *The 1999 World Development Indicators*. CD-Rom. Washington, D.C.

World Bank (2000). *The 2000 World Development Indicators*. CD-Rom. Washington, D.C.

Wößmann, L. (2000a). Schooling Resources, Educational Institutions, and Student Performance: The International Evidence. Kiel Working Paper 983. Kiel Institute for World Economics, Kiel.

Wößmann, L. (2000b). Specifying Human Capital: A Review, Some Extensions, and Development Effects. Kiel Working Paper 1007. Kiel Institute for World Economics, Kiel.

Wößmann, L. (2001). Why Students in Some Countries Do Better: International Evidence on the Importance of Education Policy. *Education Matters* 1(2): 67–74.

Index

Kiel Institute for World Economics

Symposia and Conference Proceedings

Horst Siebert, Editor

Towards a New Global Framework for High-Technology Competition
Tübingen 1997. 223 pages. Hardcover.

Quo Vadis Europe?
Tübingen 1997. 343 pages. Hardcover.

Structural Change and Labor Market Flexibility
Experience in Selected OECD Economies
Tübingen 1997. 292 pages. Hardcover.

Redesigning Social Security
Tübingen 1998. 387 pages. Hardcover.

Globalization and Labor
Tübingen 1999. 320 pages. Hardcover.

The Economics of International Environmental Problems
Tübingen 2000. 274 pages. Hardcover.

The World's New Financial Landscape: Challenges for Economic Policy
Berlin . Heidelberg 2001. 324 pages. Hardcover.

Economic Policy for Aging Societies
Berlin . Heidelberg 2002. 305 pages. Hardcover.

Economic Policy Issues of the New Economy
Berlin · Heidelberg 2002. 251 pages. Hardcover.

Tübingen: Mohr Siebeck (http://www.mohr.de)
Berlin · Heidelberg: Springer-Verlag (http://www.springer.de)

KIELER STUDIEN · KIEL STUDIES

Kiel Institute for World Economics

Editor: *Horst Siebert* · Managing Editor: *Harmen Lehment*

More information on publications by the Kiel Institute at http://www. uni-kiel.de/ifw/pub/pub.htm, more information on the Kiel Institute at http://www.uni-kiel.de/ifw

Tübingen: Mohr Siebeck (http://www.mohr.de)
Berlin · Heidelberg: Springer-Verlag (http://www.springer.de)